Merry
to

2001

We love you
Donna : Bob

BY THELMA MARTIN ANDERSON

The Golden Lad

Where Coyotes Howl

Where Coyotes Howl

Thelma Martin Anderson

THELMA MARTIN ANDERSON

MORRIS PUBLISHING
3212 E. Hwy 30, Kearney, NE 68847

MORRIS PUBLISHING

3212 E. HWY 30

KEARNEY, NE 68847

DESIGNED BY DEANNA O. PETERS

MANUFACTURED IN THE UNITED STATES OF AMERICA

ISBN: 1-57502-102-1

This book is dedicated to my grandchildren:
Kyle and December Peters.

This book is dedicated to my grandchildren:
Kyle and December Peters.

ACKNOWLEDGEMENTS

I extend my heartfelt thanks to the wonderful people who helped me with my book. You all helped make it better.

Thank you, Karel Reimann, Midland's city librarian, for helping me when I needed historical information.

Thanks Harvey Madsen for telling me frontier tales, some grim, like the story of the jockey hanging from the cottonwood tree and some funny, like the automobile race which took place in the Midland Stockyards.

Thanks to Harry F. Thompson, Curator and Managing Editor of The Center For Western Studies at Augustana College at Sioux Falls, for graciously reading my book and writing the commentary for the back cover.

And, thanks to my daughter, Deanna Peters, for all the hours she spent editing and designing my book.

--Thelma Martin Anderson, Author

INTRODUCTION

I began this history of my family with my grandparents who came from Norway in the period between 1850 and 1875. It is a story of hardships and triumphs, happiness and sadness.

After growing up in Iowa and spending several years on a homestead in eastern Dakota Territory, my grandma Juliana Bertelson followed her sons to Midland, South Dakota and homesteaded on Bad River.

As I searched through the pages of old newspapers. I had the eerie feeling that I walked with pioneers. I watched floods sweep away their homes and possessions and sometimes their lives. I lived with them the good years, the blizzards, the droughts.

As I grew up, I saw deserted homestead shacks where lights had gone out never to be lit again, where dreams had died with the dry and sifting earth.

I ended my account in 1938, the year I graduated from High School. I lived through the "Great Depression" and "The Dirty Thirties" when dust blotted out the sun and dirt settled thick inside our houses. I saw the hordes of grasshoppers eat our crops and gardens into the ground.

I have tried to make this account as accurate as I could. I apologize for any mistakes I might have made.

--Thelma Martin Anderson, Author

CHAPTER 1
A New World

Rumors of the abundant homestead lands in America drew my Norwegians ancestors like a giant magnet. Norway was over-populated and having economic problems. Elder sons inherited the family farm. America's vast homestead land sounded like a dream waiting to be fulfilled. A wave of immigration crossed the Atlantic, peaking in the 1880's. The immigrants came in great sailing ships, bringing their faith, their furniture and their keep-sakes.

My Grandma, Juliana Bertelson, was one of these immi-grants. Born in Nordland, Norway July 10, 1854, the third of four children born to Great-grandparents Hauge, she spent her earliest years among friends and neighbors who left behind the country of their birth for the newer, less settled lands in America. For her parents, superstition played as great a part in their migration as the promise of free land.

Juliana had three brothers, Lars, Nels and Joachem called Jake. Nels was born with a shirt on. This shirt referred to the thin membrane that sometimes covers a baby's face at birth called a caul. Seen as a good omen by some cultures, this was not the case for Great-Grandpa and Grandma Hauge. A caul meant that Nels would meet an untimely end. In addition, he slept with his eyes open. Both were signs that his life would end by drowning.

Because of this Great-Grandpa Hauge decided to take his family to America, far away from the fjords and oceans of Norway so Nels could not become a fisherman and go to sea. The move could not alter fate. Nels drowned in an Iowa lake as a young man.

Juliana was seven years old when her father and mother packed their belongings, said good-bye to family and friends and embarked on a ship bound for America. Among these belongings was a wooden box about six inches square that had been hand pegged with tiny wooden pegs by a long ago ancestor. The date carved on the bottom was 1640.

They also brought a chair hand-crafted from a three-foot chunk of hollow cottonwood log with a rounded back like a barrel. These chairs often remained in the same family for four hundred years or more. The chair was used for many years until my husband, a frugal Scotsman, attached it to his hay rake for a seat. It was more comfortable than the iron seat that had come loose.

Great-Grandpa Hauge had a beard that ran from ear to ear under his chin. His face was clean shaven. Great-Grandma Hauge parted her long hair in the center and wore it in a bun on the back of her head, letting the hair at the sides fall over her ears. No smiles marred the sober faces on their photograph. The Hauge family arrived in their promised land in 1861 and settled among their Hove and Hauge relatives on a farm near Lake Mills, Iowa.

To the dismay of her parents, Juliana fell in love with a young man when she was sixteen. They wanted their daughter married to a settled man of substance. As many parents did in those days, they arranged a marriage for Juliana. Dutifully, she bowed to their wishes and married Daniel Bertelson Nepstad.

Daniel came from a place called Nepstad in Norway. He was born in 1828, the son of Bertel, making him Bertel's son.

12

Sometimes he called himself Daniel Bertelson and other times Daniel Nepstad, which was confusing to postmasters and business people.

Daniel had been married in Norway. His wife bore five children all of whom died. His wife died also. A lonely Daniel took ship for the United States. He settled on a farm two and one half miles southeast of Lake Mills.

When Daniel married Juliana, she was a pretty young girl of seventeen with dark brown hair and brown eyes. He was forty-three. Grandpa Daniel wore a clipped beard, but no mustache. "A man that wears a mustache has something wrong with his upper lip," he said with a grin.

The Bertelson farm had a two story white house with an ornate chimney. The L shaped house had four large bedrooms upstairs, a kitchen, pantry, parlor, and one bedroom downstairs. An open porch supported by round colonnades was built into the L. Large windows looked out on a wide expanse of lawn that reached to the trees sheltering the farmstead. There were barns, hog houses, corncribs and poultry houses. Cattle, horses, and sheep grazed the lush pastures. Hogs rooted in the hog yard.

Bertina, called Tina, Telina was born there on February 27, 1872. Albert Daniel joined her August 26, 1876 and Edward Oscar arrived February 19, 1881.

Grandpa Daniel plowed his fields with oxen to raise corn and oats to feed his milk cows, hogs, driving and riding horses. He taught his sons and daughters to curry and brush the horses before riding or driving the animals. No Bertelson horse left the barn with mud or manure clinging to its slick hide. No one returned to the house to rest and eat without first grooming the animal used.

Grandma Juliana stayed up until the wee hours of the

morning, working while her family slept. She scrubbed her floors every Wednesday and Saturday night on her hands and knees, working sand over the floors to make them white and beautiful. She carded wool and spun it into cloth to make clothing for her family. She washed clothes on a scrub board in a tub and ironed them with a sad iron heated on the kitchen range, wrapping the iron handle with cloth to keep from burning her hand. She canned vegetables, meat and fruit.

Tina, at a very young age, learned to help with the work. Idle hours were few. A traveling seamstress came and stayed several weeks to sew dresses, blouses, skirts and coats for Juliana and Tina. She made shirts, pants and coats for the boys and Daniel.

In the spring of 1886, Daniel caught homestead fever. He wanted to go west and homestead in the wild Dakota Territory. Homesteading made no sense to Juliana. They had a lovely home. They had barns and fields, cattle, horses, hogs, and sheep. They made a comfortable living. Relatives and friends lived all around them, and Daniel wanted to leave it all for a new life in a country where neither house nor barn waited.

Their oldest daughter Tina was fourteen, growing into a tall slender young lady. Albert was a sturdy ten-year-old. Mischievous Edward was five, and Juliana was pregnant with her fourth child. She didn't want to leave her beautiful home in Iowa for the uncertainty of the wild and hostile Dakota Territory where bands of painted Indians were likely to pass by.

But Daniel's mind was made up. He rented out the Iowa farm and loaded household goods, food and machinery into the covered wagon. He hitched two yoke of oxen to the wagon and headed west. Tina and Albert mounted horses and drove the cattle. A driving team trailed the wagon.

Daniel cracked the whip over the backs of the oxen and the

14

wagon creaked along the road. Juliana looked back with tears in her eyes as her home with the green lawn, trees, and fields waiting to be planted, faded into the distance. The baby in her womb kicked, and she wondered what kind of world the child would come into.

Daniel found his homestead along Elm Creek in Buffalo county near the town of Gann Valley. Claim shacks dotted nearly every quarter. Twenty Norwegian families homesteaded along Elm Creek so they soon made new friends. The mournful call of the turtle dove came from the prairie. Orioles serenaded the ducks and muskrats swimming in the creek.

Many homesteaders built sod houses and barns. Shacks had walls three feet thick and were papered on the inside with newspapers. Some people put hay down for floors, taking out the old hay, sweeping the dirt floor and laying a new batch of hay once a week.

Daniel built a cabin and barn near Elm Creek. Chamberlain lay some twenty miles to the south and the mighty Missouri River about fifteen miles east of his homestead.

The Norwegian community on Elm Creek held a big celebration on the Fourth of July. Dances and spelling bees entertained the homesteaders. Traveling ministers had church in different homes. The Bertelsons attended church whenever they could.

On July 17, Juliana went into labor. They had no midwife. Daniel paced the floor.

"I'll take care of Mama," Tina said. She went into the bedroom where her mother lay on the bed. "Tell me what to do," she said.

With instructions from her mother, Tina delivered her baby sister. She washed the baby and dressed her in the long white gown her mother had made. She wrapped the baby in a blanket and carried her into the bedroom. "Isn't she pretty, Mama?" Tina laid the curly black-haired baby beside her mother. They named the baby Nina Amanda and shortened it to Amanda.

In August, Daniel and Albert worked in the hay field, cutting hay and hauling it to the barn. Tina herded the cattle as they grazed in the tall prairie grass. On a hot August day, she ran around the cows to turn them back. A buzz sounded. A rattlesnake struck, his fangs sinking into her leg through her woolen stockings. She raced to the house, screaming, "Mama, Mama, a rattlesnake bit me."

Juliana ran to the hay field to get Daniel. Terrified, Tina ran after her mother while her heart pumped the poison through her body. Daniel carried Tina home. The poison was taking deadly effect. Her pulse was weak and rapid. She shook so violently that her skirt danced around her ankles. Daniel cut the wound and applied poultices to draw the poison out of her system. They prayed for her to recover, but had little hope that she would.

A drinking buddy of Daniel's offered to ride to Chamberlain for a doctor. He rode hard and pulled his lathered horse up at the doctor's office. The doctor shook his head. "There is no use for me to go. She will be dead before I can get there."

"Can you give me some medicine for her? I will take it back."

"Take it," the doctor said, handing him a small bottle, "but you'll not find her alive."

Daniel's friend rode the long trail home. He gave Daniel the medicine. "How is she?"

"Not good," Daniel said.

Tina, her leg swollen and purple, swallowed the medicine Daniel gave her. Her tongue swelled until she couldn't close her mouth. Her convulsions shook the bed. They feared she was dying. Four heart rending days passed and she slept. She awoke feeling better and recovered completely. In later years, she said, "An old drunk saved my life."

Families all up and down Elm Creek were haying. One woman trampled the hay her husband pitched into the rack while their babies rode in a burlap bag tied to the back of the wagon.

Daniel hitched his oxen to the plow and plowed fields. Some farmers walked barefoot behind their plows as the black furrows turned. They raised wheat and flax, sacked the grain in canvas bags and hauled it to Kimball some twenty miles east of Chamberlain, a long haul in wagons pulled by oxen or horses.

Daniel hauled water from the creek for drinking, cooking, washing clothes, and bathing. Wild fruit grew in abundance: grapes, plums, and chokecherries to pick and can . They ate the buffalo peas that grew thick on the prairie.

Juliana worried about the painted Indian warriors, riding bareback on their horses, roaming the country as they passed from one reservation to the other. Indians often camped beside the creek, and she feared they would go on a rampage and kill settlers. The Battle of the Little Bighorn in which General Custer and his troops were wiped out was barely ten years past and still fresh in people's minds. The Indian Ghost Dancers with their magic shirts and talk of an Indian messiah made settlers uneasy.

One day when Daniel was gone, the children spied riders on the horizon. They ran into the house, shouting, "Mama, Mama, Indians are coming. Indians are coming."

Juliana grabbed baby Amanda. "Hurry, we will hide by the creek." She ran out the door with Albert close behind her. Tina grabbed Edward's hand and they rushed to the creek. Juliana lead them into a chokecherry thicket.

Hearts beating against their ribs, they hunched down in the bushes and peered through the dense foliage. "You must all be quiet as little mice," Juliana said. "If the Indians come, we will jump into the creek." Grandma Juliana planned to drown her children to keep them from being captured and tortured by the Indians. They hid in the bushes until darkness fell, but no Indians came.

The winter of 1887-1888 was one of extreme cold and deep snow. Daniel tied a long rope between the house and barn so he could grab the rope and follow it to the house if blizzard winds blew so hard he couldn't see where to go. The winter winds that howled out of the northwest could turn the country into a mass of swirling snow that blotted out everything.

A spectacular display of sun dogs on January 11, 1888 indicated a change in the weather. Gale winds out of the southeast blew all day and roared into the night. The wind swept across the prairie, piling the fast falling snow into huge drifts. The temperature was 20 degrees below zero. Many people dared not go to the barn to do chores in the blizzard. They thought tomorrow would be a better day, either cold and still or the south wind would bring a warm spell.

Thursday morning, January 12, the sun rose in a clear sky. The wind had died, replaced by a warm breeze from the southwest. The temperature was 32 degrees above zero. The day was so mild people thought a Chinook wind was in the making. The snow sparkled like diamonds. Huge snow drifts nearly leveled the draws.

Some farm buildings were almost buried in snow. Doors had to be dug out. The snow was so hard it had to be cut out in blocks with a spade. Farmers headed to town to get needed supplies. Albert and Edward trudged off to school on the hard snow.

About ten o'clock, the wind switched to the northwest. Daniel went out to feed and water his livestock. Snow so bright it hurt his eyes lay in shimmering mounds to the far horizon. He walked to the creek and dug down through the hard snow to clear a space for the cattle to drink. He cut a hole in the ice and turned the cattle out of the barn. He followed them as they wallowed through six foot drifts to the creek. The cattle crowded around the hole, drinking their fill of the icy water. Suddenly a cow raised her head and sniffed the air. With a snort, she turned and ran toward the barn. The other cattle scurried after her. With a mighty roar, wind and snow enveloped them. Blinding, choking snow filled the air. Daniel grabbed the tail of the last cow and hung on.

The snow was a great white wall, shutting out the buildings and the trees along the creek. Daniel could see nothing except his hand on the cow's tail. Tiny ice particles pelted his face. Running and stumbling through the snow, Daniel clung to the cow's tail as she dashed for the barn and safety from the bitter, screaming wind. The cattle ran into the barn. Daniel leaned against the wall, gasping for breath. He blinked and wiped the snow from his eyes. The cattle began eating. Daniel closed the barn door and edged around the barn into the suffocating snow. Sharp pellets stung his face. The bitter wind almost snatched his breath away. Daniel felt his way along the barn wall and found the rope. Holding to his lifeline, he struggled through the blowing snow to the house. He burst through the door.

"Papa,"Tina said, "we were afraid you were lost in the blizzard."

Daniel looked like a snowman. Snow clung to his eyebrows and beard. Amanda toddled over and touched his coat.

"I am glad you're here, Daniel," Juliana said. "I hope the teacher didn't send Albert and Edward home."

The teacher had sent the pupils out to go home before the storm caught them. As they rounded the schoolhouse, they saw a strange rolling cloud coming. The temperature dropped rapidly from 32 degrees above zero to 30 degrees below. The teacher called the children back into the schoolhouse. The blizzard hit with staggering force, wiping away all landmarks.

Some teachers turned the children out to go home because there was no food in the schoolhouse and little fuel. Many children never reached home. One teacher dismissed his pupils and nine of his eleven students perished. Their bodies weren't found until spring. One brother and sister were found clasped in each others arms when the snow melted in spring. A thirteen-year-old boy froze to death in his father's arms. Because so many children perished in it, the blizzard of 1888 was called "The Children's Blizzard."

Some teachers kept the children in school. When the fuel ran out, they burned desks and chairs. One young teacher kept her pupils in school until the fuel was gone. Darkness was coming. She knew they would freeze to death in the schoolhouse. She tied the children to herself and each other in a long line. She led them along a fence that stretched all the way to a farmstead. The children stumbled after her. The older children helped the small children up when they fell. They arrived safely at a grove of trees and then at the house.

One man and wife started to school with food, clothing and a shovel. They lost their way. The husband buried his wife in a snowbank and tramped around the spot until morning. All night they called to each to keep their spirits up as the deadly wind blew. The next morning, he dug her out of the snow, and they went to the schoolhouse.

A man, riding home from Armour, became lost in the blizzard. He chanced to bump into a schoolhouse. He lead his horse inside. Another man came to the school to get his children, but the wind changed his mind. He took his team into the schoolhouse with him. The men, the teacher, the pupils and three horses shared the schoolroom through the storm.

The storm raged all day and all night. The sun rose on a morning that was still and intensely cold. Hills and ravines had flattened out, covered with dazzling white. An eerie silence hung over the land. Smoke rose straight into the clear sky. The homesteaders dug into their barns. When the door was opened, a cloud of steam poured out. Snowdrifts were so hard steps had to be cut in the snow to let the cattle out of the buried barns.

The blizzard was the worst in the history of Buffalo County and the west. The storm raged from Idaho to the east coast. Most stock loose in the blizzard died. The death toll of people known to have died in Dakota was over one hundred. West of the river cattle barons lost whole herds of cattle and horses. Sheep men had no sheep left to herd.

Yet, spring came. The snow drifts gave up their dead. Elm Creek ran high. Ducks returned to swim in the creek. Orioles sang from the woods, and mourning doves called from the prairie again.

Daniel hitched up his oxen, worked the soil and planted seed. Albert learned to drive and care for the oxen and became his father's right hand man. Edward, too, had his chores.

Summer brought an abundant harvest of wheat and oats. The Bertelson family enjoyed picnics and horse racing, bowery dances and spelling bees with their neighbors. In 1889, Dakota Territory was divided into North and South Dakota. The Bertelson homestead was in the new state of South Dakota.

The asthma that had plagued Daniel in Iowa was worse in South Dakota. The Post Office got his mail mixed up, irritating Daniel. In 1890, he decided to go back to Iowa. He hitched his oxen to the wagon and the long trek back to the farm near Lake Mills began. Juliana was happy to head back to her beloved Iowa farm. She would see her family and friends again. There would be no more painted Indians, no more fear that a prairie fire would whip through the tall grass.

Baby Amanda was four years old, a doll with bright, black eyes and curly black hair. Edward was nine with dark hair and brown eyes that sparkled with mischief. Albert was a strapping lad of fourteen, growing tall, Tina a slender young lady of eighteen.

Juliana Bertelson holding Tina about 1873.

(Seated left) Grandma Juliana Bertelson, (Standing) Tina, (Seated right) Amanda.

22

CHAPTER 2

Home Again

Back home in Iowa, Grandpa Daniel was good to his family, but he loved his whiskey. Grandma Juliana, tired of his drinking, had him black-balled at the bars and liquor stores so he could no longer buy liquor.

Daniel was so desperate for a drink that he asked Tina to buy him a bottle one day as they rode down the street in the buggy. Tina said, "No, Papa, I will not buy you any whiskey." He glowered at her, but said no more, and she drove the team on down the street.

Tina was Daniel's favorite child. One day at dinner, he said, "Pass the bread."

Tina picked up the bread plate and said, "Say, 'please', first, Papa."

He glared at her while forks stopped mid-way to half-open mouths. Her stunned brothers and sister waited for an explosion. "I don't say please," Daniel said. Aghast at what she had done, Tina passed him the bread. The other children said nobody but Tina could have talked to their father like that. She said she never did again.

One of Daniel's friends was a surly giant with a black beard who whipped his wife if she displeased him. Daniel was one of the few men he liked, probably because most men were afraid of him and Daniel was not. Daniel never dodged a fight. In one brawl, he whipped the Champion of the Norwegian Navy. Daniel was visiting his friend during the early evening. The man's wife came into the house, looking frightened. She said, "I can't find the milk cows." Her husband looked at her. "Come here, you know what you get." He grabbed her and was going to turn her over his knee and spank her.

"Hold on," Daniel said. "This time you will not whip her." The man glared at Daniel for a moment, then laughed and let her go.

On November 10, 1891, Juliana gave birth to a blue eyed baby boy. They named him Alvin Oscar. On April 26, 1894, Dina arrived. She was not given a middle name. On her birth Daniel was sixty-six years old, Juliana nearly forty.

Daniel hired a man to help with the farm work. The hired man liked Tina, but she ignored him. Disgruntled, he said, "Tina is too tall to be human and too short to be a witch." The comment didn't phase Tina who was enamored by a young man whose family had moved from Primrose, Wisconsin to a farm near Forest City, Iowa when he was eighteen years old.

Carl Olson, called Charley by everyone, was a handsome young man with dark hair and brown eyes who stood about five feet nine inches tall. His brothers Olaf and Robert were both bigger. Although Charley wouldn't fight, he loved to wrestle, taking on all challengers and regularly pinning his brothers. His younger brother Rob, who was several inches taller and a good fifty pounds heavier, never stopped trying to throw Charley. They had their last match in Rob's corn field when Charley was past seventy and Rob around sixty. Cornstalks cracked and popped, and suddenly Rob found himself flat on his back again.

Charley had four living sisters; Mary, Anna, Addie and Lisa and three brothers; Olaf, Levi and Robert. One sister died

24

when she was thirteen. Lying on her deathbed, she opened her eyes and said, "I see Jesus. Mama and Papa must come. All my brothers and sisters must come." Then she was gone.

Charley was a devout Methodist and Tina was Lutheran. Charley figured Catholics were on the wrong track and Lutherans were right behind them. He lived for eighty-seven years without changing his mind.

Charley told us that he rode the train to Lake Mills to see Tina and when he left, "Tina almost wouldn't let me go. She wanted to get on the train with me." This story made her indignant which made him laugh. Young ladies of that day did not chase men.

Tina and Charley were married June 12, 1892 at Forest City, Iowa. Uncle Charley said Aunt Tina was so thin when they got married he had to "shake the sheet to find her." We thought this hilarious, and he roared with laughter.

"Oh, Charley," Tina said, her voice disgusted.

If a man had a bossy wife, people said, "She wears the pants in her family." Uncle Charley said, "I wear the pants in this house." He declared, "I'm the head of this household."

Smiling, Aunt Tina said, "Yah, but the neck turns the head."

After living on several farms in Iowa, they settled on a farm near Buffalo Center, about twenty miles west of Lake Mills. Charley changed his name to Myrland, the place his parents came from in Norway, because his mail got mixed with another Carl Olson's mail.

Amanda, Edward and Alvin graduated from the eighth grade in the small country schoolhouse two and a half miles from their farm in District 6, Norway Township, Winnebago County. Tina and Albert only went to about fourth grade as they had to work at home.

Dina's first teacher was G.E. Honesy, a handsome, dark-haired young man who taught the District 6 school in 1901 and 1902. Dina stayed with Tina and Charley one school term, and Tina brought her home to Lake Mills for the summer. Tina returned that fall to take Dina back with her for another school term. Dina was packing her clothes when Alvin called her aside. "Please stay here, Dina. Don't go with Tina. I don't have anybody to play with." Dina stayed home and went to school with Alvin.

Summer days were busy with corn and oats to plant and tend, hay to make, cows to milk, horses, hogs and sheep to care for. Spring brought calves and colts, lambs and litters of pigs. Chickens scratched in the dirt. Turkey gobblers gobbled and strutted around their harems.

Dina and Alvin loved to go with Albert in the hay rack as the team trotted to the hay field. The patient horses plodded from one haycock to the next while Albert pitched the hay into the rack. Dina and Alvin chased the field mice and cottontails that ran away from the haycocks. Striped garter snakes, blue racers and gray bull snakes slithered through the mown field, catching mice. When the rack was half full, Dina and Alvin climbed up on the hay. They ran round and round, packing the hay. With the hay mounded above the rack like a loaf of bread, they headed home.

Dina sometimes fell asleep on the fragrant hay as the load swayed along the trail. Albert stopped the wagon beside the haystack and winked at Alvin. He stuck his pitchfork carefully under Dina and heaved her and the fork full of hay toward the haystack. Dina woke up, flying through the air. She landed on the soft hay and sat up. Alvin and Albert laughed. They loved to tease her.

Dina and Alvin roamed the fields and pastures and played

in the woods. When fall turned the leaves to red, yellow and brown, they picked black walnuts and hazelnuts in the woods.

One day Dina and Alvin went into the storehouse to play. Alvin took the top off the wooden sugar barrel. Standing opposite each other, they dug their hands into the sugar, threw the white grains into the air and watched them rain back into the barrel. Alvin's tosses grew wild. He dug deeper into the barrel and threw the sugar full in Dina's face. Sugar stung her eyes. She put her hands over her eyes as the tears came. Alvin was horrified. "Don't tell Mama. Don't tell Mama." They put the lid on the barrel and slipped out of the storehouse, and Dina didn't tell.

Although Dina was eight years younger than Amanda, they played together with their dolls. Dina had a small wooden rocker, but Amanda's rocker had a padded seat. Dina's small blond doll seemed dwarfed beside Amanda's gorgeous porcelain doll with her white buckskin body, beautiful face, dark hair and brown eyes that closed when she was laid down. She wore a stylish gown.

A furniture store owner in Lake Mills, captivated by Amanda's snapping brown eyes and black curls, gave her the doll, a doll bed, and the padded rocking chair. Dina wished for a doll and chair like Amanda's, but she didn't get them.

A fast buggy team was the pride and joy of many families. Buggy races were common. No speed limits were posted on their roads. The best buggy teams carried Standardbred blood. They could make the buggy wheels sing. The Bertelson driving horses were of the Hambletonian strain of Standardbred. Tina never allowed another team to pass her. When a buggy drew up behind her, getting ready to pass, she let the lines out and her horses whistled down the road. Dust flew, making the other team "eat her dust."

One fellow tried to pass her buggy. She let the lines out.

Her horses extended to full trot. The teams raced neck and neck down the dusty road. Tina's team pulled away. He whipped his team, but they couldn't catch her. Many a man was chagrinned at being beaten by a woman. Tina thought it was great fun. Not lady-like, but fun.

Dina and Alvin loved to go home with Tina in the buggy behind her fiery half-Arabian horse. Prince was chestnut with a white spot in his forehead and a burning desire to beat every horse on the road. Dina and Alvin liked to speed down the road with Tina, feeling the breeze blowing past their faces and Prince's mane and tail streaming in the wind.

Prince was Tina's favorite driving horse. When she yelled, "Come, Prince," he ran to her from wherever he was in the pasture. Tina would wind his mane around her fingers and lead him into the barn where she rewarded him with corn or oats.

When Prince was hitched to the buggy, he arched his proud neck and pranced. He would follow Tina anywhere. She was driving him on a buggy one day when they came to a bridge that frightened him. He stopped, snorting and refused to step on the bridge. Tina stepped down from the buggy and took hold of his bit. "Come, Prince." She pulled. Prince stepped lightly onto the planks. His nose touching Tina's shoulder, he followed her across the bridge.

One day Tina went to the barn to ask Charley to go to Buffalo Center. Charley said, "No, we can't go today." He wanted her to coax him, then he would go, but instead Tina went back to the house. Charley was so angry he hitched Prince with one of his draft horses and drove to the field to cultivate corn. Prince was not a plow horse. He pranced down the row as if he were pulling a buggy. This threw him ahead of the larger horse, making him pull most of the load.

Prince danced and pranced as sweat broke out on his sleek chestnut coat. Tina, watching from the house, worried about Prince. She knew the gallant horse would drop before he quit. When she could stand it no longer, she went to the field and tried to talk Charley out of his foolishness. She asked him to take Prince back to the barn.

Charley pouted and drove on down the row. Tina ran in front of the team, forcing them to stop. Charley took the horses back to the barn. I don't know whether they went to Buffalo Center, but they probably did.

When bicycles came into popularity, Charley bought two. He and Tina rode merrily to Buffalo Center on their "wheels."

No doubt Tina inherited her love of horses from her mother Juliana. They owned side saddles and loved to gallop their horses with the wind blowing in their faces, their long black riding skirts draped over their legs.

Once Juliana was riding home after dark. The trail passed through a deep woods where a man had been murdered a few days before. Someone had heard him pleading for his life. Juliana slowed her horse when she came to the spot where the man died. The woods were black as pitch. She felt uneasy, knowing that when the horse smelled the blood, he would get excited. She pulled the horse to a walk and rode past the dreaded place. Safely past, she let her horse break into a gallop.

The horse thundered down the trail. Suddenly, he leaped high and sideways. Juliana tightened her legs against the leg rests and hung on, fighting to control the frightened horse. As she pulled him to a canter, she knew she had been mistaken about the murder location, but the horse knew.

Grandpa Daniel died in 1901 at the age of seventy-three. Juliana was left with a farm to run. Dina was seven, Alvin nine.

Albert and Edward were young men of twenty-five and twenty. They took over the operation of the farm with their mother.

Edward was a tall young fellow, but not as tall as Albert who was called "The Big Fellow." Edward was a laughing young man with a shock of brown hair. He loved to tease Amanda and the neighbor girls almost to distraction. Aunt Amanda told us, "Edward teased too much."

When the haymows were empty, farmers had dances in the hayloft. Edward played his violin for barn dances. He loved to dance, and he loved to fight. The town boys fought the country boys. The Norwegians scrapped with the Irish and Germans. Someone was always looking for a scrap and Edward was always willing to oblige.

Alvin had his troubles with the town boys. One day a gang of boys caught Alvin alone in Lake Mills and gave chase. Alvin sped down the railroad track for home with the Lake Mills boys yelling and throwing rocks at him.

An Irish family lived on a neighboring farm. The father was dead so the boys ran the farm with their mother. The Irish family was largely ignored by their Norwegian neighbors, but Albert and Edward were friends with the boys.

Albert's friend was considered to be a bit dense. He told Albert, "When Pa died, the priest came and wanted money to pray Pa out of purgatory. We gave him the money. He came again wanting more money. He said Pa was nearly out of purgatory, but he still had one foot caught. I didn't give him any more money. I said, 'I know Pa. If he's only got one foot caught, he'll get out by himself.'"

Edward and Jack, the younger boy, went to dances together. Edward took Amanda along. Jack danced with the pretty girl with the dark curls and flashing brown eyes. They fell in love and

30

wanted to marry.

When Grandma Juliana found out, she was terribly upset, as was the rest of the family. They couldn't have Amanda, a Lutheran, marrying an Irish Catholic. "It's my fault," Edward said with tears in his eyes. "I shouldn't have brought Jack here." Amanda gave in to their wishes and broke up with Jack. Dina thought it was a shame.

Snow often fell deep in Iowa, laying a thick white blanket over field and meadow and piling huge drifts between the buildings. Cattle, sheep and horses were snug in barns. Hogs had their houses, and chickens were locked in chicken houses. Sleigh bells rang as frisky horses pulled bobsleds and sleek cutters over the creaking snow.

One winter the wind built an enormous drift between the house and barn on the Bertelson farm. The path to the barnyard ran over this hard snowdrift. The men walked over the path many times each day, carrying milk from the barn and slop to the hogs. Working like a pair of badgers digging a den, Alvin and Dina dug snow rooms in the drift, tunneling all the way through.

The unsuspecting hired man plodded along the path one frosty morning, carrying two buckets of slop for the pigs. He stepped on the tunnel. The snow gave way. Slop spilled over him, soaking through his clothes to his skin. He struggled out of the snow with potato peelings and assorted pieces of garbage clinging to his clothes. His breath came out in a little cloud, a cloud that was rapidly turning to smoke. Albert promised to speak to Alvin and Dina. He told them, "You mustn't make any more tunnels under the paths." His face was serious, but there was a twinkle in his eye.

In winter young people gathered at the lake to ice skate. Grandma Juliana's brother Jake cut a hole in the thick ice and put a post in the hole. He lashed a long pole horizontally to the post with one end longer than the other. He hitched a horse to the short end and a sled to the long end of the pole. As the horse went around the post, the sled whistled around the outside. The faster the horse went the more dizzying the ride.

In summer the lake was a gathering place for swimmers, waders and boaters. The Hauge boys were excellent swimmers, often swimming across the large lake. Women might hitch up their skirts a bit and wade. One day Nels and another man dived in to take one last swim across the lake. They swam with strong sure strokes until they were dots to the people watching from shore. In the middle of the lake, Nels went down and drowned. The other man swam to shore.When asked where Nels was, he said, "I thought he was right behind me. I didn't know he was in trouble." Some people thought he would not have helped Nels anyway. Thus the prophecy made at Nel's birth was fulfilled.

The Bertelson Family: (Standing) Edward and Amanda, (Seated) Albert, Alvin, Mother Juliana, Dina and Tena.

Albert Bertelson.

Tena Bertelson Myrland.

The Bertelson Family: (Standing) Albert, Edward and Tena (Sitting) Father Daniel, Alvin, Amanda (Standing) Mother Juliana and Baby Dina.

Charlie and Tena Myrland.

CHAPTER 3

Free Land and Large Dreams

The newly opened homestead land west of the Missouri River in South Dakota was a favorite topic of conversation in the early 1900's. Grandma Juliana's brother Jake boarded the train and went west to Draper, South Dakota. The small town was bursting with homesteaders. Jake found his homestead north of Draper on White Clay Creek in 1903. He built a two story frame house close to the creek.

Albert and Edward listened to Jake's glowing reports of the vast country with grass rippling across the prairie--free for the taking. Even though Grandpa Daniel left his family well provided for with a productive farm, a herd of milk cows, horses, pigs, everything they needed to make a good living, his boys, like their father before them, caught "homestead fever." They went west to build new dreams in a new land.

Albert and Edward helped Jake load his cattle, horses, machinery and household goods into immigrant cars on the Milwaukee Railroad, said good-bye to family and friends and boarded the train with the Hauge family. Twelve-year-old Alvin and the hired man were left to run the Iowa farm.

When the Milwaukee Railroad pulled into the depot in Draper, Albert and Edward helped drive Jake's cattle to his homestead near the new town of Van Metre on the Bad River. Jake, his wife Amalia and four small daughters Alma, Olga, Nora and Clara

34

settled into their new home while Albert and Edward rode horse-back to Midland about twenty miles west on the north side of Bad River. Here they found a growing frontier town.

Midland was founded in 1890 by J.C. Russell as a trading post, sixty miles from the nearest railroad. Until the homesteaders arrived, J.C. 's customers were cowboys, ranchers and Indians . Located on the Spotted Tail Trail from the Pine Ridge Indian Reservation in southern South Dakota to the Cheyenne and Standing Rock Reservations north of the Cheyenne River, Midland was a half-way point for Indians going between the Rosebud Reservation and Cherry Creek. They traveled up and down Brave Bull Creek in horse drawn travois that were later replaced by spring wagons with dogs and extra ponies following.

Indians had traded with J.C. Russell since 1890. At times as many as two hundred in a day passed through Midland and traded at the store. Gus Stormer, one of the early stage drivers, had a pregnant Indian woman among his passengers from Ft. Pierre one day. Some miles out they came to a creek, and she asked him to stop and let her out for a while. She disappeared in the woods. Half an hour later, she came back with a newborn baby in a blanket. She boarded the stage, and they continued on to Midland.

Albert went to work for Tom Jones on the W-M wagon and rode on the spring and fall cattle round-ups. Cowboys earned $35.00 to $45.00 per month. June 23, 1904, the W-M wagon had a herd of over four thousand cattle rounded up ten miles northeast of Midland. The cattle had been cut into half a dozen herds according to ownership and were held by fifty cowboys.

The herds of long horned and mixed breed cattle had grazed the free range all winter. Now the calves were to be branded. Tents were set up for the crew. Cooks were busy at the canvas covered cook wagons. Cowboys rode around the nervous, bawling cattle, keeping the herds separated and bunched.

Albert glanced at the menacing clouds building in the west as he edged a cow back into the herd. The clouds grew darker as they rolled and churned across the sky. Driven by hurricane winds, the boiling clouds raced toward the herds. Cattle sniffed the air. Cows bellowed for their calves, and cowboys worked frantically to keep each herd bunched so they wouldn't mix with other herds.

The wind hit with sudden fury. Lightning flashed. Tents blew down and whipped across the prairie. Canvas tore from wagons and sailed through the air like giant kites. Cattle snorted. Cowboys yelled and fired their pistols in a vain attempt to keep the cattle together. It was useless. The cattle stampeded, scattering across the prairie. Herds mixed with other herds and ran southeast for miles.

The round-up had to be done over again. According to The Western Star, Midland's newspaper, "It was a bigger job to separate them again than it had been the first time." Homestead shacks were also blown over in the storm. Three shacks along Mitchell Creek were reduced to kindling wood.

Edward worked for his mother's cousin Olaf Hauge on a sheep ranch operated by Olaf and his brother Jim Nelson. He herded sheep, worked at the dipping tanks when sheep were dipped for scab and helped with haying the lush grass. The Nelsons ran sheep on the vast stretches of government land where large herds of horses and cattle also roamed.

Jim Nelson headquartered at the mouth of Brave Bull Creek where Brave Bull flows into Bad River. Olaf's camp was near Witcher Holes Creek miles to the northwest. This creek was named for a freighter who got his wagon stuck in the creek in heavy mud. Witcher got another team and tried to pull his outfit out of the creek. His freight wagon wouldn't budge. He got down in the mud and dug holes around his wagon and got the outfit moving again. The Creek is still called Witcher Holes.

Albert and Edward liked this new country. Homesteaders were required to build a shack, plow five acres and live on their homestead six months per year. They could prove up in five years, pay a small fee and own the land, a wonderful opportunity. They flocked into the country. Tar paper shacks, sod shanties, log cabins and homes dug into a hillside like a coyote den sprouted across the country like mounds in a prairie dog town.

Ample rain fell. Lush grass covered the land. Hay was plentiful; mowers few. Ranchers said they had never seen grass so high so early in the year as it was in late June of 1904. Plums, chokecherries and grapes hung thick on trees and vines along rivers, creeks and draws. People drove buggies and wagons out for an afternoon of fun, roaming over the bluffs, picking fruit.

A bounty of $100.00 was put on grown wolves and $10.00 on pups because wolves were killing livestock all over the country. Wolves killed "More livestock than the rustlers stole." Wolves could kill a cow or horse and were murder on calves and colts.

Midland was the hub of a large trading area, boasting stores, hotels, restaurants, land offices and a newspaper. The Western Star, housed in a lean-to on Russell's store building, was a staunch supporter of the Midland community. Editor Frances Gueffrey kept up a running duel with the editor of the Mitchell paper because he called the country west of the Missouri River "a barren wasteland." Cowboys who carried pistols and participated in gun play came under fire from Gueffrey as well. He suggested that the gunslingers "talk it out like men with sense instead of shooting at each other."

Editor Gueffrey had high hopes for the west river country and Midland. He urged people to subscribe to his weekly paper for the bargain price of $1.50 per year and make it the leading news-paper west of the Missouri River. In the July 4, 1904 issue, he proudly proclaimed, "Don't forget, we are here to stay. We confi-dently expect to be here when railroads, trolley lines, electric lights, etc. adorn the streets of Midland."

The railroad came and electric lights arrived, but no trolley ever set wheels in the streets of Midland whose total population never exceeded four hundred residents. In the early 1900's, how-ever, many people echoed Gueffrey's sentiments about the country that was settling up fast. Rates at Mrs. Hall's Midland Hotel were $1.00 per night but rooms were so scarce people had to sleep three in a bed with strangers. J.C. Russell's store was expanding. New businesses opened nearly every day. Advertisements for a good blacksmith and wagon maker to locate in town were posted. More tar paper shacks, sod shanties and dugout houses appeared across the prairie. Some people with money built two story houses with kitchen, parlor and bedrooms. They had come to stay.

Harry Hopkins added a new addition to his Government Hotel located midway between Ft. Pierre and Hayes so he could better serve the many transients coming into the country. Ozro Stroup ran a stage line from Ft. Pierre to Midland, a two day trip. A stage went west to Deadwood and the gold fields.

This was a versatile country. Some farmers ran huge herds of hogs with no fenced hog pastures. Mrs. Leonard Bower came to Midland looking for a drover for the large herd of hogs they ran on Dry Creek southeast of town. Otis Addison herded the ornery crit-ters for a week for his board, but when Mrs. Bower cut his food down, he quit.

Editor Gueffrey said, "He's looking for greener pastures" and he found them on Brave Bull Creek where he homesteaded. J.C. Russell saw a new market here. He had a herd of brood sows and sold weanling pigs to homesteaders for $2.00 per head. He bought an incubator and hatched chicks to sell.

John Putnam came in from his homestead and wanted to buy an incubator from J.C. Someone told him that some of the chicks hatched had wooden legs and the rest were woodpeckers, so he decided he didn't want one of those contraptions. Russell's incubator eventually hatched three hundred baby chicks, none with wooden legs and not a woodpecker in the lot.

John Denton, who homesteaded over southeast of Midland, claimed he found a beer spring on Dry Creek. Editor Gueffrey said, "Either the story is a rank fake or the neighbors have already drained it."

Bad River was up and down many times that summer. George Munson delivered mail to Nowlin eight miles upriver from Midland, then drove to check things on his claim south of Bad River. When he returned a few hours later, Bad River was roaring deep. George tied his team to his cart and spent the night underneath.

The July 4th celebration at Stewart's Hall northwest of Midland on Mitchell Creek drew families in buggies, wagons and on horseback. They came from every direction. Cowboys and single homesteaders galloped in to join the festivities. A good time was had by all except the people from south of Bad River. Heavy rain Saturday and Sunday sent Bad River rampaging and dangerous to cross so everybody south of the river had to stay home.

Along about sundown, the dance started. Albert and Edward no doubt were there, waltzing and square dancing with the ladies. Since there were four or five men to every girl, the ladies were mighty popular. No wall flowers graced the benches at pioneer dances. Sometimes the men drew numbers to see which girl they would get to dance with and how many times. Sleepy children were put to bed on blankets in the wagons while parents danced until the sun came over the horizon.

Rivers and creeks were so high during August that the Linder Brothers who ranched on Bad River four miles west of Midland took a week to haul their wool to Pierre. Farmers and ranchers were putting up a bumper hay crop. J.C Russell bragged about the strawberries, green peas and new potatoes from his garden. He was proud of the twenty-five acres of corn growing tall on the river bottom, the leaves whispering in the slightest breeze. His good crops made both he and his customers happy. Harrens bought a wagon load of roasting ears and hauled it home to their log cabin on Ash Creek.

The Sioux Falls Argus Leader bragged that a cornstalk in eastern South Dakota measured nine feet tall. A traveling salesman took a ten footer from J.C. Russell's corn field and displayed it in Ft. Pierre. The Stock Journal of Ft. Pierre said, "The Mitchell knockers cannot stuff their campaign rot down people who have seen for themselves." Flour was up to $6.20 per barrel.

A carload of horses sold for $75.00 per head in July. In September it was hard to sell anything but prime beef in the Chicago market. Prime cattle only brought $2.00 to $3.50 per hundred weight. R.A Dawson and Mike Quinn from up Ottumwa way took a carload of beef cattle to Chicago and said they were happy to get back alive. Dawson bought a pair of overalls for forty-nine cents, and Mike Quinn blew nineteen and a half cents on a new straw hat.

Albert and Edward met Waldemar A. Steien, called Walt, a young carpenter from Pepein, Wisconsin. Walt built houses and anything else anyone wanted built.

Walt's ad in The Western Star read: "If you need any carpentering or log houses built neatly, call on W.A. Steien, contractor, Midland, S.D." The Western Star said Walt's latest handy work, the J.D. Snow "Mansion" in east Midland, was "a model of perfection."

Walt and Editor Gueffrey were friends. Walt had built the lean-to onto Russell's store building that housed the printing office and was the first subscriber to The Western Star. Their friendship thrived outside work-related activities. When Chris Larsons threw an afternoon tea party at their homestead eight miles up Mitchell Creek, Walt and Editor Gueffrey took part in the hunting contest held there. Editor Gueffrey won with three cottontails, some woodpeckers and a huge hoot owl. Walt Steien got second with a mud hen and a large hawk.

Walt homesteaded on Mitchell Creek about four miles due north of Midland. He lived in a dugout in the side of a hill with his corrals down below. Mitchell Creek meandered through the northern part of his land, providing excellent winter shelter for livestock. Walt was also a surveyor and photographer. His Kodak camera used glass negatives and is in mint condition today.

Business boomed as more homesteaders arrived. J.C. Russell hired Walt Steien and Matt Bakken to haul lumber from Pierre to build an addition on his store. They left Midland on Tuesday morning with three teams and returned Saturday with three heavy loads of lumber, excellent time for a trip of over one hundred twenty miles.

Walt then went out to help Walt Tygerson in the hay field. Walt Tygerson's homestead was on Mitchell Creek above Walt Steien's homestead. They spent long hard days in the field in the hot August sun. Sweat ran down their faces and their shirts got sopping wet. Rattlesnakes were numerous and angry during the "dog days" of August, so one had to keep a sharp eye out for them.

41

Haying was tedious. A mower pulled by two horses makes a slow five foot swath around a hay field. They raked the hay with a dump rake, pitched it on the hay rack and hauled it home to be stacked by the barn or corral. The hay was pitched off the rack, too, unless the farmer had hay ropes to lay across the bottom of the rack so the team could roll the load off the hay rack into a stack.

Runaways were common. Horses ran away with plows in fields and wagons on the road. Fences were few, but if a runaway team hit a new barb wire fence, the results were usually disastrous. Theodore Peterson was mowing on the Mitchell Creek bottoms above Tygerson's when his team spooked and ran away. The horses kicked and trampled Theodore. The mower ran over him nearly tearing his clothes off. He was found bleeding and unconscious by a neighbor who took him home.

Walt Tygerson decided to dam Mitchell Creek between rains so he would be assured of a good water supply. He walked behind his team in the hot sun, plowing sod, scraping up loads of dirt and dumping them in the creek bed. He finished the dam just in time. The rains came down. The creek came up and Tygerson's dam went down to Bad River. He gave up on the dam and went to the meadow to haul hay to the barn. The team ran away with the hay rack, leaving him standing in the field with a pitchfork full of hay. The team roared into the creek and dumped the hay rack upside down in the creek, damming the creek again with his wagon and hay.

In June of 1904, a Government order said all cattle in this part of the country should be dipped for Texas itch, commonly called scab. The disease came with the thousands of longhorn cattle that were brought from Texas. Ranchers across western South Dakota from the Missouri River to the Black Hills built dipping tanks.

42

A group of ranchers decided that Midland needed a dipping tank. In August a teamster with a four horse team hauled a load of lumber from Ft. Pierre to build the pens. Leaving the team standing in front of J.C. Russell's Store, he went inside. The team spooked and ran away. They tore down the street, scattering lumber with every jump. Dust flew and men jumped out of their way. Roy Bean galloped up and stopped the frenzied horses just as they were turning to avoid the fence east of The Hotel. The team wasn't injured, but lumber was scattered for half a mile.

The lumber was gathered up and hauled to Jack Daly Creek two miles west of town near the junction of Jack Daly and Bad River. The dipping tank, holding and sorting pens were built on the wide flat west of Jack Daly. Walt Steien built the Booth Hotel on the bank of the creek to house the men who worked at the dipping tank.

CHAPTER 4
Homestead on Bad River

Creeks and rivers ran high several times that fall. Mail from Ft. Pierre to Midland was two days late because Bad River was too high to cross. A large number of Indians were forced to put up their teepees and wait for the rampaging water to go down.

When the autumn leaves were turning to orange and yellow the time had come to cut the tall corn and bring the shocks to the barnyard. George Gunderson and John Snow thought they could rig a corn cutter on an automobile and cut the corn faster and easier than with horses. The contraption was suspended in space like an aerial hammock. With John driving and George in the back to run the cutter, they headed into the corn field. The car roared down the row in low gear, but the cutter didn't work. They had to abandon their splendid machine and hitch up the trusty team.

A heavy yield of potatoes was also being harvested. A new bridge had been built across Plum Creek at the Stalley and Paige ranch about forty miles northwest of Midland. Civilization was on the way.

The paper said a farmer sent this note to a local merchant: "Send me a sack of flour, five pounds of coffee and one pound of tea. My wife gave birth to a big boy last night, also five pounds of corn starch, one screw driver and a fly trap. It weighed ten pounds and a new straw hat."

Upriver from Midland, Scotty Philip, the man who saved the buffalo, had one hundred and sixty buffalos in his pasture near Nowlin.

Cattle were still coming to the dipping tanks in great herds, "a sea of cattle," and the round-up wagons were being readied for the fall round-up. Albert Bertelson rode out with the W-M wagon again. Road ranches were doing a big business with all the freighters, homesteaders, ranchers, speculators and people seeking new locations for businesses and professions, flooding the country.

Walt Steien was busier than a beaver with a major leak in his dam. Stewart Hall was torn down, the lumber used to build a new dance hall in Midland. By December Walt had finished a house for J.D. Addison on Brave Bull Creek and was rushing to work on the new Town Hall across the street and east of Russell's store. Walt took time out during the building to haul a load of Christmas goods from Pierre for J.C. Russell's Store, then headed out to J. Stipes to build a barn. Many homesteaders were going home for the winter, having spent the required six months on their claims.

Albert had been watching a choice homestead on Bad River two miles east of Midland. The claim, belonging to Edward Heide, had a one room log cabin on the east bank of the river. Heide had been gone since summer. He was last seen at Ft. Pierre attending court. He then went east with a shipment of horses and disappeared. The presumption was that he had been killed in some accident, perhaps a train wreck. Heide's cattle, machinery and other property were sold by Sheriff's Sale on December 10, 1904. Some cattle only brought $16.50 per head on mortgage sale, but Walt Tygerson had received $49.50 per head on a carload of cattle in Chicago. Heide's property went to pay his mortgage. The land was there, ripe for the picking.

45

Albert went to Ft. Pierre and contested the Heide claim. On March 6, 1905, he went before the County Judge in Ft. Pierre and took over the claim. Edward was hauling hay for Hauge and Nelson during January of 1905.

Crews were sawing chunks of ice and loading the blocks on wagons to be hauled to the ice houses. February turned bitterly cold. Two inches of snow covered the ground. The temperature dropped to 38 degrees below zero. A young lad herding sheep for Charles Shaft over on Dry Creek bet he could run five hundred yards barefoot. The temperature stood at 38 degrees below. He took off his shoes and socks and sped across the snow covered prairie. The lad won his bet, but he was laid up with severely frozen feet. Perhaps he was tired of herding sheep in that frigid weather and wanted to sit by the fire.

A storm roared in with more snow, blowing it into the draws, which made good grazing for livestock. By February 24, a foot of water ran over the ice in Bad River. By March the river was running high. Everybody was ready for spring.

Homesteaders were in fields and gardens, plowing the soil in April. Occasionally someone reported a team running away with the plow dragging, and the homesteader yelling some choice words as he ran after the horses.

Albert had time to do some work on his homestead before the spring round-up started. Albert and Edward had persuaded their mother to come to South Dakota and look at a homestead up for relinquishment. They looked forward to her visit in the summer.

The spring of 1905 heralded a wet summer. Field work came to a halt when a warm rain began to fall May 2. Rain fell for two days. Draws and rivers ran full from north of the Cheyenne River to south of Bad River. On the afternoon of May 4, the wind

46

switched to the northwest. Rain turned to snow, huge wet flakes that fell like feathers from a broken pillow. Snow fell until the night of the fifth, dumping twelve inches on the already soaked prairie. The wind changed to the northwest, bringing one of the most disastrous blizzards in western South Dakota history, the Blizzard of May 4 and 5, 1905.

The wind howled out of the northwest, driving wet snow in a blind fury. Range cattle and horses caught out in the storm drifted with the screaming wind and snow. There were no fences to stop the drifting livestock. Wet snow clung to the noses and eyes of cattle so they had trouble breathing and couldn't see. The shrieking blizzard drove them into draws, creeks and rivers where thousands perished. Thousands of cattle drifted over the Badlands wall and crashed to their deaths many feet below. Cattle from behind pushed those in front over the wall, then staggered after them, blinded by the ice and snow that covered their eyes.

One herd of long horns had been recently shipped to South Dakota from Texas. The herd was held on a large flat where Wall, South Dakota now stands. Cowboys tried to keep the cattle bunched, but the force of the wind and snow drove the longhorns over the wall. A young cowboy was caught in the press and went over with them. After the storm subsided, Leo Barry, a young cowboy later married to Aunt Essie's stepmother, rode down with several other cowboys to look for him. The cowboy and his horse were buried in the mass of cattle. His body was never found.

The loss of horses was also enormous. Many homesteaders had turned their horses and cattle out of barns and corrals to feed on the range. These animals had shed their heavy winter hair. Shed livestock losses were extreme.

Then the weather turned warm. The snow melted, cascading into draws and creeks. By Sunday afternoon May 7, Bad

River was half a mile wide. Mitchell Creek carried a load of water nearly half a mile across in places. People coming from the east reported seeing fifty dead horses between the Mathieson ranch east of town and Midland. Over four thousand cattle perished along the upper Bad River. Some ranchers lost nearly their entire herd.

Every draw, creek and river gave up its dead livestock. The smell of decaying carcasses rode on every breeze. If the wind blew the odor toward shacks or houses, the smell was overpowering. The stench from the thousands of decaying cattle and horses was almost unbearable. Those cattle and horses left their bones for the bone gatherers. Bones were about all some farmers had left. They picked up wagon loads of bones and hauled them to railroad towns to sell.

The thaw brought green grass and flowers. Bluebells, white star flowers and yellow violets added their exquisite beauty to the green grass of spring as far as the eye could see.

Walt Steien had been supervising the building at the Graham ranch on Brave Bull Creek before the blizzard roared in. When Bad River went down some, he decided to finish his carpentering. He took the box off his wagon, tied a long rope to his buggy and hitched his horses to the wagon box. He climbed into the box, drove into the river and floated across with the long rope trailing. He unhitched his team from the wagon box, tied onto his buggy rope and clucked to the horses. The team pulled the buggy into the water. The current caught the buggy, jerking it downstream. The rope broke. Walt grabbed his lariat and ran along the riverbank, dodging trees while trying to rope his buggy. The water swiftly carried the buggy away. He couldn't catch the bobbing thing.

Editor Gueffrey said, "that old reeling buggy that has been an eye sore and a menace to the fairer sex is on its way to the great southern gulf." While his buggy floated toward "the great southern gulf," Walt went to the Graham ranch and finished his work there.

By June Albert Bertelson was riding for the Tom Jones W-M wagon as they worked the mouth of Brave Bull Creek. W-M territory reached from Philip to Wendt on both sides of Bad River, a distance of some fifty miles. By the middle of June, cowboys held over three thousand cattle at Jack Daly draw, waiting for dipping.

For meat to feed his crew, Tom bought stock from the herds they trailed in, paying the critter's owner $10.00 for a calf, $17.00 for a yearling and $19.00 for a two year old. The animals were butchered on the prairie.

Tom went into Midland, looking for overalls big enough for his cook and told about killing a large wolf on the round-up. Cattle dipping was in full swing. Foreman J.D. Snow and the dipping crew drove a thousand to fifteen hundred head through the tank every day. The cowboys looked forward to the 4th of July celebration in Midland as they kept the restless cattle from mixing with other herds.

The Midland 4th of July ad in the paper read: "Come to Midland for the 4th. If you expect to get drunk and fight, stay home."

A small town had sprung up at Jack Daly draw composed of cowboys, cooks, waitresses and people who dropped by to look and to listen to the bedlam of bawling cattle and shouting men. A couple of real estate agents drove around the country in a new Cadillac, scaring horses half out of their wits.

The rains kept coming. A June rain brought Bad River up twelve feet in fifteen minutes. On Saturday evening, July, 2, 1905, the sky clouded and rain began falling steadily through the night.

Sunday morning the clouds grew darker and thicker, hanging near-ly to the ground. Rain poured all day.

In the afternoon, Bad River began to rise at an alarming rate. People began moving possessions that might be swept away in a flood. Livestock was cut loose to find shelter on the hillsides. By eight P.M., Bad River was bank full and rising a foot an hour.

Brave Bull Creek rolled out of its banks toward Bad River. Water ran a foot deep through the Tom Jones house, forcing Mrs. Jones, three small children and the hired man to seek refuge in an old pole shack on higher ground.

The water swept away corrals, stables, wagons, harness, everything in its path except the two room log house. The house stayed while water two feet deep coursed through.

J.D. Addison, farther up Brave Bull, lost his stables, sheds, corrals, wagons, buggies, saddles and harness. His possessions floated down the creek past the Jones ranch. Fortunately, his new house, built on higher ground, stayed.

The roaring flood waters gathered homestead shacks, chicken houses, barns, whatever rocked loose went with the water. George Nitcy had livestock including a splendid stallion tied in his barn when the flood swept down the river. Deep water ran through the barn, threatening to drown his animals. Nitcy's hired man tied a rope around his body. With George holding the rope, he waded into the barn and brought the animals to safety.

Arthur Austin, a young man who homesteaded about three miles north of the dipping tank, was on the dipping crew. He watched the flood rolling down the Jack Daly valley and worried about what was happening on his claim. He decided to ride across Jack Daly Creek, now half a mile wide, swift and dangerous, and go home. The other men warned him not to attempt a crossing.

The wide flat was a sea from break to break, but Arthur

was determined to go. He mounted his horse and headed up the draw. Alphonse Koob, his neighbor, rode with him. A mile upstream, Arthur decided to cross. "I wouldn't go in that water, Arthur," Alphonse said. "It's too deep."

"I'll make it." Arthur plunged his horse into the water. The current caught the animal, jerking him around. The saddle turned. Arthur sprawled into the treacherous water. He caught a small willow waving in the water and yelled, "Help!"

Before help could reach him, the willow broke. He was carried downstream. Koob saw him surface once about twenty feet from the willow, then he disappeared beneath the muddy water. After a day long search, Arthur Austin's body was found about a mile downstream, not quite back to the dipping tank.

While the men were trying to dry their clothes at the Booth Hotel, Frank Linder rode up. The cook stepped outside to throw coffee grounds away and yelped. He was standing in water. Bad River was over the flats, too.

The dipping tank crew and the women who worked in the hotel gathered blankets and a piece of canvas and headed for the hills to the northwest. They spent the night huddled, shivering in the cold rain.

The flood waters ran over the dipping tank and swirled around the Booth Hotel, tearing the building loose and floating it three hundred yards southeast. The hotel came to rest almost over the embankment into the Bad River flood plain.

A mile upriver, M.A. Linder reported the water ran four and a half feet deep through the kitchen. He and his mother carried most of the furniture upstairs. The house held.

By Monday morning July 3, Bad River raged across the flats, running six to eight feet deep over corn fields, and lowland gardens. J.C. Russell lost sixty acres of "as fine a crops as were ever seen anywhere in the country." The rushing water swept Jim Snow's new "mansion" in east Midland along in its path, but the family escaped to higher ground.

Albert and Perry Rifenberg, Fred Trumbo and Ed Cook were caught in the Rifenberg brothers' house on Bad River when rising water surrounded the house. The men saddled their horses and anxiously watched the river rise until water ran three feet deep through the house. Afraid to wait longer, they mounted and headed for higher ground a half mile across the tumbling water.

The strong current caught the horses and swept them down stream. The force of the water knocked Albert Rifenberg from his horse. He grabbed the struggling animal's tail and hung on. The horse swam past a tree with only the swaying top above water. Albert grabbed a branch and pulled himself into the tree where he spent a terrifying day and night. By Tuesday afternoon, the water had gone down enough so he could wade to an island where Trumbo's horse was marooned. He rode out of the flood area and went to the W-M wagon for help. Perry Rifenberg, Fred Trumbo and Ed Cook all drowned.

A mile west of Midland, Mrs. Jim Nelson and four children were marooned in the house, surrounded by the rampaging water of Brave Bull Creek. Bad River and Jack Daly added their water. Nelsons spent several harrowing days, waiting for the water to recede.

Uncle Jake and his family went to bed Sunday night and woke up floating down White Clay Creek. Jake felt the house moving and rushed to a window to look outside. The house was bobbing down the creek toward Bad River eight miles north.

Amalia and the girls jumped out of bed and came to look. They watched the flood from an upstairs window as huge trees, chicken house, sheds and dead animals were carried along on the flood.

The house hit the rushing waters of Bad River, shot into the fierce current and whirled around, heading east toward the Missouri River fifty miles away. Water flowed into the downstairs. Praying for help, Jake and Amalia watched as the house sank lower and lower.

"What will we do?" Amalia asked. The frightened children pressed close to their parents.

"Get on the roof," Jake said. "The water'll come in here next."

"How can we get on the roof?" Amalia looked at the roiling water and the roof edge above her head. She shivered.

Jake shoved the window up. "Climb on the windowsill. I'll boost you on the roof."

Amalia climbed onto the slippery window sill while he steadied her against the movement of the house. She grasped the roof edge. He pushed. She scrambled out the window and climbed onto the peak. Perching on the gable, she reached down to help as Jake boosted the girls, then climbed up and joined them. Straddling the roof like they were riding a giant horse, they floated down the river as the house continued to sink.

When the house floated past Wendt, they saw people on the shore. They yelled and waved. Someone on shore saw them perched like a row of chickens on the ridge of the house. The house had settled so far into the water that only the roof was still above the muddy water. Men launched a boat and rowed to the house. Jake handed his children and wife to safety and climbed aboard himself. The men rowed toward shore. With a final gurgle, the house was sucked beneath the churning water.

The mighty flood rolled on towards the Missouri River. The flood waters roared into Ft. Pierre, catching people at their breakfast tables. Water poured through their houses. Terrified families climbed to the roofs of their houses and looked across the vast sea. Water rose, shaking small houses, breaking them from their foundations, sending them along in the flood. Larger houses gave way to sweep along on the current. The entire city of Ft. Pierre was under water.

Down the valley over the already ruined district, a mighty wave came, roaring and crashing. A floating house struck the new $4000.00 steel bridge spanning Bad River. The bridge groaned and tore loose to sink below the turbulent water.

Rescue boats plucked people from roofs and tree tops. Ft. Pierre south of Bad River was carried away. Water flooded Main Street, filling the basements of stores and other businesses with water. Ft. Pierre was fortunate. Only one drowning was reported while upstream two women homesteaders drowned.

The flood waters receded. People began to rebuild. Uncle Jake took his family back to the homestead and built a four room log house on higher ground.

Clara and Nora Hauge, the little girls that went down Bad River on their house in the 1905 flood.

Lena Hove's claim shack near Van Metre. Gathering includes the Jake Hauge family, the Peterson family and the Harmon children. Lena Hove and the Harmon children were Dina Bertelson's cousins.

CHAPTER 5
Another Homestead on Bad River

Dipping was resumed three days after the flood. Cowboys drove cattle through the muck into the corrals and holding pens. Cattle again came to the dipping tank in large herds. Dipping was finished in August after around thirty thousand head had dunked in the tank and gone back to the range.

The flatland was dotted with ponds. Every slough and lake bed was full of water. Thousands of ducks hatched during the wet season and swam on the ponds. By the first of August, ranchers and homesteaders were putting up the abundant hay crop. Walt Steien was building an addition on the Jarman brothers home in Nowlin.

Due to the flood, Midland postponed the July 4th celebration until August. A large crowd came for the dance, baseball game and fireworks. Midland's baseball team was ready to play all comers. Ottumwa's new team was eager to take on Midland and Hayes.

The W-M wagon finished the season August 1 and disbanded. Albert went to work for a freight outfit hauling out of Ft. Pierre. His twelve-year-old cousin Nestor Nelson drove one of the wagons. They left Ft. Pierre with loads of livestock feed billed to Midland. As Nestor climbed aboard his wagon, Albert said, "Your seat is too far forward, Nestor. If something happens, you'll pitch over the wagon and get run over. Better move it back." Nestor moved the seat back and sat down. The freight wagons lumbered down the muddy street. Nestor's team bogged down in front of The Rowe Hardware Store. Another teamster unhooked his team, hitched to the front of Nestor's outfit and pulled him out of the mud hole.

Albert said, "The creeks and draws are running, and some are boggy, Nestor. You have to hit them hard and fast, or you'll get stuck again. Whip up your team, and you'll go right through." Young Nestor popped the lines against the backs of his team and hit the mud holes with speed that showered team, wagon and boy with mud and water, but he didn't get stuck again.

The freighting trail went through Ottumwa and then southeast to Midland. Nestor was a proud boy when he drove into Midland with his muddy wagon and load of shorts.

The summer of 1905, Juliana Bertelson took the train to Draper. She went to Jake Hauge's homestead and on to Midland. Albert and Edward were happy to see her. Albert showed her the homestead they had told her about. She bought the relinquishment. Her homestead joined Albert's homestead, running across Bad River in a southeasterly direction. A one room log cabin stood on a small flat not far from a high river bank, a location safe from floods.

Albert and Juliana went back to Lake Mills to sell the farm and get ready for an auction in the spring. They kept horses, cattle, poultry, hogs, enough livestock for the new farm, furniture, and machinery. Edward came home for one last visit during the winter but returned to South Dakota in April of 1906, again to work for Olaf Hauge. Albert and Julianna sold the farm to Tom Johnson, and after the auction, Albert returned to South Dakota.

He learned that vandals had broken all the windows out of the Booth Hotel at the dipping tank and damaged furniture and other property. The town was growing in ways that were negative as well as positive. J.C. Russell's new $15,000.00 store building stood tall and proud two stories high and advertised everything to eat, wear and use. The building was to stand for the next sixty years. Midland had been staked for a town site. The town boasted lumber yards, four stores, the promise of a telephone line, and the railroad track was coming closer every day.

Midland had two new saloons. Johnson and Nabours built one; Gordon and Bradshaw the other. Midland had a spanking new steel span bridge across Bad River. Walt Steien had built a new house on the Tom Jones ranch on Brave Bull and was building one on Mitchell Creek for Horace Howes a mile down the creek from his homestead.

A spring blizzard in March had dumped snow across the prairie. The snow melted quickly and rivers and streams ran bank full. Grass was coming green. Wind upset some homestead cabins, during a rainstorm.

Albert rode out with the W-M wagon. Albert and Edward were happy that soon their mother, Alvin and Dina would come to South Dakota. They would all be together again.

Sheep dipping was in full swing. In July under a scorching sun, Edward was hauling water to the dipping tank at Hauges. He stopped the team by the fence and watched sheep splash into the water, disappear, then surface blowing and sneezing. They clambered out the other end of the tank, dripping wet, but minus the ticks. Edward didn't feel good. He had a cold and a touch of the grip.

"I'm sick," he told Olaf. "I'm going to the house." He climbed down from the wagon and went to the dugout house where he sank down on the bed. By Sunday afternoon, Edward was worse. Olaf sent someone to get a doctor. Edward Bertelson died of pneumonia Monday afternoon, July 16. He was twenty-five years old.

Olaf Hauge told Edward's mother, "Edward was fully aware of his impending death. He was up on Sunday but then he got worse."

The tall laughing young man with the shock of dark hair and the merry brown eyes who loved to tease the girls, dance, play his violin and fight with anyone who cared to test his mettle was gone.

Albert and Olaf loaded Edward's body in a wagon, hauled it to Murdo some fifty miles southeast and boarded the train for Lake Mills, Iowa. Edward was laid to rest in a Lake Mills cemetery beside his father.

Lars Hauge and family from Lake Mills had been visiting the Jake Hauge family. Both families caught the train at Pierre to go back to Iowa for Edward's funeral. Lars was the auditor of Winnebago County and had a real estate office, dealing in farms, farm loans and city properties.

Amanda told a strange story about her brother's death. She and Dina were upstairs. Amanda looked toward the doorway and saw Edward on the stairs. Startled she said, "Why, Edward!" The next moment he was gone. Later they received the telegram about his death. Many years later, an old man in Keister, Minnesota, who had been Edward's undertaker, claimed he removed a bullet from Edward Bertelson's back. If so, Albert must not have wanted his mother and sisters to know what really happened to Edward.

After the funeral, Dina boarded the train in Lake Mills with her Uncle Jake, Aunt Amalia, Alma, Nora, Olga and Clara. Dina was twelve years old. She was excited about going to this new country that she had heard so much about from her brothers.

The train rumbled over the tracks, clicking off the miles. The girls watched out the windows as the velvet green pastures and peaceful milk cows, the corn fields and tree surrounded farm-steads of Iowa faded into the distance. They slept and awoke to look out at the rugged hills and wide open prairies of South Dakota, a wild unfenced land where herds of horses and long horned cattle grazed, antelope raced over the prairie and coyotes made their dens. They disembarked at Pierre and boarded Olson Brothers' ferry to cross the Missouri River, the widest river Dina had ever seen.

At Ft. Pierre Jake got the team and buggy he had left at a livery stable, and they headed for the homestead. The team trotted across the prairie with Uncle Jake, Aunt Amalia and little Nora on the front seat, the girls on the back seat. Several hours later, the team splashed across a creek. Jake stopped the team. "We'll fill our drinking water can here," Jake said, jerking the cover off the can.

"You aren't going to drink that muddy water after driving the team through it, are you?" Dina was horrified. She was used to drinking clear, cold water from an Iowa well. She didn't want to drink water that horses had walked in.

Uncle Jake laughed. "Yah, we are. All the water we have to drink comes from creeks and rivers. The mud will settle. We have to drink it. You will, too."

"Yah," Alma said. "We drink out of the creeks in the sum-mer, and we drink snow water in the winter." Dina made a face, but she learned to drink when she had a chance, mud or not. Wells were scarce and the water often too alkali to drink.

Dina and the Hauge girls were happy to get home. The girls showed Dina around the farm. She met Uncle Jake's hired man, a German lad named Hans. Hans called Dina, "Dinah" and teased her, saying, "You got a darkie name." Shy Dina was embar-rassed that he didn't pronounce her name correctly. Hans owned two spirited saddle horses. Since Dina didn't have a horse, he said she could ride his horses. Dina loved to gallop over the prairie and feel the wind in her face.

"Can I ride one of your horses, Hans." Alma asked.

Hans grinned and shook his head. "No, you ride your father's horses."

By September Grandma Juliana was ready to move to South Dakota. Albert had bought more cows to go with her herd of good milk cows. They loaded cattle, horses, red sows, harness, furniture, machinery and household goods into immigrant cars on the Milwaukee Road. Juliana, Amanda and Alvin boarded the train and rode to Draper.

Grandma Juliana felt sadness at leaving her lovely home, her prosperous Iowa farm and her many friends and relatives, but her sons wanted to try a new land where coyotes howled and the wild wind blew. Where her children were, she would be also. Amanda was leaving the heartbreak of Iowa for a new country. Perhaps she was glad. God was leading them to a new and greater adventure.

They unloaded the cars and took everything to Uncle Jake's farm. The Hauge family moved into two rooms of the log house so Juliana and her family could use the other two rooms. Charley went to Oregon to look for land, and Tina came to stay with them.

The Bertelson family stayed the first winter with the Hauge family. Dina went to school with the Hauge girls in a small log schoolhouse. They could buy groceries and get mail at Koll's Store two miles south of the farm.

When spring came, Albert and Alvin drove the cattle overland to the homesteads. Dina watched them ride away, wishing she was going along, but she had to finish school. The railroad had arrived in Midland in December, so Juliana, Tina and Amanda rode the train. One frosty spring day, Uncle Jake sent Dina to bring some horses from the pasture. Scattered patches of snow dotted the hills and the north slopes were icy. Dina galloped the horse around a hill and saw the horses. Her horse nickered. The other horses raised their heads, then nickered and flashed away. Dina's horse grabbed the bit in his teeth and raced after them. She couldn't hold him. He hit a patch of ice and went down. Dina flew over his head. Her face cracked against the ground. She got up with her nose bleeding. A short distance away, her horse waited. She mounted and rode home, blood running down her face and the front of her coat. She left the horse at the corral and went to the house.

"For goodness sakes, Dina, what happened?" Aunt Amalia asked.

Dina shook her head. "I don't know. I rode around the hill, looking for the horses. When they saw me, they ran. My horse ran after them, and I couldn't stop him. He fell, and I don't remember anything else." Aunt Amalia helped Dina out of her blood spattered coat and washed her face.

"I'm dizzy. I don't feel good," Dina said. "Can I go to bed?"

"No, no, you mustn't go to sleep, Dina," Uncle Jake said. "You have to walk around. I'm afraid you have a concussion. If you go to sleep, you might not wake up again." They kept her walking around, but all she wanted to do was lie down and sleep. Albert came. He looked at Dina and said, "Let her go to sleep." She was all right when she awoke.

In March a blizzard blew across the prairie, dumping piles of snow. Some people gave up on the country and left. Homestead relinquishments were advertised for $100.00.

The first passenger car had arrived in Midland April 7, 1907, disgorging one hundred and twenty-three passengers. The first through passenger train to Rapid City went through Midland

August 15, 1907, linking the west to markets and towns east of the Missouri River. Dina was happy when school let out in May, and Amanda came to Van Metre on the train to get her. The train was due in Midland at 2 PM.

Dina could hardly wait to see her new home, even though it was only a one room log cabin on the banks of Bad River. The steam engine tooted a long whistle, and the train rattled past East Midland and pulled up at the depot, steam belching from the engine. Amanda and Dina walked out with the crowd of people jostling each other to leave the car. Behind the passenger cars, immigrant cars waited to be unloaded. The horse drawn Cole and Bailey dray wagon rumbled down the street to take freight from the train.

Dina and Amanda stepped down from the train and headed uptown on the boardwalk. They passed the new two story Town Hall built by Walt Steien. A fine hall for dances, plays and meetings was upstairs. Ralph Hanson had a store downstairs. Dina and Amanda turned and continued up the boardwalk built by Al Nabours from his saloon to the depot. The first three signs Dina saw on Main Street advertised saloons. She turned to Amanda in amazement. "Midland is all saloons." Amanda laughed and pointed out the many business places on both sides of the street. Midland was growing rapidly with thirty-seven substantial businesses.

The thirty-three room Bastion Hotel and Hellekson's General Store were on the south side of the tracks. Both were later moved to the north side. A two story hotel stood on the south side of Main. Midland had two barber shops, a butcher shop, several livery barns, the Bank of Midland, three lumber yards, Russell's General Store and The Western Star newspaper.

Three restaurants offered a good meal for twenty-five

cents. Hotel rooms were $1.00 per night, but one might have to share a bed with strangers. Julia Talledge came to town on the first passenger car in April and shared a bed with a woman and child. Fourteen women and children slept in the room, some on the floor. Dan Bastion shuttled people between his hotel and the depot in a three seated buggy.

Dina and Amanda walked down the boardwalk to Russell's Store. The Grindstone Bulletin called Midland, "the muddiest place on the globe," so the boardwalk was welcome. The slur angered Editor Gueffrey. He wrote, "Midland is the busiest place between Pierre and Rapid City." (Grindstone was a tiny settlement some forty miles northwest of Midland.)

Amanda told Dina about the fire in March that destroyed several business places. Signs of the damage remained. The fire started in the second story of the Schrader and Knoer Hardware Store on the south side of Main, supposedly from a gasoline lamp. Fire ranged from building to building while men formed a bucket brigade to bring water from across the street. J.C. Russell manned the pump. Buckets passed from man to man past about three hundred men. The last man threw the water that hadn't splashed out on the fire. The fire was getting away from them, so men lifted several small buildings and turned them away from the fire, among them Snow's Confectionary Store. Most of the buildings burned, but Midland still had candy.

In the seventeen years since J.C. Russell opened his small trading post on the flat where Mitchell Creek joins Bad River, Midland had grown to a lively trading center. Midland drew trade from seventy-miles away. Like spokes in a wagon wheel, seven roads led to Midland.

Scattered across the prairie were stores started by enterprising homesteaders; stores that became neighborhood gathering places with a post office and town hall. Some grew into towns.

Ottumwa, fifteen miles up Mitchell Creek, had been a stage and freight station and a roadhouse on the trail between Ft. Pierre and The Black Hills. Many of these towns were to grow until they had stores, banks, hotels, and blacksmith shops before they faded into only a memory in the minds of people who lived during that exciting time.

Albert came with a buggy to take Dina and Amanda home. Some of the round-up wagons were moving out. Walt Steien had hired out to the Tom Jones's wagon to move cattle for Mike Dunn who ran great herds in the territory before the homesteaders came.

Grandma Juliana Bertelson in front of her house on the Iowa Farm. The horse is wearing a sidesaddle.

Edward Bertelson

CHAPTER 6
The Homestead Becomes Home

Dina was bursting with excitement as the team trotted south out of town. They crossed Bad River on Midland's new $3,650.00 steel span bridge. The river had roared past twenty-two feet deep the first part of May and was still flowing fast. The trail angled southwest for a mile and a half across the Bad River valley. They passed the Jim Nelson home, splashed across Brave Bull Creek and headed across a large prairie dog town. Dina laughed at the prairie dogs scurrying for their dens and diving inside. The little animals popped back out to bark in indignation at the people crossing through their domain.

Albert stopped the team beside Juliana's log cabin. Dina ran inside to hug her mother. Albert's cabin was across the river a half a mile northwest. The flood of 1905 ran through his cabin several feet deep. There Bad River made a bend and ran south, enclosing a broad meadow on the level below the cabin. Spreading cottonwood and elm trees dotted the meadow. Ash trees grew along the river. Beaver built their dens in the banks and dammed the river with sticks and mud.

A small flat surrounded Grandma Juliana's house with the Bad River breaks rising to the south. No trees grew on this high plateau. At the age of fifty-two, Grandma Juliana began a new life far from the fjords of Norway and far different from the green fields of Iowa. This vast land of prairie and grass was rapidly fill-

65

ing with homesteaders. Once again she was in South Dakota. This time there would be no going back to Iowa except to visit. She was thankful for the railroad that would carry her swiftly back to visit relatives and friends.

Some of her cousins homesteaded near Midland, too. Jim Nelson and family were about a mile down river. She had Hauge and Hove relatives on homesteads in her brother Jake's locality. Her niece Alphia Hauge, daughter of Lars, homesteaded near Van Metre.

Juliana and the girls slept in her cabin, and Albert and Alvin in Albert's cabin while they waited for Juliana's house to be enlarged. During those first years, Grandma Juliana must have thought often of her pleasant roomy house in Iowa with the broad expanse of green lawn and the sheltering oak trees. When the hot summer winds sizzled across the prairie, and heat waves shimmered and danced along the horizon, she must have wished for a drink of cold water from her Iowa well. Water here came from Bad River, water so muddy at times that it had to set for a day or more to settle the silt dirt.

Sometimes in winter, the wind howled across the prairie. Driving snow filled the air like a white wall. Sometimes temperatures plummeted to the bottom of thermometers, going to twenty to forty degrees below zero like in the winter of 1904 when the foolish young man ran barefoot through the snow and froze his feet.

South Dakota was where her children were so South Dakota was where she would live. All of her children were with her except Edward who slept in a Lake Mills cemetery. The pain still tore at her heart.

To Alvin and Dina moving west was the start of a great adventure on the wild frontier. They heard about Frank Linder shot by a transient gambler named Harry Brooks. Brooks and Linder got into an argument at a drinking and gambling party. Around midnight Frank mounted his horse to go home. As he rode down the street, a shot flashed out of the dark. The bullet passed through his arm above his elvow and severed a major artery. He rode to Pat Gallagher's house and yelled, "I'm shot."

Gallagher came to the door, saw Frank and said, "You're shot in the belly with a bottle of whiskey." He slammed the door and went back to bed.

Frank Linder had a habit of saying, "I'm shot," when he drank too much whiskey. This time his play on words cost him. He fell from the horse and bled to death in front of Gallagher's house.

A $200.00 reward was offered for his killer. Harry Brooks was arrested and confessed. Johnny Snow was put in charge of him until the sheriff would arrive. Snow put Harry Brooks on his honor to stay around until the sheriff came. Being a prudent man, Brooks mounted his horse and high-tailed it out of the country.

Mrs. Linder and her sons Alfred and August had home-steaded a mile upriver from the Bertelson homesteads. August operated the Eagle Restaurant in Midland. Dina and Alvin laughed at Albert's story of Alfred Linder and the coyote. Alfred trapped a coyote the winter of 1905. He killed the animal, slung the beast over his shoulder and headed home. The coyote came suddenly to life and bit Alfred in the leg. Alfred howled and dropped the coy-ote. The coyote streaked for the hills. Leo Hollis raced past Alfred on horseback, lariat whirling. He roped the coyote, and that was the end of that varmint.

For Amanda, Midland offered a chance to start a new life and forget Jack, the Irish lad she had loved and given up. Tina waited for Charley to come home so they could start a new life either here or in faraway Oregon where she did not want to go. Albert was happy. His dream of building a cattle ranch was beginning, and his family was close by.

To Dina and Alvin, the valley of the Bad River was a delightful place. Birds sang as the sun burst over the horizon on a spring morning. Squirrels chattered from the trees. Coyotes howled from the hills. Dina and Alvin were fascinated with this new country where cowboys rode the range with six shooters on their belts. Walt Steien carried a forty-five revolver. Six guns were becoming unpopular with some people.

An item from Nowlin in "Olney's Occasions" column said, "We wish the Honorable Tom Jones would keep his reckless cowhands on his own creek where he can manage them, for they come over on the river with their big Colts (revolvers) and scare the river people in a shameful manner, even some of the ladies. The circle riders are the worst......." Albert was a circle rider.

Mail began to arrive by train in February of 1907, and Olney started a stage between Midland and Philip. The fare was $2.50. The stage was short lived because the railroad went all the way to Rapid City that summer.

Unlike many homesteaders, Bertelsons had money from the sale of their property in Iowa. They had milk cows, riding and driving horses, hogs, poultry and machinery. Albert and Alvin were ready to start farming as soon as they built a larger house, barns, corrals, hog houses and other outbuildings. The first thing Grandma Juliana wanted was a larger house so she could get her family under one roof. Albert hired the carpenter and contractor Walt Steien to build the addition.

The trees along the creeks rang with the sound of axes and saws and the crash of towering cottonwoods as Albert and Alvin felled trees and sawed them in lengths for the addition. They hitched a team to the logs and dragged them to their mother's house. Working from sunrise to sundown, they made ready for Walt.

Walt was a stocky young man of thirty-five. He told them he rode horseback from Pepein, Wisconsin to Lake Preston, South Dakota, stayed with an uncle for a time, then mounted his horse and headed west again. He came to Midland in 1898. In 1902 he rode with the Jones wagon on the last big cattle round-up of western South Dakota. The great herds were rounded up from the Missouri to the Black Hills and from the Cheyenne to the White, roughly one hundred miles by one hundred seventy miles.

The Bertelson family moved into Albert's cabin while Juliana's was being enlarged. The women slept in the cabin while the men bedded down outside. The small cabin was crowded at mealtime. As Walt worked to expand the Bertelson house, he found his eyes often turning toward the lovely Amanda. Editor Gueffrey put Walt on his list of admirable and eligible bachelors. Of these bachelors he wrote, "Every one of them is a gentlemen and those girls that can win a place in their hearts would indeed be lucky." It was soon clear that Amanda had won that place in Walt's heart. What she would do about it remained to be seen.

Dina and Alvin found Walt amusing. He had bow legs and bow arms and walked with a lumbering gait that made them laugh. When Walt rode a horse at a trot or gallop, his arms flapped like a crow flying leisurely toward a corn field.

Alvin and Dina laughed about the story of Leo Hollis breaking a horse for Walt. Leo taught the animal to buck if the rider flapped his arms. Walt climbed aboard his newly broke horse and loped off a hill above Mitchell Creek, his elbows bent and his arms flapping. The horse bowed his head and bucked. Walt sailed over his pony's head and lit on the ground.

Dina thought Walt looked like a big gorilla, rolling along elbows stuck out and arms bowed. She and Alvin would walk behind him, mimicking his every step, stopping instantly, if he looked their way.

Amanda didn't think Alvin and Dina were funny. She told them to quit mocking Walt and mind their own business. They couldn't understand why she got so upset, but they stopped imitating Walt.

Albert and Alvin helped Walt lay the logs to make another room on the cabin. They chinked the logs with cement. They hauled lumber from Midland to build an upstairs. By fall the house was finished with two bedrooms upstairs, a kitchen and a parlor downstairs. They moved the kitchen range, the round oak table with matching chairs, the dishes and utensils into the kitchen, and the house began to look like home. The round cottonwood chair that came from Norway was installed in the parlor. Juliana, Albert, Alvin, Amanda and Dina lived in the new house. Tina lived in Albert's cabin until Charley came back from Oregon that fall.

Walt was a frequent visitor as he courted Amanda. He told about finding a horse and mule that had strayed from Brown and O'Neill, railroad graders working on the roadbed as track was laid west of Midland. Walt collected a $50.00 reward, more money than was earned by a cowboy in a month. Some homesteaders walked to Midland, worked on the track until late fall, then walked home. Their families were left at home without a word from the men until they walked in the door months later.

Albert and Alvin cut ash posts and poles and built a large square corral and a small round corral with snubbing post in the center to tie up broncs. They built hog houses, a chicken house, corncribs and barn, using logs and lumber.

The Bertelson homestead was not a lonely place like some

70

of the early homesteads had been that were far out on the prairie miles from town or neighbors. Midland was two miles east, Nelson's a mile down the river, Linders a mile upriver. Mrs. Linder was some years older than Juliana, but they became dear friends. I remember Mrs. Linder as a lovely lady with hair like spun silver.

Up Brave Bull Creek was the Tom Jones ranch, the Charles Anderson homestead and the J.D. Addison ranch. Tar paper shacks or sod houses stood on nearly every quarter of land. Homesteaders sometimes fenced gardens or small corn fields, but the country was largely unfenced. Cattle of many colors roamed the prairie; long horns from Texas and dogies from Minnesota. Many an angry homesteader chased the range cattle and horses away from garden or field.

When evening came, cheery lights twinkled from every hillside. Most homestead shacks were cheaply made temporary housing, often papered with newspapers. The shacks were small enough so they were cozy with a fire going, but if the wind blew or the fire went out, the cabin got mighty cold. Sod houses were warm because the walls were from eighteen to thirty-six inches thick.

Alvin and Albert sawed firewood with a two man saw and hauled water from the river in a stone boat, a rough sled of planks with strap iron on the runners. The stone boat was used for hauling wood and posts, too, summer and winter. In addition, Alvin and Albert had cows to milk and hogs to feed. Chickens filled the chicken house and turkeys roosted on the corral. Ducks and geese swam on the river, sharing the water with beavers, fish and turtles. A large snapping turtle could make a meal of a baby duck. Sometimes a hapless duck limped back to the barnyard because a turtle had snapped off part of its foot.

Dina and Alvin liked to sit on the high river bank and

watch beavers swim up and down the river on a moonlit night. If they tossed a pebble into the water, a beaver tail slapped the water, and every beaver disappeared, but they couldn't stay inactive for long. Soon beaver heads poked above the surface again and the busy little animals went back to work.

"Man works from sun to sun, but woman's work is never done," was certainly true of pioneer women. They never lacked for something to do. Grandma Juliana made soap by melting tallow in a huge, three-legged iron pot setting on a bonfire. Water was leached through ashes and added to the tallow mixture. This boiled while Dina or Amanda stirred it with a big stick. They poured the yellow soap into wooden trays and cut it into bars.

Dina helped wash clothes. She scrubbed soiled clothing on a scrub board and dashed them with a funnel shaped dasher on the end of a handle. If Dina dashed the clothes long enough and hard enough, they got clean and she got muscles, tired muscles. Tina had a glass scrub board which was easier on the knuckles than the metal ones were.

Albert bought his mother a wooden wash machine which lightened the load. The agitator looked like a cow's bag with four teats hanging down into the water. A wringer was turned with a crank. No more wringing clothes by hand. The agitator was powered by a long handle on the side of the washer. Pushing the handle back and forth was Dina's job. After ten minutes of pushing the lever, clothes were clean and Dina was puffing. She rested while she turned the handle to wring the clothes. Alvin and Albert spelled Dina on the washer when they came in for dinner. I can see Alvin showing Dina how fast he could push the agitator handle until his mother said, "Alvin, you go to fast. You'll break the machine."

Men's clothes had grease spots rubbed with butter and

72

kerosene and were scrubbed on the washboard before going into the washer. The clothes hung on lines outside to dry, except in frigid weather when they hung on lines across the kitchen. A copper boiler sat on the range, boiling white clothes to make them whiter. Hot clothes were transferred from boiler to washer with an old broomstick. Nobody threw away old broom handles. Dresses, shirts, blouses, pillow cases, and dresser scarves were sprinkled, then placed in a basket to be ironed the next day.

Late fall was butchering time. Hogs were turned into hams, bacon, sausage and pork chops. Beef was butchered late enough so the quarters could be hung in a cold room to freeze for winter use. In spring left-over beef was canned. This was often a family project with Amanda, Tina, Dina, Alvin and Albert all pitching in. The meat was packed in jars and boiled for hours in the boiler on the kitchen range. Potatoes and canned goods were stored in a cave dug into a hillside. The wild fruit that grew in abundance along the creeks, river and draws was coveted as were the June berries that ripened on the high breaks. In late July, chokecherries hung in purple clusters from the bushes. Next came tart buffalo berries and plums.

Berry picking was fun. They came home with buckets and baskets of fruit and chigger bites that itched like crazy. Sometimes young people organized fruit gathering picnics and went out to gather wild fruit. Jars of delicious jams, jellies and sauces appeared on the shelves in the Bertelson storage cave.

If a woman sat down to rest, she could always pick up something that needed mending. Dina learned to darn a sock so it was as good as new and to patch Alvin's bib overalls or Albert's moleskin pants. Grandma Juliana still scrubbed her floors with sand every Saturday and Wednesday night to make them clean and white. None of her daughters continued this practice. None of them had lovely white floors either.

A cold April rain made gardens late, but by summer crops were lush. The cows had dropped calves. Litters of red piglets romped and squealed in their pens. Hens scuttled about, scratching in the dirt for worms and bugs to feed their chicks.

Bertelsons milked cows and sold cream. The skim milk went to the hogs and chickens. The chickens loved sour milk. The squealing, crowding pigs liked any kind of milk or slop.

C.D. Joy was buying butter and eggs in Midland. Setting eggs were advertised for .75 to .80 for thirteen eggs. Grandma Juliana sent her cream to Ft. Pierre on the train. Midland was growing, almost by the day. Doctor Chambers, a dentist, and Doctors Vincent and Edwards, medical doctors, had offices in town. Dr. Minard arrived and set up practice. There were lawyers, land agents and a new millinery shop where ladies could buy stylish hats.

Russell's Store had a sale on calico for seven cents a yard, so a lady could make a dress for about forty cents. Women made calico sunbonnets for themselves and their daughters. They wore long sleeves to keep their arms white. No tan would darken their hands or face, if they could help it.

Amanda and Albert Bertelson in front of Juliana Bertelson's house.

CHAPTER 7
Wedding Bells

Midland's 1907 Fourth of July Celebration drew over a thousand people. Buggies and wagons were parked wherever there was space for them. Patient horses tied to wagon boxes, munched hay and switched their tails at the flies that pestered them.

Dina and Amanda donned black riding skirts and white blouses and rode to town. They joined other riders in the colorful parade that reached from one end of Main Street to the other. The twelve piece Midland Cornet Band with all horns blowing led the parade. Next came twenty-two Sioux warriors in full dress--beaded fringed leather shirts, feathers and feathered headdresses.

The Midland Fire Department entry rattled along directly behind the Indians. It consisted of a wagon running gear with a short ladder on the reach. An old pail and a lantern hung on the back end. A horse and cow hitched together pulled the contraption. Somebody was spoofing the fire department which was actually a volunteer bucket brigade. After this came horseback riders and buggies and wagons decorated with red, white and blue bunting.

Dina and Amanda rode their horses around town to various events. In the afternoon, they sat their horses by Russell's Store, waiting for the horse races. The race course ran from Mitchell Creek up Main Street and ended on the flat west of Russell's Store, a distance of a little over half a mile.

A pistol shot rang out. The Men's Horse Race was on. The

horses tore up the road. Twelve-year-old Elmer "Swede" Anderson, blond hair streaming in the wind, led the field. His horse gained with every leap, speeding down Main Street and flashing across the finish line to win. Dina watched the Women's Horse Race and wished she had entered. "I'm going to ride in the Women's Horse Race next year," she said.

Amanda smiled. "I am, too."

They rode to the stock yards to watch the bronc rides. Since there were no bucking chutes, a rider led a wild bronc, snubbed tightly to his saddle horn, into an open space. Another man stood in a stirrup beside his horse, leaning across his saddle. He "eared the bronc down" by grabbing an ear and chewing on it. Oddly this distracted the horse so he stood like a statue to be saddled and mounted.

The bronc was turned loose, mad enough to blow smoke out his nostrils. He erupted into a squealing mound of horse flesh. The crowd cheered. The pickup men caught the bronc and brought him back to the yards when the ride was over. The show went on. The action was slow, but exciting.

July 6, a violent storm ripped through Midland and the surrounding countryside. Hurricane winds blew black clouds across the sky. Rain poured down. Hens scurried for shelter with their broods running behind them. Gathering their chicks into any shelter they could find, the hens spread their wings to save their young from the killing rain. Hail as big as hen eggs battered houses and beat gardens and fields into the muddy ground.

Hail tore through the rubberoid roofs that covered many houses in Midland and the tar paper covered shacks on homesteads. Julia Talledge sat on the cot in her claim shack a mile north of Midland with an umbrella over her head while rain streamed through the roof.

The hail battered forty-eight windows out of the Bastion Hotel and broke every window pane out of buildings on the south side of Main Street. Wind blew the front wall out of the post office. Water poured into buildings through windows and tattered roofs. A few days later, people were repairing their roofs with cedar shingles, supplied by Midland's four lumber yards. The hail ruined crops and pastures, but the moisture brought the grass back quickly.

Amanda homesteaded on a quarter of land that stretched east to Brave Bull Creek and south from her mother's land. She hired Walt Steien to build a shack on her land. She moved into her tiny house, and Walt came courting. He told her he couldn't even bake bread. He had baked a batch and the bread was so hard he couldn't cut it with a knife. "I took a loaf to the chopping block," he said. "I was getting ready to hack it to pieces with the axe when a lady rode by. She sure laughed at my bread." Walt began squiring Amanda to dances and socials.

The first part of November Amanda was thrown from a horse and seriously injured. They took her by train to St. Mary's Hospital in Pierre. She came home several weeks later, completely recovered and eager to live on her homestead again.

While Amanda was gone, Walt helped Dina get acquainted with some of the neighbors. They rode across Brave Bull Creek and visited Okie Morford on her claim southeast of the Bertelson place.

Homesteaders were still flocking into the country. Immigrant cars arrived daily from the east to discharge passengers and freight.

One Saturday the train pulled in from the east and stopped with the caboose on the bridge that crossed Mitchell Creek. Thinking the car was at the depot, Conductor Mellette stepped out of the caboose and fell twelve feet to the bottom of the dry creek bed. He landed among the rocks, breaking his jaw and causing other injuries. The engine was hitched to the caboose and took him back to Pierre to the hospital. The train sat on the siding and waited for the engine to return.

The railroad bridges were a temptation to people who wanted to cross Mitchell Creek or Bad River when they were running or even when they weren't. Dr. Vincent started across the Mitchell Creek bridge. He was halfway across when the train roared around the curve. Dr. Vincent was caught too far from either end to get off the bridge. He climbed down and hung by his hands off the edge of the trestle. The train thundered across the bridge. The bridge shook. Dr. Vincent held on for dear life, but the rumble shook him loose. He fell fifteen feet into the dry creek. The Western Star said he limped for a while.

Up near Nowlin, one of the Philip girls started across a railroad bridge when Bad River was running deep. Two hound pups tagged along. The train caught her in the middle of the bridge. Grabbing the pups, she climbed through the iron uprights onto a piling. Sitting on the piling, she clutched the pups in her arms. The river raged below them. The train thundered onto the bridge. The bridge vibrated like a plucked mandolin string. As the train rumbled across the bridge, she clung to the terrified pups. They chewed on her arms and struggled to get loose, but she didn't drop them. When the train had gone on its way, she stampeded off the bridge with blood running down her arms. The pups scampered beside her.

Dina and Alvin visited Rachel, Anna, Nestor, Oliver and Ingwal Nelson and got acquainted with Myrtle and Elmer "Swede" Anderson who lived up Brave Bull Creek. To Dina and Alvin, the prairie was a delight. They could ride for miles and never open a gate. They roamed the rugged hills and valleys and explored Bad River. They rode under the tree where a man had been hanged for doping a horse back in the 1890's.

Alec LaPlante, who lived east of Midland on Bad River, raised race horses. He built a race track and challenged all comers to a matched race against his fleet Quarter Horse stallion, the fastest horse in his stable. The horse's fame grew. A man from Minnesota accepted the challenge. He arrived at the LaPlante ranch with a fast Thoroughbred and a jockey to ride him. The horses danced at the starting line. The gun banged. The horses leaped into full gallop. The Quarter Horse took the lead and beat the Thoroughbred handily.

The man from Minnesota cried, "Unfair." The track was poor. His horse could win on a good track. He challenged LaPlante to a return match in Pierre on a decent track. LaPlante accepted. The horses were lined up on the Pierre track. Bets were laid. The crowd waited. The gun banged and the horses raced away. They thundered down the track. The Thoroughbred pulled ahead. He left the Quarter Horse behind. LaPlante had to pay.

He decided his horse ran a sluggish race because the other jockey had drugged the animal. The jockey was found some time later, hanging from the branch of a cottonwood tree on what was to become the Bertelson ranch. How he got there was a mystery, but people had their ideas about what had happened.

Walt pressed his suit with Amanda. They were married February 5, 1908 in Ft. Pierre. Now Dina and Alvin knew why Amanda got angry when they poked fun at Waldemar A. Steien whom she called Walter.

The Western Star said: "Walter Steien and Miss Bertelson were married in Pierre last night and went from there to Wisconsin on their wedding trip. They will return later and make their home on Mitchell Creek. The bride has resided in this community since last spring. She is a young lady of sterling worth, and during her residence here has made many friends. The groom has lived here about ten years and is regarded as an upright and industrious young man. Their many friends are offering congratulations in which The Star joins."

They boarded the train and traveled to Pepein, Wisconsin to visit Walt's family. A month later, Walt and Amanda returned from their honeymoon. They moved to Amanda's homestead to stay the required fourteen months. A homesteader could prove up in fourteen months instead of five years by paying a small amount of money.

Since Walt was half Swede, he took some good-natured kidding from Alvin and Albert for not being pure Norwegian. A little ditty went: "Ten thousand Swedes ran through the weeds pursued by one Norwegian."

Dina and Alvin watched for rattlesnakes wherever they went. Alvin could grab a rattler by the tail and snap the snake's head off. He said, "You have to catch the snake when he's crawling. Grab his tail with your hand coming back. Snap him forward. His head will pop right off." Dina didn't try that trick, but she wasn't afraid to pick up a bull snake. She found one crawling around upstairs. Her mother, Tina and Amanda were in the kitchen. Dina threw the snake down the stairs. It landed on the kitchen floor. She heard somebody scream. Laughing, she went downstairs and threw the snake outside.

Every paper carried stories about rattlesnakes seen and killed and occasionally biting someone. A rattlesnake bit a two-year-old girl. The doctor was in the middle of an operation and couldn't come. Prompt care by her parents saved her life.

Miss Harnsberger had a harrowing experience with snakes

80

when she came to her claim after an absence. Being tired, she went straight to bed. She awoke to find three rattlesnakes coiled on the floor, sticking their tongues out at her. She dodged the snakes and rushed outside. She grabbed a spade and killed the snakes. The next morning, a rattlesnake was coiled around a turpentine bottle at the head of her bed. She demolished the snake with the spade. That afternoon she discovered a fifth rattlesnake in her shack. That was too much. She went to a neighbor's to stay.

Tina was happy when Charley came back from Oregon and decided to stay in South Dakota. Charley found his homestead on land relinquished by earlier settlers, among them Walt Tygerson. Charley gave Tygerson $1.00 for a quit claim deed on forty acres. He bought a patent from the United States on a hundred and sixty acres for $80.00. His homestead was strung out in forty acre plots, a mile long and a quarter of a mile wide, a mile above Walt Steien's place. Tina and Amanda would be close neighbors. Charley's great-niece Sharon Englehaupt and her family live there now.

Charley and Tina chose their building spot on a beautiful meadow in a bend on the south side of Mitchell Creek. Charley could dig like a badger, and the second bench above the creek was an ideal place for a house and outbuildings. The slope was sharp and leveled quickly into a wide plateau reaching a quarter of a mile west to the hills. With spade and shovel, Charley attacked the slope. He dug into the east slope to make the house and went around the end to dig into a north slope for the outbuildings.

The farmstead was effectively protected from the howling northwesters of winter. He roofed the outbuildings with poles covered with earth, making dark, yet snug barns for livestock and poultry. The dugout for the house was walled with rocks gathered from the surrounding hills. The roof was rough lumber covered with tar paper and cedar shingles. Later they added a frame kitchen, living room and bedroom with tar paper on the outside. Vines climbed an open porch on the south. Two rows of tall holly-hocks with pink and red flowers grew on either side of the walk, making a lovely lane to the house.

In February of 1908, the railroad brought the first tractor to Midland for O'Farrell and Son's Store. The Hart-Par two cylinder machine burned either gasoline or kerosene and could pull a two bottom plow. O'Farrell and Son's unloaded and demonstrated this wonder machine. The Western Star said: "The Hart-Par had a cough like an old cow with a potato stuck in her throat." Five farmers from the Pheba neighborhood north of Midland bought the tractor and proudly drove it home. Some farmers thought that such a contraption would never take the place of a good four horse team. They were wrong. Tractors continued to invade the country. The Standard Oil Company put in two large storage tanks to supply fuel for the new machines.

W.W. Ness advertised a fine looking trotting stallion named Heggie at stud at the Star Feed Barn in Midland. Heggie stood a majestic seventeen hands and weighed a thousand three hundred and fifty pounds. Frank Calhoon stood a beautiful black Percheron at his livery barn. The horse had been shipped from France and commanded an impressive stud fee. Terms were $4.00 cash and $4.00 when the mare was in foal. Alvin and Albert looked these fine stallions over.

Alvin broke a bay mare for Dina. Dina loved the gentle mare and named her Nellie. She spent many happy hours riding Nellie up and down the rugged hills and over the meadows. She taught Nellie to sail like a deer over ravines and fences. Alvin tried to teach his horse to jump ditches, but the horse couldn't get the hang of it. To Alvin's disgust, he stepped into the ravine and hopped out. If Dina rode someplace and wanted Nellie to go home, she turned the mare loose. Nellie made a bee line for home, jumping any fences in her way.

On a lovely afternoon in May, Amanda and Walt entertained friends with an ice cream and cake lunch. Bertelsons had plenty of cream, milk and eggs to make the ice cream. Walt, Charley and the Bertelson boys turned the handle to freeze the delicious dessert. Ice was available from the ice dealer in Midland, if one didn't have an ice house.

Over fourteen hundred people thronged the streets of Midland for the 1908 Fourth of July Celebration. Frontier celebrations often lasted for several days. People from a distance brought tents and set them up along the river. Thus they had access to water, and bushes nearby made convenient toilets. However, such facilities posed a problem for women and girls with their long skirts and many petticoats.

Dina rode Monte, Albert's bay horse, around town with her friends. The business places were decorated with yards of red, white and blue bunting. Flags flew from every building. A volley of rifle fire proclaimed the beginning of events.

The Midland Cornet Band, playing a stirring march, led the parade that stretched all the way down Main Street's three blocks. Postmaster Francis Ryan was dressed as Uncle Sam with his red and white striped pants, blue swallow-tailed coat and tall stove pipe hat. A gaily decorated wagon followed with teachers and their students wearing tinseled cards across their chests that represented every state in the Union.

J.C. Russell's Store wagon came next, followed by buggies, carriages and wagons all laced with bunting. The Calhoon Livery Stable carriage was literally hidden under a covering of bunting. Riders on prancing horses followed.

Dina waited eagerly for the horse races. At 1:30 the riders gathered near Mitchell Creek. Monte pulled at the bit and danced as Dina lined him up with the other riders. The starting gun banged.

Monte leaped forward and sped toward town. He led the field down Main Street past hotels, restaurants and stores while the crowds along Main cheered. Monte raced across the finish line west of Russell's Store. Dina collected $5.00 first prize.

Another wonderful crop year was shaping up. Fine barley crops were ready to cut the first part of July. A heavy rain in late July gave corn and flax a boost. Crops were growing well on the Bertelson acres that had been plowed on the river flats.

Barley was cut and shocked on many farms during the hot days of July. A man driving a four horse team on a binder, cut and bound the grain into bundles. Sometimes the whole family shocked grain.

In late July, according to the paper, Walter and Amanda and Grandma Juliana entertained "a large company of friends and neighbors on Sunday." Neighborhood gatherings were fun for everyone. Children played along the river while their parents visited. Men played horseshoes.

Jake Hauge and family, Juliana's niece Alphia Hauge and cousin Lena Hove came from Van Metre on the train. The women baked many cakes, and the men froze gallons of ice cream.

That summer the Chicago and Northwestern Railroad had a special fare for people from "back east" to come west and visit. Walt's father Louis Steien and Walt's sisters Olga and Lottie came to visit Walt and Amanda. The girls decided to stay. Olga went to work at The Bastion Hotel. Lottie spent the summer learning to ride swiftly over the prairie with Dina. The Western Star said, "Lottie Steien is becoming an expert equestrian." That fall Lottie went to Ft. Pierre to work in the hospital and become a nurse.

The year was shaping up to be a good one for farmers. The paper said, "A wonderful crop should be harvested through August. Barley is in the shock. Wheat soon to be cut and flax and corn crops give promise of being the heaviest yet."

August brought temperatures above a hundred degrees that ripened wheat, oats and barley that stood in shocks waiting for the threshers. Threshing started in August and continued until all the crops were harvested, sometimes lasting into October.

When the steam engine puffed onto the field pulling the thresh machine, neighbor gathered to help neighbor with the harvest. Walt and Charley helped at the Bertelson place. The bundle racks rumbled to the field. Men jumped out of their racks, pitchfork in hand. The horses plodded from shock to shock and bundles flew into racks. The men raced to see who could get the first load to the thresh machine.

Tina and Amanda came to help their mother and Dina cook a huge dinner of chicken and mashed potatoes, gravy and pie. Threshing a good crop was a time of comradeship, joking and laughing. The men washed at the washstand outside the kitchen door and sat down to the wonderful meal cooked for them.

Winter wheat made twenty-five to twenty-seven bushels per acre, and The Midland Grain Company was paying $1.00 per bushel for wheat. A good yield for a good price. Most farmers had only ten or twenty acres of wheat. Today's farmer may have thousands of acres. Field crops weren't the only bumper crops. Hustons from southeast of Midland claimed they picked a forty pound watermelon.

A soaking rain in August boosted the bumper corn crop that was coming. Albert went up to help Walt put up hay on his Mitchell Creek homestead about six miles northeast as the crow flies from Amanda's homestead.

If they rode across the hills and valleys at the right time they would see the stage going or coming between Midland and Ottumwa on the Mitchell Creek Trail. The stage went every day except Sunday.

Ottumwa had a post office, a general store, a blacksmith shop, harness shop, meat market, two hotels, a pool hall, two feed barns, school and churches. Today Ottumwa is only a memory and a graveyard.

Two wheeled, single horse road carts crowded the roads along with buggies, wagons and a few automobiles. Sometimes an angry buggy driver would let his team out to full trot and keep ahead of the smelly automobile for a while.

Bad River quit running in August and by September the corn crop was ripening. Albert and Alvin cut their corn and stacked the shocks by the barn to be used in winter for cattle and hog feed. They put up hay on the river bottoms. The cows sneaked into the corn field, and Dina rode after them. She galloped back and forth behind the cattle, herding them out of the field. The cows nipped at the corn. The horse stumbled and fell, rolling over Dina. She got up, dazed and bruised. Her shoulder hurt and she was scratched by cornstalks. She caught her horse, mounted and drove the cattle home. Battered and disheveled, she limped into the house.

"Dina, what happened?" Albert asked.

"My horse fell and rolled right over me," she said. "My shoulder hurts, and my jaw feels like it's broken."

"When a horse falls with you, Dina," Albert said, "get on your hands and knees and crawl out of his way as fast as you can."

"I didn't have time to crawl. He rolled over me before I could even move." Dina couldn't eat solid food for a week.

With homesteaders on nearly every quarter of land, cattle and horses were being squeezed off the range. Homesteaders were angry because cattle and horses roamed their land. The days of wide open free range were passing. Still many large herds of cattle and horses ranged over the unfenced land and were gathered for branding in summer and market in fall. Under pressure from irate homesteaders, the South Dakota legislature passed a law that cattle, horses and sheep must be kept under fence during the summer months. Livestock could roam the prairie during the winter.

People in town and country turned their dry cows and the horses they weren't using loose to graze on the hills and meadows in winter. Some animals roamed the streets of Midland and grazed on unsuspecting farmer's wagons that were parked in front of stores while the owners bought supplies.

The cows and horses broke into flour and feed sacks and ate the delicious contents. They had to eat fast before the farmer or merchant charged out of the store, bellowing to chase them away. The paper advised merchants to "declare war on loose cows and horses."

Dina liked to watch the great herds of long horned cattle go by in the fall. Cattle of many colors, spotted, roan, brown and white, followed the old cattle trail to Midland. Mrs. Nelson didn't want all those cattle trampling the grass so close to her house and garden. She walked out and told the first cowboy she saw to trail his cattle some place else. The cowboy smiled and tried to explain that the cattle were following an old cattle trail. They couldn't be changed now. The herd moved on, horns and hoofs clicking, straight across the meadow toward Midland.

Mrs. Nelson walked beside the cowboy and gave him a piece of her mind until the cattle had passed by and gone on their dusty way.

The days of unlimited free grazing were gone. Cowboys were moving farther west to Wyoming and Montana. The railroad brought hundreds of new homesteaders every day. Sometimes the line of people waiting to pick up mail at the Midland post office stretched half a block down Main Street.

The editor of The Western Star was proud of South Dakota. He bragged: "Men grow bigger in South Dakota, women more matronly and children healthier, while boys are 'chips off the old block.' Fruits and vegetables come earlier and remain longer than in New England. Birds sing sweeter, sunshine comes nearly every day of 365. South Dakota is a big state different somewhat from eastern states where one must keep dancing around all the time to keep inside the state's boundaries. One can get a big bunch of productive land in this state now for a few dollars."

The time was to come when you couldn't give this land away.

Amanda and Walt Steien in the buggy that replaced the one that went down Bad River.

Taken around 1910. (Standing) Alvin and Albert Bertelson and Charlie Myrland. (Seated) Amanda, Grandma Juliana and Tena.

CHAPTER 8
A Foxy Pair of Grays

The fall of 1908, Dina rode down river to school in the Nelson living room. Walter Mack taught Dina, Rachel, Anna, Nester, Oliver and Ingwal Nelson and two neighbor boys. Dina finished the eighth grade that year. The fall before she rode two miles to Midland and attended school for a few months in the Presbyterian Church with Miss Ball teaching. Her mother became ill and Dina stayed home to help her.

Norwegian Lutheran Church was held once a month often at Nelsons or Bertelsons. Reverend Jenson came from Presho and Reverend Storm came from Philip. They came by buggy or horseback, sixty miles from Presho and twenty-five miles from Philip. When the train reached Philip, Reverend Stormo rode the train. Dina and Alvin were confirmed in The Lutheran faith by Reverend N.J. Stormo July 25, 1909 in the Nelson living room.

Bad River quit running the fall of 1908, but a four inch rain in October brought it up, so people could get good drinking water again. Walt finished building a house for Mrs. Myers down on Brave Bull Creek.

That fall a prairie fire ranged over a large area near J.D. Rogers place south of Walt's homestead. Prairie fires were a homesteader's worst nightmare, but this one stopped before burning anyone out.

Homesteaders did constant battle with the many predators

that liked to dine on unwary chickens, turkeys, fat ducks and geese.

Chickens ran like crazy for the hen house if an eagle or hawk floated over. Any chicken that got too far from home was apt to find a huge bird dropping out of the sky to grab him. Homesteaders shot at every eagle or hawk that appeared. Someone reported shooting three eagles. Bobcats sneaked into hen houses at night to snatch a meal. Coyotes lay in wait in broad daylight to grab heedless poultry and streak for the hills. Skunks, mink and weasels raided the hen coops. Farmers waged war with traps and guns to protect their valuable fowl.

The first cold spell of the season came in November, but the cold didn't stop the Brave Bull School from having a box social. Bertelsons and Steiens would have attended.

Walt and Amanda, Dina, Alvin and Albert loved to dance. Tina did, too, but Charley was a good Methodist and didn't dance. He didn't think anyone else should dance either. People came from miles around to dances at the Tom Jones and J.D. Addison ranches.

Furniture was moved out of living rooms and kitchens. Chairs and benches lined the walls for the ladies in their long gowns. When the violin, mouth organ and maybe a banjo, guitar or accordion began to play, men chose their ladies for a waltz, square dance or fast polka.

Ladies brought cake and sandwiches for midnight lunch. Dancing lasted until dawn while beds, cots and wagon boxes filled with sleepy children.

George Stoner, who was smitten with Walt's beautiful sister Olga, came from DeSmet to Midland by buggy to spend the winter on his claim on the flat southeast of Walt's homestead.

George drove two hundred and fifty miles, stayed until

January and went back to DeSmet. He came back in March and married Olga.

By December Bad River was frozen from Philip to Ft. Pierre. Alvin and Dina skated to Nelsons. The Nelson young people joined them, and they skated to Midland and back home.

The middle of December brought warm weather, and Dina's cousin Alphia married Wilmer Hollis. They lived on Alphia's homestead.

In February melting snow cascaded into creeks and rivers. Bad River ran nearly bank full. Walt Steien carpentered at the Linder ranch. From there he went to Miller east of Pierre to work on a large building while Amanda held down her claim.

Spring brought the time for setting hens and raising a new batch of chickens. Elton DeWitte advertised pure bred White Wyondotte hatching eggs for .85 for thirteen eggs. In May Barred Plymouth Rock eggs were offered at .75 per thirteen. The prairie came alive with birdsong--the cheerful call of the meadowlark, his yellow breast swelled with love; the song of the horned lark wooing his mate and the haunting cry of the mourning dove. The golden plover searched for a nesting place in the grass, and the ruffed grouse drummed as he strutted, chest puffed, for his lady. Along draws, creeks and rivers, plum blossoms perfumed the air.

Farmers were plowing sod to plant wheat, oats, barley and corn. Alvin and Albert walked for hours behind a plow, holding the handles as the horses plodded up and down, turning rich black furrows. They plowed eighty acres across the river west of Albert's cabin and forty-five acres north of their mother's cabin. The hot dusty work wet a man's shirt with sweat and sent him to bed tired at night.

Many acres were planted with a hand seeder. A man walked up and down, turning the crank as the seed (wheat, barley, or oats) fed from a canvas bag hanging around his neck scattered out onto the field. Bertelsons bought an endgate seeder that rode the tail gate of the wagon. Alvin stood in the wagon and drove his team while the seed sprayed over the field. The grain was then disked or dragged to cover the seed.

Bertelsons planted corn with a two row corn planter that checked four or five kernels into a hill. An old saying went: "One for the cutworm, one for the crow, one for the blackbird and two to grow."

Midland had some excitement when a four horse team driven by James McLaughlin spooked at the freight barn and ran away with a load of furniture. People jumped into buildings or dashed out of the way as the wagon careened down the street. Other drivers whipped their teams to get buggies and wagons out of the way. The runaways were circling The Western Star office in the Russell building when McLaughlin got them stopped.

By the middle of May, small grain was luxuriant and a lush carpet of grass covered the prairie. Range cattle, thin from a winter of grazing the hills, were gaining weight. Calves and colts frolicked on the hillsides at the Bertelson farm. Chicken and turkey hens were setting. Red sows birthed large litters of piglets. Dina worked in the garden, planting potatoes, lettuce, peas and radishes. She also carried water and feed to the setting hens.

They fooled some hens into setting on duck and turkey eggs which took longer to hatch but the hen didn't mind. She couldn't count so she sat patiently on her nest until downy bundles came out of the eggs. Hens didn't care whether they hatched ducks, chicks, turkeys or even goslings. The mother hen did her best to care for her brood even when the ducklings splashed water all over the food. She scolded, but she forgave them. They about drove her crazy when they jumped into the river and took a swim, leaving her on the bank screaming for them to come back.

Amanda was happy when Walt finished his job in Miller and came home. He went to the Howes ranch down Mitchell Creek and built a long barn with horse stalls in one end and a garage in the other for Horace's car.

Lottie came from Ft. Pierre to visit Amanda and Walt. Grandma Juliana and Tina took advantage of the nice weather and rode the train to Van Metre to visit Hauges a few days.

A dry spell in May was followed by rain in June. Bad River ran high. Corn grew taller overnight. The threatening weather kept a large crowd from attending Midland's Fourth of July Celebration.

Dina and Amanda rode in the parade and around town on a foxy pair of grays belonging to Walt. The Philip Band led the long parade down Main Street. When horse race time arrived, Dina and Amanda rode to Mitchell Creek for the Ladies Horse Race. The horses lined up. The starter fired his gun. The horses leaped away and tore toward town. Forging ahead, the grays sped down Main Street. They whistled past Russell's Store, running neck and neck. The grays raced over the finish line in a near dead heat. The Western Star said Amanda won. Dina, my mother, said the horses tied. Perhaps Amanda gave her sister half of the prize money.

A hard rain on a Saturday night in July brought welcome moisture. Farmers said the prospects for a bumper crop were never better. The prairie, still mostly unfenced, was green with tall grass as far as the eye could see.

John Peterson up Mitchell Creek from Walt's place advertised high grade Shorthorn cows and a bull for sale. Scrawny dogie cattle from Minnesota were being shipped in by cattle dealers.

On hot summer evenings people sat outside to enjoy the evening breeze. Lucky people had a porch and swing. In summer, every lady carried a fan. Some carried lovely folding fans, which worked surprisingly well.

By late July, binders were cutting wheat. In August threshers moved in and a good crop was threshed. Rain fell abundantly in August to keep the bumper corn crop growing. The country was as bountiful as Albert had said it was.

Midland was so prosperous, three tennis courts were put in at the schoolhouse. Midland teams competed with Philip, Murdo and other towns. Russell's Store advertised dress skirts that reached the floor in lovely pleats for $4.00 each. Tina, Amanda and Dina loved those. Boys could get long black stockings and knickerbockers which they didn't like. Boys dreamed of the day they would be old enough to wear long pants.

The Farm Journal advertised a five year subscription and a copy of "Horse Secrets" for $1.00. "Horse Secrets" warned the buyer about tricks to watch out for when buying or trading horses. Tricks like why a slick trader might put a lemon up a horse's nose or use turpentine to make a lazy horse lively.

Alvin and Albert found time to break horses to ride and drive. Alvin was the main bronc rider. They tied the horse, saddled him and climbed aboard. The horse bucked until either the rider was thrown or the horse gave up. If Alvin got bucked off, he tied the horse's front leg to the saddle horn and mounted again. With only three legs working, the pony couldn't buck hard. Alvin broke a pair of dapple gray geldings with blaze faces for himself and Dina. She named her horse Baldy; Alvin called his horse Favorite.

That September Walt took a shipment of cattle to Chicago and several prairie schooners passed through, heading farther west.

The new Van Dusen Elevator in Midland shipped several cars of wheat. The Chicago and Northwestern put in a large cistern at the depot. Water was hauled by tank car from the Missouri

River to fill the cistern. People hauled free drinking water from that cistern for the next sixty years.

Corn was cut, shocked and hauled to barns for winter before the weather turned cold in November and blanketed the prairie with four inches of snow.

Milton Reisling, the Hayes-Midland stage driver, spent a night in a haystack after his horses played out six miles from Hayes. Fortunately, he had no passengers. He found shelter and feed for his horses at a shack, but no heat for himself. He burrowed into the hay to keep from freezing. The next morning, he climbed out of the hay, brushed off a few straws and drove to Hayes.

A warm spell the end of November melted snow and sent Bad River running near bank full. There would be plenty of ice to cut, and the river would be frozen all the way from Bertelsons to Midland for skating again.

Midland had no high school the fall of 1909, so Dina went to Forest City, Iowa where her Uncle Lars had moved. She stayed with Lars and Susan, sons Ludolph and Alfred and daughters Selma, Marie and Lenore. Dina and Selma were the same age.

Dina was lucky to be going to school in Iowa. December, January and February brought bitter cold. The prairie lay under deep snow from horizon to horizon. Children and teachers stumbled through deep drifts to get to school or stayed home. Cold seeped into houses and cellars, freezing canned goods and turning potatoes and barrels of apples into rocks. Women put on extra underwear and stockings. They didn't wear pants in those days.

When blizzard winds howled and whistled around the corners and under the eaves of her house, Grandma Juliana must have thought about Iowa winters where snow often fell so gently that a cap of snow lay a foot deep on fence posts. If snow fell gently in

South Dakota, before long the wind blew the snowcap into millions of tiny pieces that settled into drifts on the plains and hillsides.

By January the temperature was twenty-five degrees below zero. Bad River wore a thick coat of ice. Scotty Philip lost four hundred sixty-eight cattle on his ranch near Nowlin when they crowded onto a dam and fell through twenty-two inch thick ice.

Halley's Comet appeared the last part of January, lighting the night sky as bright as day. Dina and the Hauge girls marveled at the wondrous light. Some people thought the end of the world was upon them. Some even committed suicide to avoid the coming calamity.

The light faded as the comet went on its way for another seventy-six years. Dina was here to see the comet's appearance in 1986, but Halley's disappointed us. We saw no more light than from a distant star.

In March Charley ran an ad in The Western Star that said: "See Charles Myrland, the man with the axe." He wanted work cutting wood for stoves and posts for fences. Walt finished building a house for Tom Jones and started one for Horace Howes.

The weather turned warm and the snow melted. Creeks and draws ran into Bad River. Bad River roared down and tore out the Nowlin bridge. People on the north side of the river had to drive eight miles to Midland for groceries and supplies.

Wild ducks and geese flew north. Midland prospered. C.E. Murray put a new sidewalk in front of his store. By the first of April, farmers were purchasing grain and seed potatoes in great amounts from Midland. Planting of wheat, oats and barley was in full swing.

Midland in 1908 as you look West. Dina raced her horse up this street in the horse races.

Midland, in 1909, shows the many business places of a fast growing town.

CHAPTER 9
Amanda Proves Up

Amanda proved up on her homestead and bought the U.S. patent at Ft. Pierre April 7, 1910. She sold her land to her mother and moved with Walt to his homestead on Mitchell Creek. They no longer had to travel between homesteads to see each other.

Walt and Amanda built a house of cottonwood logs with a large kitchen-living room on the south and a comfortable bedroom on the north. The cabin had big windows on the south and west. The roof sloped up from all sides and peaked at the center. Later Walt added a frame kitchen with pantry. South of the kitchen was a small bedroom. The kitchen-living room became a spacious parlor. Walt and Amanda were to live there for most of the next forty years.

Amanda helped Walt cut ash posts and poles to build fences and repair corrals. Amanda learned to swing an axe and pull her end of a crosscut saw. She helped saw cottonwood logs almost three feet thick for the heater and split wood for the kitchen range.

Walt dug a well on the flat between the creek and the corrals. He bought a windmill to pump water. The well had good water for household use as well as livestock. Towering above cottonwood, ash and elm trees, the windmill blades turned in the slightest breeze.

Walt built a square barn with a flat roof against a low rise west of the corrals. The hill and the thick woods along the creek sheltered the barn and corrals from the cold northwest wind.

Walt built substantial weather tight barns for others and slapped one together for himself. He stood twelve inch boards on end for sides and didn't batten the cracks. The wind blew snow into the barn. Rain poured through the cracks in the unshingled roof. Snow lodged on the roof, insulating it in frigid weather, but letting the snow melt drip into the barn.

The barn sheltered Amanda when she milked cows in stormy winter weather, but in spring the barn became a quagmire of manure. In rainy weather, water dripped through the roof and ran down her neck. Walt hung his saddle on the corral fence where it shrunk and cracked in the hot sun.

Amanda cared for the cattle, milked the cows and fixed fence while Walt carpentered. They never had a large herd of cattle, probably no more than thirty cows. Walt plowed forty acres on the flat east of the house around a creek bend. A mile and a half southwest of their house, George and Olga Stoner hauled lumber from town and built a three room house and a small hip-roofed barn.

Grandma Juliana and Albert continued to add to their holdings by buying land from neighboring homesteaders who proved up and left. Alvin and Albert fenced the land. They built up their herd of horses and cattle. An abandoned homestead shack was moved to the house for a living room. Walt built a large kitchen between the new living room and the log cabin, a spacious living room, and two bedrooms upstairs and two down. A magnificent stag in a forest was etched in the glass of the front door. I loved that picture. I had never seen a door so beautiful. I still haven't. The glass lasted for forty years before being broken.

The snow left a deep moisture base. Farmers looked forward to bumper crops again in 1910. Charley plowed his flats on both sides of Mitchell Creek. He planted corn and alfalfa in his fields, watermelons and muskmelons in his garden and corn field.

Charley was called "The Watermelon King" because he hauled wagon loads of melons to Midland and sold them. Small boys jumped on his wagon and rode with him as he sold his melons. Young people sneaked over the hill to raid Charley's melon patch, making Charley madder than a hornet in a bottle. What they ate didn't bother him. The destroyed and plugged melons got his dander up. He didn't want anyone tramping his melon vines, destroying the fruit of his labor.

When the harvest moon rode high, Charley lay in his melon patch, waiting for raiders. Boys slunk over the ridge. Peering at the house, its windows lighted by a kerosene lamp, they slipped toward the melon patch. They cat-footed into the patch. With a roar like a grizzly bear, Charley rose out of the patch and pounced on the nearest boy. Charley could run faster than the boys could. He rounded up the raiders and took them to the house where Tina cut luscious ripe melons, and the sheepish boys ate their fill. Pete Elrod, Ingwal Nelson and Archie and Garrett Rogers tried to raid Charley's melon patch and ended up eating melons in the Myrland house.

Charley planted corn with a hand planter. He stuck the planter in the ground, pulled the handles apart and a seed dropped in the ground. Charley claimed he ran down the row planting corn and Tina brought corn to refill the pint seed holder. He planted ten acres in one day and got the hills so straight in the rows that the corn could be cultivated both ways. Whenever he told that story, someone told him such speed and accuracy were impossible.

In April the Calhoon brothers drove into town in a new

Overland. They made the sixty miles from Pierre in three hours. A team and wagon took a day and a half in good weather. The Western Star called the Overland, "The dandiest car in town." Calhoons planned to use the car to take people around the country to locate land etc. There were already a few cars around town. Banker Sherwood owned a Maxwell.

Potatoes were eating size by July but prospects for small grain were poor. Hot winds blew across the land, and clouds were empty.

The dry weather didn't stop Midland from putting on the biggest ever Fourth of July Celebration. The Western Star said: "Three thousand people in town and not one drunk man on the street with two saloons running wide open all day. We defy any prohibition town to show a better record." The editor didn't want prohibition to come, but come it did.

Indians from the Rosebud Reservation came to Midland with their wagons, dogs and horses. A group of warriors in full dress danced to entertain the crowd.

Dina rode Monte around town. She was crossing the railroad track with a group of friends when Monte caught his foot in the ties. With a mighty lunge, the frightened horse jerked loose and limped after the other horses. Dina felt bad. Albert cheered her up. "Don't worry, Dina. We'll put Monte in Calhoon's barn and rent a horse for you to ride." He rented a horse from Frank Calhoon and Dina was horseback again. She wanted to ride the horse in the Ladies Horse Race. She asked Walt what he thought. Walt went to Frank Calhoon. "Can Dina ride your horse in the horse race, Frank?"

"Sure," Frank said. "Old Birdie is fifteen years old and can't run, but she can ride him, if she wants to."

Dina rode to the starting line down by Mitchell Creek.

Catching enthusiasm from his young rider, Birdie pulled at the bit and pranced. The starting gun banged.

Birdie leaped out in front. He laid back his ears, stretched out his old neck and ran. He ran like his tail was on fire and a pack of wolves were snapping at his heels. Dust scattered behind his flying hoofs. Dina leaned forward into the wind rushing past her face. They flashed past the Bastion Hotel, past restaurants and stores, past the bank and Russell's Store and on to victory.

The Western Star said, "Dina Bertelson won $5.00, riding Calhoon's Birdie." Dina accepted the first prize while old Birdie danced around as if to say, "I may be old, but I'm not dead." Dina won races at later celebrations riding Monte.

Rain was badly needed. Catfishing was still good in the river, but creeks and rivers were going down. The swimming pool at the Bastion ranch was getting much use by both men and women.

The summer of 1910 was dry from Canada to the Gulf of Mexico. By the end of July, farmers were worrying about the lack of moisture and lamenting because hay cutting time was upon them and there was no hay to cut. Beef cattle were being shipped to Chicago a month earlier than usual. Someone advertised Hereford bulls for sale. Better cattle were coming into the country.

The Midland Opera House put on a minstrel show. The Lutheran church began holding church in the Presbyterian Church in Midland. James Faubel started a new hotel on the south side of Main Street a block east of Russell's Store. The Midland Produce was buying cream, and land seekers were still flooding into the county on every passenger train.

Indians, trading in town, stole a bolt of silk and one of calico from C.E. Murray's Store while Mr. Murray was out to lunch. When he got back to the store, Murray got the Deputy Sheriff and they hurried to the Indian camp. They searched wagons and found the silk and calico. The thieves were jailed and fined.

The heaviest rain of the season fell the middle of September, filling dams and water holes. Creeks and rivers ran, and people had water again.

Some people raised good Early Ohio potatoes in spite of the dry summer. By November Midland's new sidewalk project was finished. The Western Star bragged: "Midland has the best sidewalks of any town in the country." No one had to walk in the mud to cross Midland's streets anymore. The ladies could cross the streets without soiling their long skirts and high button shoes. The crosswalks were rounded so cars and wagons could cross with a slight bump.

Lumber yards sold coal so there was something to heat houses with besides wood, twisted hay and buffalo chips.

Women still couldn't vote, but they were pushing hard for the privilege. William Howard Taft was President. The United States had decided to stop letting foreign countries scour their prisons and asylums in order to send their inmates to America.

In September Olga Stoner had a baby boy with sister Lottie, now a practicing nurse, on hand. George sold his homestead to Walt and took his family back to Lake Preston.

I never understood why Uncle Walt didn't move that handsome hip-roofed barn to his farmstead and replace the monstrosity that roosted against his hill. Aunt Amanda could have milked cows without rain running down on her head. His sister's barn and house remained empty landmarks for forty years before being torn down.

Midland built a two story schoolhouse on the hill north of town. The school only had first through ninth grade so Dina stayed home that fall.

The drought of 1910 was bad, but the drought of 1911 was worse, a rude awakening for the homesteaders who had been raising tall corn, bountiful grain and large potatoes and mowing the tall grass for winter feed. Not much snow fell the winter of 1910-11, not even enough to stop a prairie fire north of Midland from burning a large area.

Even so, Bad River gave a bountiful ice harvest for next summer's ice cream. The weather warmed so much the last part of January that flies buzzed about outdoors. People went for drives in their automobiles like it was June instead of January.

Several business men put hitching posts in front of their stores in the spring. No more runaways while the homesteader was buying groceries.

So many automobiles chugged around that Calhoon Brothers enlarged their garage and built an oil house. The Midland State Bank proudly announced a capital of $1,000.00.

The Chicago and Northwestern Railroad drilled an artesian well at Capa to provide water for the steam locomotive that pulled the train. A free bathhouse with a large plunge was built. People flocked to Capa and soaked in the hot water.

The Poler Hotel in Capa built a plunge in the hotel. Hot water from the well flowed through the plunge and supposedly cured many an ailment. Midland wished for such a well, but the railroad didn't oblige.

Rain fell in May and crops looked good. Ample soil moisture gave farmers hope for a crop. Rain didn't fall again until the end of May. Another dry summer was shaping up.

Grandma Juliana and Amanda took the train to Van Metre to help Alphia and Wilmer Hollis celebrate their first wedding anniversary.

Bad River quit running. Catfish as big as Dan Bastion's

hogs were sighted in water holes on the river. Everybody wished the river would run and bring fresh water. In June heavy rains southwest of Midland sent flooding creeks to dump their load into Bad River. The river ran with Badlands mud so thick and white the water was unfit for man or beast until the water cleared.

Ice was in high demand. Iceman Jones had a runaway while delivering ice around town. One team spooked at the railroad track and ran down Main Street, scattering pedestrians in every direction. Another team ran away from a farmer who was disking a garden in town. The farmer fell off the disk. The team tore up the street, disking all the way. The sharp disks ran against one horse's legs, cutting him so severely he had to be destroyed.

In July a gale wind blew a barn down, and a good rain fell, but it was too little and too late for grain crops. Hay prospects looked fair.

In March an immigrant train unloaded more land seekers in Midland. By July homesteaders were "throwing up their tails and leaving." Beaten by the dry weather and the hot winds that shriveled their meagre crops and left nothing to harvest, homesteaders packed up and left in droves. Some sold their claims; some abandoned or relinquished their land. Some left everything for the banks to gather and sell.

Discouraged homesteaders left their hopes and dreams in a sod shanty or tar paper shack. The wild and lonely wind rattled flapping screen doors. Coyotes howled at the doorstep. Bobcats prowled inside, catching mice and voles that had taken the shack for their own.

Cattle and horses trampled inside to fight the flies that plagued them in the summer or take shelter from the biting wind in winter. Windows fell out. Rain came in. Snow blew through broken windows and sifted over broken dreams.

With the passing years, dirt drifted over the ruins until nothing was left but a dent in the ground where a root cellar had been and a mound where the soil had been thrown. Even these signs were grown over with grass.

Sometimes a piece of furniture or a child's toy was left behind. Deserted homesteads were places to be explored. We found Indian head pennies, buffalo nickles and liberty head dimes. Once I found a china egg used by a long ago homesteader to coax his hens into laying eggs in the nest where it was placed. Another time I found a shaving mug.

Grandma Juliana and Albert added to their land whenever a claim near them came up for sale until they owned a thousand acres. Bad River wound across the northern part, providing excellent winter shelter for cattle and horses.

The Western Star tried to cheer people that dry summer with this reprint from The Miller Press: "For ten years South Dakota has produced more wealth per capita than any other state. One bad year shouldn't be held against her."

Corn took a spurt after heavy rains fell in August. J.C. Russell reported that his corn had ears "as long as a short man's arm and would make twenty bushels to the acre." People were out along draws, creeks and rivers, picking plums for jelly, jam and sauce.

A hard rain brought creeks cascading into Bad River until the river ran ten feet deep. Farmers were cutting a short hay crop and expecting a good potato crop. Albert and Alvin cut hay on the bottoms and had corn that would make some feed.

The Norwegian Lutheran Church met at Bertelsons in July and Nelsons in August. Everybody brought baskets of food for a potluck dinner.

In September Tina caught the train to Van Metre to visit the

Hauge family and other relatives. Walt and Amanda took the train to Pepein, Wisconsin for his mother's funeral.

That fall Walt finished work on living quarters added to the rear of Hellekson's Store and was in charge of the Robertson Lumber Company for a while in October.

Dena started school in Midland October 10, 1911. She was seventeen years old and in the tenth grade. She had changed the "i" in her name to "e". Nobody mispronounced her name anymore. She studied English II, Latin II, History and Geometry with grade averages of 97, 91, 97 and 96 according to her report card.

Dena and Alvin loved to dance. They attended dances from Nowlin to Van Metre and Belvidere to Moenville. Vivacious Dena with the laughing brown eyes and infectious laugh was the "Belle of the Ball" according to her admirers. Her dance card was always full.

Foot stomping dancers crowded the Opera House in Midland every Friday night. At a dance in March, the dancers went to The Midland Hotel for lunch at midnight. The management thought the dancers were gone for the night and locked the dance hall. The dancers came back after supper eager to waltz and polka. They found a locked door. Someone got a key and the dancers went in and danced until morning.

The corn crop was fair in spite of the dry summer. Alvin and Albert cut and bound their corn and hauled the shocks to the barn to be husked during winter.

A blizzard howled across the country in November, dumping snow and building drifts in draws and fields. Dena had to ride through the drifts to get to school. Cows were turned into corn fields to browse on stalks left standing. Farmers worried about gray wolves seen along the Cheyenne River. Midland installed Coleman gas street lights. No more dark streets, if the lamplighter made his rounds.

The winter of 1911-1912 was severely cold. The northwest wind brought blizzards that sifted snow through the cracks in many a claim shack. Some people couldn't even keep warm in bed. Everyone hoped for an early spring.

Dena didn't always get to school. The Nelson children went to school in Pierre. Their mother had moved there because Midland's school didn't have eleventh or twelfth grade for Rachel and Nestor.

A warm February melted snow and sent draws rippling toward rivers. Spring finally came with its promise of green grass, flowers and singing birds. Three days of heavy soaking rain brought smiles to farmers' faces.

J.C. Russell rigged an irrigation system for his ten acre truck farm. If the summer was dry, he would pump water from Bad River to his garden. One of Myrland's hogs took advantage of the balmy spring weather and strolled three miles up Mitchell Creek to the August Peters place. Tina walked after the wandering sow and shooed her home.

Albert put an ad in the paper saying a month old roan calf had strayed to his place. A brockle faced brown cow strayed from the Bertelson herd.

Alvin saddled his horse and rode south across the rugged Bad River breaks, questioning homesteaders about the brown cow. He stopped at one homesteader's corral to ask the owner if he'd seen anything of a brown brockle faced cow. In the middle of the pen, lay the brockle faced cow's head.

Alvin turned around and rode back home. Nothing was ever done about the butchering of the brown cow. Bertelsons figured the man needed the meat to feed his large family.

A soaking rain came in May. Seed corn was $3.00 per

bushel and the time had come to plant. W.J. Elrod had started buying cream in Midland so there were several cream buyers in town.

In June The Western Star became The Midland Mail and reported that crops never looked better. Heavy rains came again in July, forcing the Midland Fourth of July picnic into City Hall.

Calhoon Brothers Livery Barn advertised a choice of team and buggy or automobile for rent to drive over the country. Maxwell automobiles sold for $1,085.00.

Tina, Dena and Amanda went to C.E. Murray's Store to see the ladies shirt waists on sale for .69 each and the four hundred pairs of shoes to choose from.

That summer Dena went to Ft. Pierre and took a test to get a second grade teacher's certificate. In the fall, she rode off to Center School, her home school. Her chocolate brown hair was coiled in a bun at the back of her head. She loved teaching and the children liked her. She taught in log school houses and tar paper shacks, teaching eight grades and often more than twenty students. Teachers were paid in warrants which they sold to merchants at a discount.

Dena wore a divided skirt when she rode horseback. No lady would be seen wearing a man's pants. Her skirt had a panel across the front that could be unbuttoned for riding and re-buttoned when she dismounted.

One icy day, she was riding down the slope from the barn to the house when her horse slipped and fell. Dena and the horse slid beside each other for several feet. Dena got up and found the panel neatly ripped from her skirt.

Schools had large fenced yards and sometimes warm barns for horses. Dena rode to school in the frigid cold, her horse fighting through snow drifts. Snow fell deep that winter.

Corn crops were good, renewing people's faith in the country. A fine potato crop was harvested in September.

In November Walt helped build a bridge across Mitchell Creek a few miles upstream from his homestead and another wild creek was tamed. South of the Bertelson ranch, a prairie fire raged west of Brave Bull Creek, burning a large area. Also in November, Woodrow Wilson was elected President of The United States.

A March blizzard roared in, blowing snow into drifts. Snow reached almost to the top of J.C. Russell's two story store building.

The Bert and Wilmer Hollis families who had moved to Canada came to visit Bertelsons. They were back to stay. South Dakota was better than Canada.

According to The Midland Mail, Walt and Amanda adopted a twelve-year-old girl whose last name was Spooner. I don't know what happened to her. I had heard they tried an adoption that didn't work.

Bountiful rain promised a wonderful crop. People bragged once again about what a great country this was. Cars were competing for the roads. Calhoon Brothers advertised Ford cars for sale at their Midland Auto Agency. Ford touring cars sold for $550.00 FOB Detroit. The price was later reduced to $490.00. An International truck purchased by Marve Young appeared on the streets of Midland. Dray horses would soon be part of the past.

Farmers drove Overlands, Model T Fords, Maxwells, Franklins, Elgins, and Metz. The smelly contraptions still scared the living daylights out of horses.

In August The Midland Mail reported that England had declared war on Germany. Prices would go up. Midland was sending hundreds of cans of cream east on the railroad, shipping $8,000.00 worth of cream in July.

Kruse Madsen built a bowery on his ranch on Bad River, three miles east of Midland. He hired a fiddler and banjo player and advertised three nights of dancing. Dena and Alvin went the first night. People were square dancing, waltzing and having a fine time when two men showed up drunk. Kruse got so angry he cancelled the dances.

Sometimes young people hijacked the railroad handcar to go to a dance in Van Metre, Capa or Nowlin. Dena, Alvin and a couple of friends lifted the handcar onto the track in Midland one night. The men pumped the car ten miles down river to Capa and back to Midland. If the train chanced to speed down the track, they jumped off the handcar and lifted it off the track and the train roared by. Then, they put the handcar back on the track and pumped merrily on their way.

The fall of 1913, Dena taught the Rollins school in Lyman County, which at that time included Jones and Jackson Counties. She stayed at the Hauge place. Albert and Alvin drove their cattle to the Hauge ranch and wintered there, also caring for Jake's cattle while Hauges were in Norway. The Hauge girls sent Dena postcards from Norway. Grandma Juliana never went back to her homeland.

March roared in like a lion, dumping a load of snow. Hauges came home from Norway. Bertelsons moved back to Bad River.

Heavy rains in May sent Bad River out of its banks. Two people drowned when the creek they lived on overflowed and took their house. People needed to learn not to build so close to rivers and creeks. Peaceful meadows could change to roaring flood ways in minutes.

1914 was another good year. Milk cows sold for $65.00 to $85.00 each. Beef cattle brought $110.00 per head in Chicago.

111

Midland grew. The Farmers Cooperative Association put in a cream station to help take care of all the cream coming into town.

Charley raised a bountiful melon crop. Claude Flom from up north of Midland said he planted a third of an acre of potatoes and got ninety-six bushels in return.

Those were prosperous years. Crops were excellent. Grass grew tall. Prices were good. Anyone with cattle, hogs and horses made a good living especially if they had money to buy out their neighbors who proved up and sold their land. The open range increased as more people left their homesteads. Many found they could not make a living on a hundred and sixty acres. Hardships were often intense. Lights on the hillsides went out never to be lit again.

But, the Bertelson ranch prospered. They had over a hundred and twenty acres in corn, wheat, barley and oats. Their cow herd was growing. They began to run Hereford bulls with their cows. Alvin and Albert built barns, corrals, hog houses, corncribs and sheds.

In August Japan entered World War I on England's side. Also in August, Alvin Helm shot Midland Depot Agent Hunter through the heart in an argument over a freight bill. Agent Hunter ran into the depot and telephoned Dr. Minard. When Dr. Minard arrived, Agent Hunter was almost gone. He died a few minutes later.

Fords were selling "like hot cakes." Calhoon Brothers sold four Fords in one week. They were getting competition. Midland had a Metz dealer, a Maxwell dealer and an Overland dealer. C.E. Murray bought a new car and advertised his buggy for sale. Uncle Walt bought a Metz.

Automobiles were faster than horses and perhaps safer. Little Margaret Beiler fell over the front of her father's buggy when he got out to open a gate. She was not seriously hurt, but a woman and child were killed when the team ran away with their buggy while the father was opening the gate.

Alvin was squiring Irene Flom to dances around the country. Irene taught school near Powell up the river from Nowlin. One evening Alvin rented a two seated rig from a livery barn in Midland. He hitched his horse and a horse from the livery barn to the rig and headed for the Belvidere dance twenty miles south. Irene sat beside him; Dena and Swede Anderson rode on the back seat.

The horses trotted down the graded road, over the steel span bridge on Brave Bull Creek and on along the road on the west side of the creek. The road had no gravel and became impassable in spring and during rainy spells. The road is now overgrown with grass, a dim line across the prairie.

The buggy clattered down the road. With a loud snap, a single tree broke, hitting the horse's hind legs. The team jumped. "Whoa! Whoa!" Alvin held the lines of the plunging horses.

Irene screamed, leaped from the buggy and rolled in the grass. Alvin calmed the horses. Swede jumped down and unhitched the team. "What are you doing?" Dena ran to help Irene. Irene got up, looking foolish. The girls brushed the grass from her dress.

"I'm still nervous since my buggy accident," Irene said.

"You could break your neck, jumping out like that," Dena said.

Alvin and Swede pushed the buggy off the road. They all walked behind the team to the Kaiser farm.

"We broke a single tree," Alvin said "Can I borrow your buggy?"

Mr. Kaiser didn't want to lend his buggy. "We'll have it

----

back tomorrow," Alvin said.

"Well, all right, but you be sure you get back here with it tomorrow." Alvin hitched the team to the borrowed buggy and drove to Belvidere. They danced all night, and Alvin returned the buggy to the skeptical farmer as promised.

Another time Dena, Alvin and Irene rode to a dance with Swede. On the way home, Alvin and Irene sat in the back, paying no attention to Swede and his driving. Swede talked to Dena while the lines dangled nearly to the double tree behind his team.

The buggy hit a rut on a steep hillside. The uphill wheels left the ground. "Here we go," Dena said.

The buggy tipped over, spilling everybody out on the grass. Swede dropped the lines. Alvin lit on his feet, ran around the buggy and grabbed the lines before the horses could run away. Swede was still rolling on the ground. The girls got up and brushed grass off their dresses. The men tipped the buggy back on its wheels and they went home.

Dena taught the Highland Center school south of Nowlin the fall of 1914. She rode ten miles home from school one Friday afternoon, ate a quick lunch and changed clothes while Alvin saddled another horse for her. They rode across country twenty-five miles to the Hauge ranch, ate supper, then rode about ten miles to a schoolhouse where they danced until daylight. They rode back to Hauges, ate breakfast and mounted up again to drive a herd of cattle home.

A new dance called "The Bear" in which dancers dipped to each other became popular. Someone decided this vulgar dance should not be allowed. Every time a young couple began to dance "The Bear", the police came onto the floor and stopped the dancers. Soon people of all ages were dancing the bear, so the police gave up.

Midland advertised for people with automobiles to join the Fourth of July parade in 1915. More cars were showing up on the streets all the time to huff and puff among the horses, wagons and buggies. The cars didn't usually run away like Dan Bastion's team. The team sped down Main Street without a driver.

Henry Brady bought three hundred horses from Tom Jones. Horses still outnumbered cars, but automobiles were getting cheaper. Ford touring cars were down to $440.00 in Detroit. Calhoons sold eleven Fords in seven months. Elrod and Bentley sold Overlands for $615.00. The elegant Maxwell was over $1,000.00. Calhoon Brothers put in the first gasoline station in Midland. It boasted a five hundred gallon tank. No more bucketing gasoline into automobile tanks.

Midland's celebrations lasted several days. Time was required to get in all the horse races, baseball games, speeches and bronc rides. The band played from the bandstand east of the stockyards. Indians set up their tepees in the bend of the river south of the stockyards. Homesteaders tents were scattered about. Everyone was having fun.

Sometimes a rain storm dampened spirits. Young Harvey Madsen took shelter in Addison's tent with the Addison boys, during a rain storm. The boys discovered that if they ran a finger along the tent top, water dripped into the tent. Soon they had little rivers running on the dirt floor from all over the top of the tent. Wherever they could reach, they made a river. By the time Mr. Addison showed up, mud was deep inside the tent as well as outside. He was upset.

Automobile races brought new excitement to Midland celebrations. Bill Brown raced his hard-tired International dray truck against another hard-tired truck. The trucks lumbered around the baseball field, raising a cloud of dust. A good horse could have beat them a country mile.

Automobiles were getting faster. They had pneumatic tires. Marve Young was set to race his new Maxwell against Bill Brown's old Oldsmobile at the Old Settler's Picnic in August. The eager crowd waited. Mrs. Brown and Mrs. Young wiped their eyes with white handkerchiefs. Their foolish husbands were going to smash their automobiles and get killed, and they had to watch.

Bill Brown drove his seven passenger Oldsmobile touring car onto the baseball diamond beside Marve Young's slick Maxwell. The cars roared away. Dust flew. People yelled and clapped. Hitting all of twenty miles an hour, the Maxwell pulled ahead. The Oldsmobile ate dust. Men ran out on the field and pushed the Oldsmobile, but the old car was outclassed. Even with help, the Oldsmobile couldn't catch the Maxwell. Marve Young was an easy winner. Mrs. Brown and Mrs. Young dried their eyes. The race was over. Their husbands were alive and well.

That fall Dena taught at the Highland Center school south of Nowlin. She earned $100.00 per month, an excellent salary. She bought a pair of black ladies boots, sixteen inches high and square at the top. A pair of light $2.00 spurs completed the outfit. She used saddle bags slung behind her saddle to carry books and papers.

Dena loved to read. She belonged to The Book Of The Month Club and subscribed to The American Magazine and Colliers, magazines that carried continued and short stories and provided entertainment for the family.

Dena was going with Frank Elrod, son of the Overland dealer. They planned to marry, but her family didn't approve of the handsome young man. Grandma Juliana was worried. Her headstrong youngest daughter was not another Amanda. When Dena took Frank to visit Amanda and Walt, they were upset. They decided to "have a talk with Dena." After a lecture, Walt summoned all his importance and said, "You don't need to bring that fellow out here again."

Dena's quick temper flared. "He wouldn't come here again anyway, unless it was to punch your nose."

Dena was sad about her families disapproval of Frank. Frank soon went away to see what the world was like somewhere else. He didn't write to her. She didn't know where he was or when he would come back. Dena's mother was relieved. She told Dena, "Frank is gone. He will probably forget you." Dena concealed the hurt and went off to dances with Alvin, Myrtle and Swede.

Albert had his own troubles. He had been going with a young lady homesteader. Retta Russell lived in the Myrland neighborhood and was a friend of Tina. Albert planned to marry Retta, but they broke up, and he never married.

The spring of 1916 Albert and Alvin rented several quarters of land in the Moenville country some forty miles north of their Bad River ranch. Dena mounted Nellie and helped Alvin drive the cattle to the new pasture. They unsaddled their horses and turned them loose to go back to Bad River.

Nellie went straight home, jumping every fence in her path. Alvin's horse took the long way, weaving around the homestead fences that got in his way. He arrived at the ranch a couple of days after Nellie did.

Dena and Alvin homesteaded two miles west of Moenville on Stoney Butte Creek. The land was rough. High buttes rose on both sides of the creek. They each filed on three hundred and twenty acres. Alvin and Albert built a tar paper shack on the line between the homesteads so Dena and Alvin could live in the same house while they proved up.

Moenville was a grocery and dry goods store and post-office in the Julius Roseth home. The former owner's name was Moen.

Alvin met a young man lately arrived from Sioux Falls. Henry Martin was staying with his sister Isabel "Bird" and her husband Jim Huston. Jim, Bird and their small son Jimmy lived on the Cook place in the Moenville area. Alvin introduced Henry to Dena. What Alvin liked best about Henry was the shiny black Ford touring car that Henry drove.

Alvin told Dena if she would go with Henry, they could ride to dances in his car instead of going by horseback or buggy.

Henry was eager to squire Dena with the sparkling brown eyes, dark hair and ready smile. The Ford had ample room for Alvin and his lady to ride along. When Henry asked Dena to go with him to a dance, Alvin urged her to accept. Dena liked Henry. He was a quiet fellow. He didn't talk much, but he smiled a lot, smoked his pipe and was an excellent dancer. He played the violin like her brother Edward had.

Dena taught at the Standiford school. Since she and Alvin were not yet ready to live on their homesteads, Dena boarded with Bird and Jim Huston, to Henry's delight.

Mom and Dad were married in Kadoka by a flustered Justice of the Peace J.F. Hrachovec with three witnesses: J.F. Broyles, A.C. Barnace and B.F. McNally. After the ceremony one of the witnesses asked if the groom wasn't supposed to kiss the bride. "Oh, I forgot," Justice Hrachovec said. "They can do that on the way home."

When Frank came back to Midland, his sweetheart was married to someone else for which we Martin kids are duly thankful. The Midland Mail carried the story of their marriage in the October 19, 1916 edition: "It came as a surprise to their many friends when Henry Martin and Miss Dena Bertelson autoed to

118

Kadoka Saturday, the 14th and were married. Both these young folks are well know to Midland people and they have been receiving congratulations from friends. During the height of the fair activities they slipped away to Kadoka where the knot was tied. Not until the next day was it known in Midland. Each has a homestead near Moenville and they have gone to that place to establish their home. Their many friends wish them a long, happy and prosperous wedded life."

Henry didn't have a homestead. The Federal Government decided that people in that hilly country could have six hundred and forty acres of land instead of three hundred and twenty so Alvin relinquished his homestead, which adjoined Dena's to the newly married couple.

Dena and Henry Martin in the Model T.

Henry and Dena Bertelson Martin's wedding photo.

Grandma Juliana Bertelson's house. (Left to Right) Henry Martin, Walt Steien, Amanda Steien , unknown man and child.

Above: Charley Myrland and his tall corn.

Log House Walt and Amanda Steien built on his homestead.

Above: Grandma Juliana Bertelson around 1917.

(Left to Right) Mrs. Lafe Russell, Retta Russell and Bertina Myrland.

120

CHAPTER 10
Henry

My father's parents were also from Norway. Grandpa Halvor Syvert Martin was born in Norway in 1850. Great-Grandfather Syvert Kvernerud wanted to invest some money so he sent sons Halvor and Syvert Jr. to America to see the country and its money making potential.

Halvor and Syvert sailed to the United States and took the train to Sioux Falls, South Dakota around 1870 when Halvor was twenty years old. Halvor and Syvert bought land and wrote home enthusiastically about the country around Sioux Falls.

Great-Grandpa Kvernerud boarded ship with his wife Ingeborg, sons Ole, Thomas and Gilbert and daughters Isabel, Helga and Grunda. Isabel was married. Her husband died and was buried at sea.

Dad said when Grandpa Halvor got to New York an obliging fellow sold him the name Martin for $5.00. Ole and Gilbert took the same name. Tom and Syvert became Seversons.

The family settled on a farm near Woonsocket. Syvert died there at the age of seventy-eight. Ingeborg died nine years later. She was eighty-three. They were buried in The Silver Creek Cemetery at Woonsocket.

Thomas farmed near Clark. He was married and the father of two sons and two daughters. Ole settled on a farm in the Blunt area east of Pierre. He was married with four daughters and three sons. Gilbert was a bachelor and lived on a small farm near Canning east of the Missouri River. I don't know what happened to the daughters.

Grandpa Halvor married Tilda Helgerson in 1879. Norwegians seem to have a hard time making up their minds as to who they are. Grandma Martin was called Taran, Tilda and Teldum. Her tombstone says Teldum, but Dad's birth certificate lists her name as Tilda.

Tilda was the oldest of four living children of Arne Helgerson Hagan. She was born May 4, 1858 in Iowa. Annette died very young. Tilda had three brothers, Ole, Knud and Syvert.

Great-Grandpa Arne brought his family to America from Norway in the 1850's. He settled in Iowa where a man offered him $300.00 to go into the Union Army and fight in the Civil War in his place. Arne was assured he would only have to stay three months.

With such a tidy sum, Great-Grandpa Arne thought he could buy cattle, machinery, horses and hogs and for only three months of dodging bullets. He donned the uniform of a Yankee soldier, picked up his rifle and headed into battle. The three months stretched into three long years. He came out a bitter man.

Dad said a troop of southern cavalry chased Great-Grandpa Arne. He outran the cavalry and disappeared in the woods. Great-Grandpa Arne hated southern Johnnies for the rest of his life. He left his wife and children to go into the Union Army and returned when the war was over in 1865

Arne moved his family to a farm near Canton where Tilda married Halvor Martin. She bore eleven children over the next twenty years. Three boys Arne, Henry and Halvor died in infancy. The living children were: Ida Annette born December 23, 1879, Sophia Amelia born June 23, 1883, another Arne born June 23,

1886, another Henry Syvert born January 24, 1890, Tillie born March 22, 1892, Isabel born June 2, 1894, Helen Josephine born December 8, 1897 and Gina Bertina born December 3, 1899.

Grandpa Halvor and Grandma Tilda and six children left Woonsocket in 1895 and settled on a farm near Canton. Helen and Gina were born there. Grandma Tilda died of a heart attack January 7, 1906. She was forty-seven years old and is buried in the Canton Lutheran Cemetery. Grandpa Halvor was left with five children under eighteen years old. Fifteen-year-old Tillie died the next year from rheumatic fever.

Dad said they ate gobs of fish from the Sioux River when they were growing up. Grandpa Halvor must have been a shrewd investor because he bought and sold farms until he accumulated a small fortune. Dad's mother also had money. Each child received a legacy of several thousand dollars from their mother's estate when they reached their twenty-first birthday.

When Arne got his money, he headed for the homestead lands of western South Dakota. He homesteaded south of Midland near the Harry Huston homestead. The Hustons had lately moved by covered wagon from Nebraska.

There were several dark haired, brown eyed girls in the Huston family. Mildred worked in her grandmother's restaurant in Midland. Arne fell in love with the dark haired Irish lass. He asked her parents if they could wed. Mildred was not quite sixteen. "You don't want to marry her, Arne," Mrs. Huston said. "She can't even cook."

"That's all right," Arne said. "I can cook."

Their oldest daughter Madge said, "Neither of them could cook."

Arne and Mildred, called Mit, were married in 1908. Halvor, called Hallie, was born in 1909. Arne quit the homestead

and took his wife and son to the the Sioux Falls area where he
operated his father's dairy farm. Madge was born there in January
of 1911. My father Henry came to see his new niece and said, "I'm
twenty-one today. I'm going to get my money and go west."

Henry got his legacy from his mother's estate and headed
west with his sister Isabel, called Bird. They settled in a homestead shack south of Hustons. Like the three little pigs, Henry was
out to seek his fortune, only the wolf wasn't trying to blow his
shack down. The South Dakota wind was.

Henry thought the Huston girls were pretty, too, but he did-
n't stay long enough to marry one of them. Henry and Bird soon
left the homestead and journeyed back to Sioux Falls.

Jim Huston came to Sioux Falls to work for Grandpa
Halvor. He married Isabel in 1911 and they had two sons. Henry
died in infancy. Jimmy was born in 1912.

My father, Henry, made a trip to Seattle, Washington, but
didn't care for that country. He came back to Sioux Falls and
farmed in the Canton area for several years.

Grandpa Halvor was a daring investor. He made a great
deal of money for the times in which he lived. He gave each of his
children $8,000.00 so they could make their own fortunes. For
seven children that adds up to $56,000.00.

Seeing the possibilities for good investments in the west,
Grandpa Halvor, with Bird and Jim Huston, boarded the train for
western South Dakota. Bird and Jim settled in the Moenville country. Later Bird bought a farm thirteen miles northeast of Midland
where she and Jim lived for a short time. Jimmy was a little fellow.

Jim Huston told Dad, "Come out here, Hen. This is a great
country. You just turn your cattle out on the free range. You don't
even have to feed them in the winter. Big herds of horses roam the

free range and paw the snow away. The cattle follow the horses and eat the grass. It's all profit and no work."

Henry decided to go out and see the wonderful country north of Midland. He took the train to Pierre in June of 1916 and went to Hustons. Henry didn't like to ride horseback. He went to Midland and bought a Ford touring car from Calhoon Brothers.

Arne and family were already in the Midland vicinity. They had returned in 1911 and rented the Dickson farm south of Midland. Arne put a pleasure boat on the large dam on his farm. Mit took two ladies for a ride in the boat. In the middle of the pond, the ladies got stranded. Arne swam out and rescued them.

Gina came west to visit Bird and Arne. Grandpa Halvor bought the Standiford farm of two hundred forty acres fourteen miles north of Midland, smack on the rolling prairie without a tree in sight. W.J. Standiford had an auction sale, selling fifty-seven registered Shorthorn cattle and forty-six horses.

Arne was a good fiddler. He made extra money, playing for dances with his wife's sister Wilma at the piano, her husband Carl Ravenscroft on drums and sometimes Ernie Helleckson and Pete Elrod blowing horns.

Grandpa Halvor sold the Standiford farm to Arne. In 1916 Arne moved his family into a little house across the draw because a family from Sioux Falls lived in the big house. Gina turned eighteen that winter. She stayed with Arne until spring and went back to Sioux Falls. She married Emmet McCloskey. They had one daughter Mildred and two sons John and Emmet.

Gina, Sophia and Ida stayed in the Sioux Falls vicinity. Ida worked at housekeeping jobs until she married Frank McCone. They had no children. Sophia married Emil Christopher in 1914. They had two sons Gilfred and Laurenz. Helen married Jack Behrens. They had two sons, John and Richard, and a short stormy marriage.

The family from Sioux Falls moved out of the big house and Arne moved in. He bought thirty-six Texas and Colorado cattle from Kruse Madsen. Luckily, the former owner left a huge stack of hay by the barn. Arne was set for a nasty winter.

That fall Henry and Dena were married. They settled down to make their fortune in the rugged Moenville hills.

November 7, 1916 Democrat Woodrow Wilson was re-elected President of The United States with the slogan, "He kept us out of war." In April of 1917, The United States declared war on Germany. Shortly thereafter, General Pershing stood at Lafayette's tomb in France and said, "Lafayette, we are here," and American boys began dying on foreign soil to leave their bodies in Flanders Field beneath the crosses, "row on row."

Henry and Dena moved in with Jim, Bird and Jimmy. Dena taught the Standiford school while Henry and Jim built an addition to her homestead shack.

That winter Henry sold his Model T touring car to W.L. Pier and bought an Overland from Elrod and Gerber. The Overland was bigger, fancier and more expensive, and he promised to teach Dena how to drive it. The Government decided that starting January l, 1917, all automobiles had to be licensed.

Some snow fell that winter. A roaring blizzard the last of January tied the stages up along the roads and caused a large loss of livestock.

Walt built a new bandstand in Midland and remodeled The Opera Hall stage. His cattle were safe from blizzards among the trees of Mitchell Creek and Amanda was there to feed them. When spring came, Walt, the county surveyor, was out surveying roads.

Another fierce snowstorm raged through the country in March. Hay was going fast. That spring roads were in bad condition from melting snow. Cars got stuck in mud holes on the ungraveled roads. Obliging farmers hitched their teams to the automobiles and pulled them through the puddle for a few dollars.

A celebrated mud hole about twelve miles north of Midland south of the Hamilton McCready farm trapped many a motorist. Ham kept a team ready and made a nice profit pulling motorists to dry ground. He pulled Henry's Overland through the mud hole a time or two. People said Ham hauled water into the hole at night so it would be ready to trap unfortunate motorists the next day.

Herbert Donald Martin was born June 20, 1917 in an upstairs bedroom of Juliana Bertelson's house. Dr. Minard delivered the chubby baby, "the apple of his mother's eye." Henry came in the Overland and took his family back to the farm at Moenville.

Two hundred twenty-five automobiles rolled into Midland for the Fourth of July Celebration. The new Rex Theater showed silent movies. People watched in amazement as the good guys and the bad guys galloped across the screen.

Henry and the Bertelson brothers bought and leased several quarters of land joining Dena's homestead. Alvin and Henry fenced it and put up hay for the coming winter. Albert bought a Model T touring car, and Alvin motored up from the Bad River ranch one afternoon. By horse he would have spent a long day.

In September Walt, Albert and Alvin took a load of cattle to Chicago on the train for themselves and Martins. The War was bringing prices up. Albert got $101.50 for a steer he bought for $45.00.

Henry and Leonard Grotta hauled a load of lumber out to the Moenville ranch. Walt helped Henry build a large two story house. Henry built corrals, straw roofed sheds and a chicken house.

Not much snow fell the winter of 1917-18. Dena and Henry jumped in the Overland and went to Midland to visit Dena's mother, sisters and brothers. February turned so warm that Albert got his Ford stuck in the mud up on Little Prairie Dog Creek northeast of Midland.

Alvin gathered strays along Bad River that fall and then went into the army. He was sent to Camp Fremont, California and put in a machine gun company. Machine gunners were called "suicide brigades," because they were on the front lines and seldom lived through battle. Fortunately, Alvin never went overseas. Walt mailed him The Midland Mail so he could keep up on events at home.

1918 was the winter of the flu. The flu killed as many American soldiers as the war did. Every paper carried the news of more deaths.

Oliver Nelson, who was in a camp in Wisconsin, told Alvin that soldiers died so fast in his camp that they piled the bodies up like cord wood. The bodies were left frozen until the ground thawed in spring so they could be buried.

Our Aunts, Tina and Amanda, Grandma Juliana and Mom knitted sweaters, socks and scarves for the soldiers. Hundreds of these items were shipped from Midland to the army.

By the summer of 1918, Herb was an adventurous little tyke. He played outside while Mom worked nearby. Wearing only a diaper, he crawled on top of an ant hill and sat down. The ant hill was home to thousands of half inch long, red fire ants. The ants were furious at this giant thing that dared to sit on their house, this thing with bare white belly and tender legs. They swarmed up his legs and over his bare chest. Huge ants crawled into his diaper, swarmed over his head and into his mouth. They bit.

Herb screamed like a little pig caught in a fence, but he

128

didn't move. He sat on the ant hill and howled. Mom came on a high run. She grabbed Herb and dashed into the house. She undressed him and tried to pull the ants loose. The ants were angry. They wouldn't let go. She pulled ants in half and the front half kept right on biting Herb's tender flesh. She put Herb in a tub of warm water. When she finally got all the ants loose, Herb looked like he had the measles.

Dad had wasted some of his money and spent some on cars and building a house. He bought land with most of what was left. In the fall of 1918, he borrowed money from Deaners Loan Company and bought two hundred Texas cattle and trailed them to the Moenville ranch. Albert bought two hundred Texas cattle, too, and hired Slim Welch to work for him.

In September Albert was riding on round-up south of the Howes ranch on Mitchell Creek. The hills were steep; the ground slick. He galloped his horse around a hill. The horse hit a slick spot and fell, landing on Albert's right leg. With a sickening crunch, the leg broke.

The horse jumped up and ran with Albert's foot caught in the stirrup. The frightened horse tore down the hill. Albert made a desperate grab and caught the horse's tail. He held himself off the ground as the flying heels flashed at his head. Albert's foot shook loose and he fell on the ground. The horse raced down the hill.

Albert was taken to Dr. Minard. Dr. Minard tried to set the leg, but the knee was crushed. He couldn't set it properly. Worried, Grandma Juliana sent for Alvin. A month later, he arrived home from the Army Base. He found Albert in his bedroom, his ruined leg stretched out on the bed, his face etched in pain. Alvin was angry when he saw his brother suffering with a leg that wouldn't heal.

He went to Dr. Minard and said he wanted to take Albert to

St. Mary's Hospital in Pierre and have Dr. Riggs look at his leg. Dr. Minard didn't think that necessary. Alvin called Dr. Riggs. Dr. Riggs, a nationally famous doctor, said, "I'll talk to Dr. Minard."

Alvin took Albert to Pierre on the train. His leg had already started to heal. Dr. Riggs broke and reset it. Albert spent almost a year in and out of the hospital, but his leg didn't heal.

He went to Rapid City where a surgeon removed the knee cap, leaving Albert with his right leg several inches shorter than the left. His right knee would not bend. His days of round-up riding were over. He was now a man who drove a team and buggy or a car.

For a number of years, Albert wore a shoe with a built up heel, but he eventually threw the shoe under his bed and left it there. Albert was no longer "The Big Fellow," although Alvin never stopped calling him that affectionate nickname.

Alvin was mustered out of the army at Ft. Logan January 3, 1919. He went to Moenville to care for the cattle there. Slim Welch worked at the Bad River Ranch.

The bitter winter had just begun to deal its misery.

Henry Martin's father and brothers and sisters. (Back Row) Severt, Halvor, Gilbert, Ole and Tom. (Front Row) Isobel, Helga and Grunda.

130

Grandma Tilda Helgerson Martin.

Dad's sisters, Helen and Gina.

Twenty-one year old Henry Martin ready to head west.

Henry Martin playing cowboy.

131

CHAPTER 11
The Winter of 1918-1919

In December of 1918, Mom and Dad piled blankets in the Overland, bundled Herb up and motored to Bertelsons for Christmas. Jim Huston was to look after their cattle. Grandma Bertelson's Christmas tree was beautiful with tinsel and decorations and lit with many candles. Little Herbert walked around and around his first Christmas tree, saying, "Petty, petty."

Myrlands were in Iowa for the winter. Charley wasn't going to milk cows and slop hogs that cold winter. He might help do chores in a warm Iowa barn.

A blizzard blew in while Mom and Dad were at Bertelsons. Dad's barn was divided with one side for horses and one for cattle. He kept his calves in the cow barn. Jim moved the calves into the horse stalls and left the door to the cow barn open so the cattle around the farmstead could come in for shelter.

When the blizzard whistled in, cattle crowded into the barn until they piled on top of each other. A bunch of stray steers drifted in to the corrals. They piled on top and smothered the cattle underneath. After the storm, Jim went to the barn. The strays walked out of the barn and headed out to pasture. Many of Dad's cows were dead.

After Christmas Dad went back to Moenville. Henry Jr. was born at the Moenville farm January 31, 1919 with Mrs. Nesheim attending. Albert Bertelson went to Rapid City to have

132

another operation on his leg. Grandma Juliana went home with Mom to help care for the boys.

The winter was bitterly cold. Cattle had trouble finding feed under the deep blanket of snow.

Alvin was thoroughly disgusted with his brother-in-law. When he talked Dena into dating the quiet fellow from Sioux Falls so they could ride around in his car, he didn't expect her to marry the jackass. Henry was the poorest excuse for a cattleman Alvin had ever seen. He thought you could run cattle on the open range, and if there was snow, horses would paw it away. Cows would follow the horses and eat their fill. Anybody with half a brain knew a horse grazed his pawed off spot until he was ready to leave. During the night, snow would probably drift over what was left.

Henry was so stupid he cut such a big drinking hole in the ice that some of his cattle fell in and drowned. Any fool should know you cut a hole long and narrow so a cow can drink without falling or getting pushed into the water. Alvin cussed Henry because he didn't know any better than to drown his cattle.

Horses didn't paw the deep snow away fast enough. The range cattle, long of horn and gaunt of belly, coming up from the warm south, shivered and froze in the relentless cold and driving snow.

To make matters worse, Dad was called to Pierre for jury duty. He hired Jack Rank to care for the cattle. Dad was a dairy farmer from eastern South Dakota. Jack came from Wisconsin. He had worked for Dad on the dairy farm. Neither of them knew anything about range cattle or the open range. They were used to dairy cows and warm barns.

Jack was married to Mom's cousin Louella Harman. They had a baby daughter Ramona. Jack rode every day, looking for cows to weak to get up. If a cow rolled too far onto her back or laid down with her back down hill, she couldn't get up. If someone didn't help her to her feet, she would bloat and die.

The thin hided cattle from the warm south could not stand the combination of cold, snow and too little feed. As spring neared, the cows, heavy with calf, even thinner from a long hard winter, grew weaker every day. To add to their misery, they were plagued with bugs in their ears that drove them wild.

A cow would lie down on a steep hillside, throw her head back to rub a tortured ear against the ground and be to weak to roll back. A horse can sleep all night on his feet, but not a cow. A cow beds down at night. If she can't get up in the morning, she is in serious trouble. Tailing up weak cows was an every day chore.

Alvin rode on the Bertelson cattle, getting the weak critters up to graze each day. He told me, "You tailed up a critter, then ran like hell to get out of her way."

A cow gets up hind end first. The cows couldn't get their rear ends off the ground, but a little boost was all they needed. When someone hoisted on a cow's tail, she came up with an angry bellow. She hit four feet with fire in her eyes and charged with a snort. The cowboy ran for his horse with the cow blowing on his hip pockets. With a flying leap, he lit in the saddle and raced out of her way.

Grandma was worried about the cows. She told Mom, "I don't think Jack is finding all the down cows."

Grandma took care of Herb and Hank. Mom saddled Baldy and rode out to help. When she found a cow that couldn't get up, she dismounted, grabbed the cow's tail and heaved up. The cow came up snorting. Mom dashed for her horse. With the cow bellowing at her heels, she swung into the saddle and galloped away.

One day Mom found a cow she couldn't get up. She hoisted on the cow's tail, but the cow was too weak to raise her front end. She got halfway up, then tumbled in a heap again. Mom rode to get Jack.

Jack looped his rope around the cow's neck. "I'll lift her front end and you lift on her tail," he said.

Jack lifted on the animal's neck. Mom yanked up on her tail. The cow came up, blowing fire out her nose. Jack jerked his rope off her neck. Bellowing in rage, she charged. Jack leaped on his horse and galloped away.

When green grass finally came, the range was dotted with the carcasses of dead cattle. Dad and Mom lost most of their herd. Their hopes for a cattle ranch died with their cattle. Shattered dreams blew away on the howling winds of the bitter winter of 1918-1919.

Alvin didn't lose many cattle. He ridiculed Dad whenever he had a chance. No matter what Dad did, Alvin made fun of him. Mom was caught in the middle until Dad had enough.

One Saturday night, Dad, Mom and Alvin went to a dance. Dad and Alvin drank a little whiskey. Dad confronted Alvin. "I'm sick and tired of your belly aching," Dad said. "You've been asking for trouble, and I'm going to give it to you. Come outside. We'll settle it."

Alvin was feeling his whiskey. He was happy to oblige. He was bigger than Dad, and he figured a lot tougher. They went back of the dance hall and had a bare knuckle duel. Dad knocked the daylights out of Alvin. They became friends and remained so for the rest of their lives.

With spring, snow melted and ran down the draws into creeks and rivers. Grass turned green along the edges of snowbanks, green that spread across the prairie. Tiny white flowers bloomed in the new grass, and the carcasses of thousands of cattle lay rotting amid the promise of spring.

The pitiful remnant of Dad's herd lingered near the feed yards or scattered out on the hills, trying to get a mouthful of green grass. Aside from a few bony cows dropping scrawny calves, all Dad and Mom had left the spring of 1919 was horns, hides and bones.

Dad went out to salvage what he could. He spent hours skinning the cold bodies of his dead cattle and hauled the hides to Midland. He headed for Midland one day with a wagon load of hides and picked up a young man who was walking down the road. "Are you a hide buyer?" the man asked. Dad shook his head, sadly aware of what the hides in the back of the wagon signified.

Dad didn't have enough cattle left to pay his loan. "Make the loan company take your cattle, Henry," Julius Roseth said. "Settle up and start over with a clean slate."

Dad and Mom discussed what to do. The Deaner Loan Company was generous. They offered to carry them while they built the herd up again. The offer sounded good. They would have the cattle ranch they dreamed about. Building up their herd would take time, but they knew they could do it. The toughest cows were still left.

Alvin fell in love and considered marriage, but his sweetheart had more money than he did. He couldn't marry a woman richer than he was. They broke up. Because of their stubborn pride, Alvin and Albert remained bachelors.

When Dad went to Sioux City with a load of cattle in the fall, he sent a young man to Dena with the Overland. "Your husband said to bring the car up for you. He didn't have time." He turned the car over to Mom even though she had never driven it before.

She put Herbert and Henry Jr. in the car, got behind the wheel and started up the rutty street. J. C. Russell, his clerk A.C.

Beiler, Behl who worked at Davidson Hardware, Alvin and a tire salesman stood in front of Russell's Store, watching. The motor died. "She'll never make it," Beiler said.

"Yes, she will," J.C. Russell said.

The tire salesman grinned. "She'll make it. I never knew a Bertelson who didn't get where they were going."

Mom stepped on the starter and the motor roared. She drove up the bumpy street and out to Myrland's farm on Mitchell Creek.

Uncle Arne's farm was halfway between our place and Midland on the market trail to the Midland stockyards. Having an abundance of hay beside the barn and few cattle to feed, Arne went through the winter without losing any cattle.

When fall rolled around, he sold his cattle and moved his family to Midland for the winter. Madge and Hallie would get to go to school, and he wouldn't have to go through another bad winter of feeding cattle in blizzards.

Another bad winter was brewing. Dad's youngest sister Gina came to spend the winter with Arne and family. Mom was pregnant again and went to Midland before Christmas to stay with her mother.

This letter dated December 20, 1919 from Dad at Moenville shows the stark reality of a bitter winter and too little feed.

Dear Dena and Kids:

Will answer your letter tonight. I'm getting along pretty good but wish you and the kids were home again as it gets pretty lonesome around here without you. Have had Soloman hauling corn fodder this week as I find I have about all I can do to take care of the cattle without going over there after a load. I'm feeding

137

about half the cows now. We have lost five head all told but so has everybody else up here. Len Grotta has lost his big bull and one of his full blood cows and quite a few others and Roseth lost a bull. There has been a lot of cattle lost up here the last two weeks. We lost all ours one night. It was so cold they just froze to death right where they bedded down. I have not got any papers from Deaners yet and they haven't answered my letter. I don't know what is the matter with them. It don't look like they intend to carry us till spring. I wrote to Albert and told him they had not sent papers yet. I don't think I can come down Xmas, Dena as I can't leave the cattle without anybody to look after them. Leonard has got about all he can do looking after his own. He seems to be sick every other day this winter so I don't like to ask him to look after ours while I be gone. I sure like to come and see you and the kids but I don't believe I better chance it. All that the weather has been nice this week. Am just about out of wood so I'll have to go and get some one of these days. Hope you are getting along all right and not sick. You will have to hurry and have that other one so you can come home to your old man. It gets dam lonesome sleeping alone. Well will close for this time.

Yours

Henry
P.S. It will be all right to write a check on me if you don't make it too big as my acc is pretty small.

Dad got some hay delivered by Thor Fosheim in January. The cold didn't keep Uncle Walt from work. He and Bill Crawford built a barn for Jack Buchanan east of Midland.

That winter Dad got a piece of steel in his left eye while working on the Overland. His eye became infected and had to be removed. He bought a glass eye.

That glass eye was mainly a Saturday, Sunday and company eye. One man asked Dad if he could see as good with the glass eye as he could with the other one. The glass eye was such a perfect match one couldn't tell which was the good eye. The glass eye usually resided in his pocket.

Dad was a wiry man, strong and slim. He smoked a pipe filled with Prince Albert, stashing the flat tin can in his shirt pocket. He chewed plug tobacco, too, as did Uncle Walt and Uncle Charley. They carried plugs of tobacco so they could chew off a chunk or loan the plug to a friend.

Hotels, restaurants and bars had brass cuspidors for their customers to spit tobacco juice in. We couldn't afford such luxury. Pound coffee cans were scattered about our house for the tobacco chewers. Dad and Uncle Charley could plink tobacco juice into the can from several feet away.

On a cold day in early December, Midland had another disastrous fire. The fire started in The Humphrey Cafe when a gas lamp blazed high. Humphrey grabbed the lamp and headed for the door to throw it outside. Flames leaped high. Fire scorched his hands and face, forcing him to drop the lamp.

Fire roared through the cafe and spread rapidly, engulfing a dentist's office and spreading to C.E. Murray's Store, Savage Barber Shop and Dr. Minard's office. The fire raced into the building occupied by the Lafe Russell family.

The weather was so cold that the chemical fire fighting equipment wouldn't work. They fought the fire with a bucket brigade from the well across the street. The fire was stopped from spreading by putting steel sheeting that happened to be handy between the fire and the next building.

The $25,000.00 fire cleaned out half a block. C.E. Murray had a fire sale of $15,000.00 worth of damaged goods. He built a new store on the corner of Main and Russell Avenue. That building is occupied by The Frontier Bank today.

Frank Calhoon's Midland Auto Company advertised Fords sedans for $875.00, coupes for $750.00, and runabouts for $500.00. Car prices had doubled since the war. For an extra $75.00 you could get an electric starter.

I never saw one of those starters that worked. Most cars had to be cranked. Jacking up a hind wheel made cranking easier. A husky fellow could spin the crank like a top. If the motor backfired, the crank spun backwards, sometimes breaking the cranker's arm.

In March water ran down the creeks and rivers from melting snow. An ice gorge east of Midland backed water into the stockyards.

Mom took the train to Rapid City and stayed with Alphia and Wilmer Hollis and their three children while waiting for the new baby.

I, Thelma Deane Martin, came into the world March 13, 1920 by caesarean section. I howled into the world dangling by one leg from the doctor's forceps, in a small hospital that had been a large house. Mom's cousin Nora Hauge was a nurse there. I weighed six pounds, a dainty baby girl with a mound of dark hair and large blue eyes. Dad waited on the Moenville farm. Herbert almost three and Henry Jr. barely one stayed with Aunt Tina and Uncle Charley.

After two weeks in the hospital, Alphia came and took Mom and me to their farm east of Rapid City. Anxious to see the new baby, Aunt Tina boarded the train with Herbert and Brother as they called Henry Jr. and came to see us.

Aunt Tina sat in a chair, holding me. Herb stood close to her chair, admiring his new sister. Brother backed against Mom's chair and frowned fiercely. "Isn't she nice?" Aunt Tina asked. "Aren't you glad you get to take her home? Brother shook his head. "No, no." He didn't like this new arrival who would take his place on Mom's lap. Winter was still lurking. President Wilson was awarded the Nobel Peace Prize. The 18th Amendment had ushered in Prohibition January 16, 1920. Bootleggers were making illegal whiskey in secret stills.

The rains came and grass grew tall. Dad's cow herd grew. He had three brands listed in The Midland Mail: rocker open A left shoulder horses, O bar left hip cattle and connected double H on a rail left hip cattle. Dad and Mom were proud of their small herd, the beginning of the larger herd they would have someday.

Mom now had three children to care for, two in diapers and one newly graduated from them. She washed clothes in a wooden wash machine that took muscle power to operate. Dad spelled her when he was in the house. She made soap from lye and grease like her mother did.

She still had time to play with us and dream about the ranch they were building. Herb and Brother played with a little wagon with steel spoke wheels and a wooden box.

"You can be the horse, Brother. I'll be the driver," Herb said, climbing into the wagon. He had already learned how to con Brother into pulling the wagon while he rode.

The cow herd had grown large enough to cover the mortgage so The Deaner Loan Company foreclosed and sold the cattle. Gone again was the dream of a cattle ranch, destroyed by a lying loan company. Mom and Dad wished they had taken Julius Roseth's advise and sold out two years earlier. All they had left was a herd of horses and two cattle brands.

Mom went back to teaching the fall of 1921. She taught the Liberty School where Uncle Arnie's kids, Hallie, Madge and Aline, went to school. We lived on Aunt Bird's farm about six miles southeast of Uncle Arnie's farm.

Mom rode to school on Baldy. The boys stayed with Dad. I stayed with Aunt Tina and Uncle Charley. I stayed with them so much I didn't know where I belonged. Madge and Hallie often rode horseback to visit Mom and Dad on Saturday and rode home Sunday.

Dad's sister Helen worked for Walt Breeding, cooking for his crew. Breeding lived on a farm a mile and a half south of Uncle Arnie's place. Helen had left her husband. Their sons, two-year-old Jackie, and one-year-old Richard were with her.

Aunt Ida said John and Helen wouldn't have split up if Bird hadn't meddled in their lives. I'm not so sure. John beat her when he was angry. When he came to Aunt Gina's house to get Helen, Aunt Gina ran him off with a broom.

Helen loved to gallop recklessly across the prairie on her horse with the wind blowing in her face. She became ill in December. Mom stayed with her at night and taught school in the daytime. On weekends Dad and Grandpa were there, too. Madge came and took care of Jackie, Richard, Herb and Brother in the upstairs bedroom.

Mrs. Poler and another lady came to nurse Helen. On Sunday December 10, 1921, Helen died of a massive hemorrhage. Mom said the men were in the kitchen laughing and joking while Helen died. She never liked Grandpa Martin after that.

Grandpa had already lost so much; his wife, three sons and a lovely fifteen-year-old daughter. Men were not supposed to cry. Perhaps he had to laugh to cover the pain.

142

Aunt Bird's son Jimmie got sick and was taken to the Pierre Hospital. The doctor said he would get well, but Jimmie didn't want to live. He died and his parents divorced for the second time after twelve stormy years of marriage. Jimmie was eleven. Aunt Bird married Eddie Dame, moved to Illinois and lived happily ever after.

Grandpa Martin talked Dad into moving to one of his farms in the Canning vicinity about twenty miles east of Pierre. We moved the spring of 1922. Dad's Uncle Ole Martin lived on a farm nearby. Uncle Gulick lived in a dugout on his homestead a mile away.

My only memory of that farm is the night a brown mare kicked the corncrib door open and fed corn to all the livestock.

In July we boarded the train at Canning to go to Midland because Mom was almost ready to give birth to her fourth child. Mom and Dad were going to take me, Herb and Brother to Midland to stay with our Aunts Tina and Amanda while the baby was born.

When the train pulled in to Pierre, Mom went into labor so Dad took her to St. Mary's Hospital where Juliana Edrina was born July 23, 1922. We called the dark haired baby with the dark eyes "Baby." She was the undisputed queen of the household and she knew it.

Grandma Bertelson lived long enough to see the child named after her. She died a month after Juliana was born. She was buried in The Lutheran cemetery in Lake Mills, Iowa.

Aunt Tina and Uncle Charley took me home with them every chance they got. Uncle Charley chewed tobacco at night and kept a spit bucket in front of the bed. I climbed over him in the night and fell on the bucket, breaking a collar bone. I cried and they felt bad.

We moved frequently. Once we came upon a family moving with a load of furniture, household goods and wooden crates of chickens. The wagon had broken down. The chicken crates smashed open. Chickens flew out and scattered over the prairie. A mentally handicapped boy of about twelve sat in the wagon, laughing uproariously as his mother chased chickens while his father fixed the wagon. Dad and Mom helped her catch the squawking fowls.

We moved back to Midland and stayed at the Bertelson ranch because Mom taught in the Schofield school south of the ranch.

Mom drove a two wheeled cart to school. She took five-year-old Herb and put him in kindergarten. Sitting on the cart seat with a fast horse hitched to the shafts, they skimmed over the prairie with their school books in the compartment under the seat.

Herb liked school. He was proud of his box of crayons, his new pencils and tablet. He played with the Schofield boys who walked to school from their home on Brave Bull Creek. If the Schofield children met the cart at the fork, they grabbed the tail end and ran behind as the horse trotted down the road.

One morning Mom decided to see how fast they could run before they had to let go. She let her horse out to full trot. Dust flew as the horse's feet hit the road with a steady roar. The children held fast to the cart. She didn't lose even one.

The school had a kitchen so the children could have hot lunches. Mom took potatoes and Schofields provided milk. She let the students take turns fixing cocoa for dinner. She noticed that the cocoa and sugar disappeared fast. She peeked into the small kitchen where two Schofield boys were making cocoa. They had mixed a cup of sugar and cocoa and were eating it with a spoon. She laughed to herself and thought they needed a little sweet stuff.

144

Mom and Herb had a cart runaway on the way to school one day. Mom got one leg caught in the spokes and was injured. Herb sailed through the air, lit on the ground and rolled in the grass. Mom got the horse stopped and they went to school.

Dad stayed at the Moenville farm with a few cows and a herd of horses. Brother and I chased Grandma's cat and caught him whenever we could. We petted the black dog and played with Brother's little wagon. Lillie Martin, Dad's cousin, took care of Baby and kept an eye on us.

When someone wanted a cool breeze to blow into the house, they stuck a knife between the sash and the casing to hold the window up. One day I jerked the knife out. The window crashed down on my hand, smashing the ends of my fingers. The finger tips bled. Mom bandaged my fingers, but I will never forget the pain.

Once Mom was going to spank me. I crawled under the gate east of the house and chugged down the road. "It won't do you any good to run away. I'll spank you when you come back," she said, watching me from the gate.

I turned around and ran back, got spanked and then she explained why I had to obey. We seldom got spanked, and spankings didn't hurt, but they broke my heart. If anyone scolded me, I felt like crawling in a hole.

We weren't allowed to swear or use obscene language. Lying was an absolute no, no. If we used bad language or lied, Mom washed our mouth out with soap. Soap doesn't taste good, but it gets the point across.

When spring came, we went to the Moenville farm. We were happy to be back with Dad. Lillie came to look after us.

Sometimes Mom hitched a team to the wagon. She and Lillie loaded us into the box, and we went down to spend a few days with Myrlands and Steiens. The trip took all day, but halfway along we stopped at Uncle Arnie's farm, eleven miles north of Steien's place.

Uncle Charley and Uncle Walt had their farms fenced. They ran cattle, horses and a few hogs.

Jake DeYoung's farm joined Uncle Charley's farm on the west. DeYoungs milked a herd of cows. One Sunday they came to Myrlands for dinner. Mr. DeYoung apologized because his over-shoes were muddy. "I get my overshoes all dirty, milking in them," he said, smiling at Aunt Tina.

"I milk in the bucket," Uncle Charley said. The DeYoung boys Herbert, Richard and Harold thought that was hilarious.

Uncle Charley fought with Mrs. DeYoung about her calves. The calves crawled through the fence and got into his alfal-fa field. Yelling and waving his arms, Uncle Charley chased the calves back through the fence and met Mrs. DeYoung coming after them.

Uncle Charley yelled at her. "You should keep your calves at home. They are ruining my alfalfa."

Sparks flew as Mrs. DeYoung lit into him. He went home and told Aunt Tina, "My, she did swear." He shook his head.

Aunt Tina and Aunt Amanda wore a trail between their houses, walking to visit each other. Uncle Charley built a neat wooden gate in the fence so they could cross over by opening a door.

Uncle Walt and Uncle Charley didn't get along. Aunt Amanda and Aunt Tina worried and agonized over their lack of friendship, but nothing changed. Uncle Walt bought a new Elgin car and parked the Metz on the hill west of the house. He wouldn't let Aunt Tina and Uncle Charley ride along to town in his new Elgin because he said the load would be too heavy for his car, although it had two seats.

Uncle Charley mortgaged his homestead and bought the Walton place on the flat between the Rogers sheep ranch and Steiens. He had raised a good alfalfa crop and sold the seed. He figured he could raise more alfalfa and easily pay for the Walton place.

Uncle Charley and Aunt Tina moved into the small house on the Walton farm. Uncle Charley dug cedar trees from Cedar Canyon north of his Mitchell Creek farm and planted a row of the evergreens west of his new farmstead. I could never understand why they left their lovely homestead and moved to that wind swept flat where the blizzard winds hit with all their fury.

As children we often visited Aunt Tina and Uncle Charley and Aunt Amanda and Uncle Walt and stayed for several days. On one occasion when Juliana and I were visiting Aunt Tina, two-year-old Juliana disappeared. We rushed outside. We didn't find her by the house so we headed for the barn. "My, I hope Yuliana didn't go to the barn." Aunt Tina's J's and Y's always got mixed up. She said, "yelly" for jelly and "jellow" for yellow.

Bonnie, a high-spirited bay mare, was in the yard at the barn. We hurried down the path. Bonnie stood like a statue in the middle of the corral. Juliana peeked out from between Bonnie's front legs, one arm wrapped around each leg.

The mare never moved a muscle as Aunt Tina walked slowly to her and picked up Juliana. Then Bonnie pranced away with her beautiful head high.

One day we headed for town with Bonnie and Topsy hitched to the buggy. The horses trotted across the mile of level prairie. We waved at Mr. Rogers riding his bay horse and herding his sheep. We came to the long hill that slanted down toward Bad River. Midland lay below us. We could see the houses and stores.

As the horses started down the hill, the buggy tongue fell down. Topsy stopped. Bonnie reared high, pawing the air. The buggy jerked around. "Whoa, whoa!" Aunt Tina held the lines taut, speaking gently but firmly to the horses. Bonnie's feet came down. She stood shivering while Aunt Tina got out of the buggy and unhooked the team. She put the neck yoke back on the tongue, hitched the horses to the buggy again, and we went to Midland for our groceries.

A fierce red rooster was absolute monarch of the chicken house on the Walton farm. He thought he owned the whole farm. He ignored the guinea fowl that ran chattering to the barn if a hawk flew over.

The red rooster strutted about when his ladies were out scratching in the dirt. I think he kept an eagle eye on them so if they found a tender worm or fat bug, he could grab some of their food before they gobbled it down. The red rooster feared neither man nor beast. Uncle Charley teased the red rooster by kicking dirt at him. The red rooster's hackles rose and he attacked the foot and leg with sharp claws and hard beak, making Uncle Charley laugh. "Thelma, run to the barn and tell Charley dinner is ready," Aunt Tina said.

Happy with my errand, I ran toward the barn. As I approached the chicken house, the red rooster stopped watching his hens and glared at me. I skidded to a stop, turned and ran back toward the house, my short legs churning. The red rooster gave chase.

I screamed and tried to run faster. The red rooster took to the air and flew straight at me. Both feet hit me squarely in the back. I fell headlong to the ground. The red rooster jumped on my back, digging in his claws. He beat a tattoo on my head with his hard beak.

148

My screams brought Aunt Tina and Uncle Charley on a high run. Uncle Charley chased the red rooster back to his flock. Aunt Tina carried me to the house. The red rooster lost his head and made the best chicken soup I ever ate.

Herb, Brother and I were visiting Aunt Tina and Uncle Charley. Brother and I went adventuring across the prairie on a lovely fall day. We wandered for over half a mile until we came to a draw south of the Rogers place.

Herb stood beside the house, watching us go farther and farther away. Our adventure worried him. He ran into the house. "Auntie, come see where Brother and Thelma are." He grabbed her hand and pulled her toward the door.

Aunt Tina and Herb came after us. We were halfway down the draw when we heard her yell. We knew we were in trouble. We ran back toward her. Woody plants grew on the prairie that made wonderful switches. Aunt Tina had one of those. She switched us. The switches stung our legs as she herded us home. Herb ran beside her, looking happy. We didn't run away again.

Herb could get into his share of trouble, too. He and Brother were visiting Aunt Amanda and Uncle Walt. They were playing on the windmill. Herb turned the windmill loose, but the pump rod wasn't bolted. The rod ran up and down without pumping water. Every time Herb tried to line up the holes to put the bolt through, the rod went past the hole. "I'll stick my finger in the hole and hold it so you can put the bolt in," Brother said.

He stuck his right fore finger through the hole and, swish, the rod cut his finger off. They ran to the house, crying. Aunt Amanda saw Brother's bloody stump of a half finger and nearly fainted. She called Dr. Riggs at Pierre and told him she was bringing Henry Jr. to the hospital. She wanted the doctor to meet the train. He assured her that would not be necessary. She should wrap the finger and come to Pierre and meet him at St. Mary's Hospital. Dr. Riggs sewed the hide back over the stubby finger.

Most of the time while we were growing up, we lived too far from church and Sunday School to attend regularly. Mom and our Aunts Tina and Amanda firmly believed in the saving grace of Jesus Christ and the love of God for all of his creation. They taught us their faith. Uncle Albert gave us a Bible Story book. Mom read us the Bible stories until the book wore out. We knew about David and Goliath, Sampson and Delilah, Moses and the Israelites. All the fascinating people of the Bible were familiar characters to us. I was shocked when I went to Sunday School with a friend who had gone all of her life and didn't even know who David was.

At night we prayed, "Now I lay me down to sleep, I pray thee, Lord, my soul to keep. If I should die before I wake, I pray thee, Lord, my soul to keep." It was comforting to think that God sent his angels to watch over us. Mom said we had guardian angels.

From the fall of 1923 to the spring of 1925, Mom taught at The Thompson School near Moenville. Herb went to The Stoney Butte School for his first grade the fall of 1923. Mom rode northeast over the high hill while Herb rode south across Stoney Butte Creek to a school over by Grottas where Oscar Markwed was the teacher. Herb rode a pony with a child's saddle. Roy Roseth, also in first grade, wished he had a saddle like that.

Sometimes Mom took Juliana and me to visit the school in the claim shack. Six Fosheim girls: Minnie, Olga, Clara, Emma, Anna and Tillie, went to school there. They rode two horses, three girls to a horse.

One night a skunk took up housekeeping under the school house. Mom came to school. The pupils arrived and school began.

The skunk didn't like all the commotion going on above her head so she sprayed. The smell was so fierce that Mom took the children out of school. They went to the Jack Gates ranch and held classes for several days until the skunk had been removed and most of the rank odor left.

One afternoon when Herb rode into the creek, his saddle turned. Herb fell off and the saddle tumbled after him. Bawling like a calf, he came to the house, leading his horse. Dad sent Brother and me after the saddle. We took the little wagon and trudged to the creek crossing, loaded the saddle and brought it to the house.

The Harry Huston family lived north of our place. We often played with the Huston kids. Bud and Florence, children of the first Mrs. Huston who had died, were several years older than Walter, Robert and Opal. Florence was a year older than Herb.

Bud was ornery. He sneaked up behind his stepmother and set her hair on fire. She didn't notice and kept right on turning meat. Bud got scared and put the fire out.

Florence, Robert, Walter and Opal were playing with us in the creek one day. Walter, Robert and Opal were helping Brother and I build stick corrals for our pebble cows and horses. A huge brown bull walked by along the fence a quarter of a mile south. His head moved from side to side, and he bellowed to himself as he looked for cows. "The bull will get us. The bull will get us," Florence said, running for a tree. "Boost me up the tree, Herb."

Herb boosted her into the tree and said, "I'll boost the little kids up."

"No, no," Florence said. "The bull will come. Climb up with me." She reached for his hand. Herb climbed up in the tree and they perched on a branch like a pair of owls. The bull went bellowing on his way. The rest of us played at the foot of the tree.

151

When the bull had gone over the hill, Herb and Florence climbed down.

Baby Juliana and I stayed home with Dad while Mom taught school. She took Herb and Hank with her to The Thompson School. One day Baby fell down the stairs, rolling and bumping all the way to the bottom.

Baby found other dangerous ways to get into trouble. Mom scattered Daisy Fly Killers around the house to poison the flies that buzzed around all summer. The Daisy Fly Killer was a small oblong tank with daisies painted all over the top. Every now and then one of the daisies had a piece of orange felt on it. When the tank was filled with sugar water, poison wicked up through the felt flowers. A fly perched on the tank, sipped water from the felt flower and keeled over dead.

Daisy Fly Killers would kill anything that drank the water. A little boy got into the Daisy Fly Killer in his parents groceries as they drove home from town. He sucked the fly poison from a felt daisy and died before they could get to a doctor.

Mom found Baby sucking on a felt daisy. She gave Baby an emetic and kept her awake for several hours. She was afraid if Baby went to sleep, she wouldn't wake up again. Baby got all right and didn't eat any more fly poison.

Brother and I found ways to get into trouble, too. One day Brother found a large round can lid with an edge as sharp as a knife. He threw the lid to me. I threw it back. We threw the lid to each other, watching the silver disk sail through the air. Brother threw it to me. I ran and picked it up and sailed it back.

Brother threw the disk high in the air. The silver wheel glinted in the sunlight. I watched the shining disk come straight at me. The disk curved down and hit me square in the face, narrowly missing my nose. Blood ran down my cheek.

I ran, screaming, to the house. Mom ran out to see what terrible thing had happened. She carried me into the house and washed the blood off my face. She wrapped a bandage around my head. There were no bandaids in those days. The cut healed, leaving a thin white line beside my nose. The scar faded with the years.

Mom said Dad was an efficient person. He always had supper ready soon after Mom came home from school. He wasn't afraid to do woman's work in an age when he might have been ridiculed for it. He felt bad enough because she had to earn the money that fed us. She came in the house sometimes and threw her enormous felt hat at him. We thought that hilarious.

We liked to ride horseback with Mom and Dad. When I was four and Brother five, Mom let us ride Nellie by ourselves while she stood beside the house and watched.

The hills loomed high behind our house. The horse loomed high above us as we looked up at her back. She looked at us with gentle brown eyes. Mom boosted Brother up and gave him the reins. She set me on the mare's back behind him. I clutched him tightly around the waist as we sat on Nellie's bare back.

"Let her walk," Mom said. "Don't go any faster."

Nellie walked over the bare gray earth with steps as soft as wool. We seemed to float over the ground so far below us. We were riding all alone with no big person to help us. It was fun.

"Let's go faster," Brother said. We kicked Nellie's sides. She walked faster. We kicked harder. Nellie broke into a trot. We bounced and laughed. With each step she took, we bounced farther back. Bounce, bounce, bounce. I was afraid. I was slipping and the ground was far away. I was falling!

We slid off Nellie's rear end, hitting the hard ground with a jar that shook every bone in our bodies. We cried. Nellie looked at us with her big brown eyes as if to say, "I didn't want to trot."

Mom helped us up. "I told you not to trot," she said as she dusted us off. We didn't ride anymore. Nellie was getting old. She and her bay colt stayed near the barn yard. One evening a stray dog followed Mom home from school. In the night Mom and Dad heard the dog barking.

The next morning, Dad found Nellie lying in the pasture with her colt standing beside her. The dog had chased her until she was exhausted and could no longer fight him away. She fell and the dog tore chunks out of her legs and hips. Bleeding and trembling, the old mare tried to rise, but she could not. Dad had to shoot Nellie, a horrible end for a noble horse. Mom cried. We all felt sad. Mom named the colt Finis. He was the end of the line.

Jack Gates, a retired Navy Chief Petty Officer, was our neighbor. His father gave Herb and Brother a donkey. That little jackass pulled the clothes off the line when Mom hung them out to dry. He got into the chicken house and ate the chicken feed. Herb and Brother liked him, but he wouldn't let them ride him. Mom felt like shooting him.

We lived two miles from Moenville. When we went to the store I played with Marie who was a year older than I. She had a little rocking chair like mine. She wanted me to be the baby and let her rock me. I was insulted. I wasn't a baby. Mr. Roseth had a bushel basket of hard candy sitting on the floor and Dad treated us each to a piece.

Even with Mom teaching school, they couldn't pay the taxes on the land so the county took the farm. In the spring of 1925, Dad and Mom were forced into the heart breaking decision of leaving their ranch. We prepared to move again. Julius Roseth got our house.

Grandma Bertelson and Herb.

Herb and Henry Jr. on a home made sled in early 1920.

Henry Jr. on the little wagon at the Moenville farm 1919.

Henry Jr. (left) and Herb sitting at the Bertelson ranch on Bad River. 1922.

Thelma riding her hobby horse. 1923.

Dad and Herb. 1917.

Henry Jr. at the Moenville farm, summer 1919.

Uncle Charley Myrland and Henry Jr.

Henry Jr. at the Bertelson ranch chasing Grandma's cat. Grandma Bertleson in background.

156

CHAPTER 1 2
Mitchell Creek

We stayed until school was out and left Moenville forever. Dad crammed the wagon box with furniture and hitched the team to the wagon. Our gray tabby cat jumped on the seat. Dad climbed on board and clucked to the team. They headed south, the cat sitting beside Dad. Mom drove the Overland.

We thought the Overland was the best car in the world, but it broke down before we even got to Uncle Arnie's house. We jumped in the wagon with Dad abandoning the Overland on the prairie. Mom left her seven foot longhorn steer horns on the dresser. They were to large to fit in a drawer. We arrived at Uncle Arnie's farm after dark.

When Mom and Dad went back for the Overland and the furniture, the horns were gone. Someone had stolen this last bitter reminder of dreams blown away with the cold winter winds of 1919.

Oscar Markwed and another young fellow went by and checked the gas tank of the Overland. The tank was nearly full. They figured Evan Griffith would come along and drain the tank, so they drained the gasoline out and refilled the tank with water. They went away laughing. Evan came by and put the water in his gas tank. Oscar told Mom and Dad and they all had a good laugh.

Dad pulled the Overland down to the Bertelson ranch and parked it on a hill south of the house. Working like beavers, Herb and Brother filled the gas tank with sand.

Aunt Bird's farm was vacant so we moved there, seeking a port in the storm. Uncle Walt and Aunt Amanda had visited one of his sisters at Van Couver, Washington in 1923 and liked the country. They rented their farm to Dad, got in their Elgin and headed west.

Uncle Walt's brother was a sea captain. Uncle Walt worked in the shipyards and Aunt Amanda kept house for another sea captain. We happily moved to their farm on Mitchell Creek.

Mitchell Creek was a wonderful place to play with trees, logs to cross the creek on and places to hide. Squirrels chattered at us. Uncle Walt's black dog played with us. We rode Dolly, Aunt Amanda's horse.

Mr. Rogers gave Baby and me each a bum lamb. My lamb was a ewe. I named her Lambie until she got big, then I called her Nannie. Baby called her lamb Buck. We fed the lambs milk from a pop bottle with a nipple on it.

One day I tied Lambie to a post by her tail. Lambie tried to follow me back to the house and jerked the end of her tail off. Mom lectured me. "You must never tie Lambie by her tail." I knew that now. Her tail was still in the knot.

We had chickens and turkeys. Red pigs ran and played around the barnyard. Baby and I wanted to catch a velvety baby pig and play with it, but the piglets were about weaning size and husky. They wouldn't let us catch them.

Dad said, "A pig will lay down and stay there if you rub his stomach."

"Will he just lay there and not run away?" I asked.

"Yah. Rub his stomach and he'll lay there and grunt."

Baby and I watched the little pigs sunning themselves in the big corral. The day was warm. The piglets looked contented.

Best of all, they looked sound asleep.

We sneaked toward a small pig, stretched out on his side. His eyes were closed. Like a cat stalking a mouse, we stole across the pen. I touched the pig's stomach. The pig jumped up. I grabbed his tail so I could hold him while I rubbed his stomach. He squealed like a banshee and pooped on my hand. It was disgusting. I didn't try to catch another pig.

Rain was short in 1925, but Dad raised a good corn crop. Uncle Charley raised a fine crop of melons and hauled several loads to town to sell. Uncle Charley had plenty of melons for any social occasion. Mom and Aunt Tina served melons at Ladies' Aid. We loved to go to their house and eat all the watermelons our stomachs would hold.

With the Overland out of commission, we needed another car. Dad tried out a shiny black Buick with a canvas top and side curtains. We headed home via the town well on the Rogers flat so we could get drinking water. Dad stopped by the well, filled the can and the shiny Buick wouldn't start.

I made up my mind right then that I would never buy a Buick. Dad returned the Buick and bought a black Model T Ford touring car. The Model T had a canvas top and side curtains with icing glass windows. You could lay the top back and sit in the sun and breeze. The top and sides wore out from flapping in the wind.

The first summer we were at the Steien place, Mom and Herb, who was eight, rode back to the Moenville country to get our horses. Herb got tired on the forty mile ride. They stayed overnight with Mr. and Mrs. Lee Tole. Dad and Lee had played for dances together on the accordion and violin.

Herb watched Mrs. Tole empty cream almost as thick as butter from crocks into cans. She scraped the cream off the inside of each crock with her forefinger, then licked the cream off the fin-

159

ger and went to the next crock. Herb had never seen anything like that before. His eyes looked like saucers. Mrs. Tole stuck a cream coated finger in his face and said. "You want a lick?" Herb back away, shaking his head.

Mom and Herb rounded up about twenty horses and drove them to Mitchell Creek. Herb rode right along, bringing up the rear as Mom wrangled the horses down the trail.

Herb thought he was man enough to handle any of those wild horses. One day, Mom, Dad, Baby and I went to town. Herb chased the horses into the corral. "Let's break one of these colts to lead," Herb said.

"No," Brother said. "They'll whip us when they get home."

"They won't even know it," Herb said.

"What if they find out?"

"Don't worry. I'll take all the blame," Herb said.

He needed a rope. He went to the barn and got a harness line. They drove a soggy sorrel two-year-old into the round corral. Herb roped the sorrel colt with his harness line. The husky colt tore around the corral and out the gate. Herb and Brother ran after him.

The colt ran around the big corral with the harness line dragging. He was still evading two little boys when we got home. Brother tore to the house. Mom and Dad saw the horses in the corral. Herb walked slowly toward the house.

"It was Herb's idea," Brother said, puffing. "He said he'd take the whipping all by himself."

Herb agreed. What Brother said was true. He got all the punishment. He didn't try to halter break any more colts.

Brother and I tried to catch the birds that flitted around in front of our house. Mom said if we sprinkled salt on a bird's tail, we could catch him.

160

Brother got the salt shaker. We sneaked toward some birds hopping about in front of the house. Every time we got within a few feet, the birds flew away. We never got close enough to sprinkle salt on their tails.

Once Brother and I were playing in the snow near the ash tree that stood at the head of a draw running down to the hen house. We saw a black thing about a foot long in the snow.

We ran to the house, shouting, "Mom, Mom, we saw a snake."

"It couldn't be a snake," Mom said. "Snakes don't come out when there is snow on the ground."

"It was a snake," I said. "I know it was a snake because it had hair all over it." I didn't see what was so funny about that, but Mom had a laughing fit.

That fall Mom taught the Lone Tree School, sometimes called Little Prairie Dog. Herb and Brother went with her. They stayed at school during the week. Baby and I liked to visit school. We got acquainted with Ella who was in Brother's grade. Brother told us, "Ella can eat flies."

Our eyes grew big. "Do you really eat flies?"

"Sure," Ella said.

A fly was buzzing around on the window. Brother caught the fly and Ella ate it for us. We were impressed. When Ella got sick and died and we felt sad.

While Mom and the boys were at school, Julian and I stayed home with Dad and often visited Aunt Tina and Uncle Charley on their farm up the creek.

We were there when Mom came down with Scarlet fever in February. The doctor quarantined her. When anyone caught a contagious disease such as scarlet fever, small pox, measles etc., their house was quarantined, usually for twenty-one days. A paper

161

was nailed to the front door, warning people to stay away. Mom, Dad, Herb and Brother had to stay home, and we couldn't go home.

Julian and I worried because Valentine's Day was approaching and we wanted to exchange valentines with our brothers. "What are we going to do?" we asked Aunt Tina.

"Don't you worry," Aunt Tina said with a merry smile. "We'll yust make some valentines and take them to the fence and you can trade with the boys. We'll have our Valentine's Day ayet." Aunt Tina had all of us saying "ayet" for "yet". I was in high school before I realized "ayet" was not a word in the English language.

Valentine's Day afternoon, Aunt Tina, Julian and I trudged over the hill to the fence that divided Uncle Charley's land from Uncle Walt's. Herb and Brother came from home. We happily passed our valentines through the fence and traded with our brothers.

We went to the school picnic on Little Prairie Dog Creek that spring when school was out. Two old ladies sat under a tree and smoked clay pipes. Some old men had bushy mustaches and beards that reached to their belts.

The lambs we got from Mr. Rogers grew fat and wooly. Lambie matured into a gentle ewe. Buck grew into a handsome brawny buck with large horns that curled around his eyes and a fierce temper. He wasn't afraid of any troll under a bridge, and he certainly wasn't afraid of any Martin kids. Come spring Nanny had a lamb so there was a new Lambie.

Buck liked to chase kids. He chased us and knocked us flat at every opportunity. Nanny watched with a smug look on her wooly face. Buck knocked Baby down. She bumped her head on a piece of iron and cried.

Dad said, "Lay down when Buck chases you. Then he won't hit you."

We learned to keep one eye on Buck as we ran from the house to the Model T south of the house to the garage and then to the Metz on the hill southwest of the house. When Buck lowered his head and tore after us, we ran for the nearest safe haven.

Buck caught me and Baby between the house and the Model T one day. We flopped belly down on the ground and lay scarcely breathing. We knew if we got up Buck would knock us down again. Waiting Buck out was scary, but we stayed on the ground still as mice in the bushes until he sauntered away. Then we got up and dashed to the Model T where we waited till he was far enough away so we could run to the house.

Buck cornered Mona Howes in the garage one day. Buck, Nanny and Lambie kept her cowering in the corner until Herb dashed in with a stick and bravely chased the sheep away.

Uncle Charley lost the Walton place because his alfalfa crop didn't make a seed crop so he didn't have the money for his payment. Mr. Walton asked when he would have the money. In those days it was a terrible insult to ask a man for money that he owed. Uncle Charley got angry and told Mr. Walton that he would have the money come fall or turn the place back. He didn't have the money and lost the farm.

I was eager to go to school so I could learn to read. I was sure that I would be able to read immediately, if I could go to school.

The fall of 1926, Mom taught at the Highland Center School south of Nowlin, and I got my wish. Mom took Herb, Brother and me to school with her. We stayed in the teacher's cottage near the small white school house during the week and went home Friday night. Baby stayed with Dad. Sometimes she came to school with us.

I was in first grade, Brother in second and Herb in fourth. We Norwegians found ourselves in the middle of a Bohemian settlement. The parents spoke broken English. Mr. Dolezal would say, "My wife, he milk the cows."

Mom taught eight grades and about fifteen kids. The play ground had swings, teeter-totters, and a giant stride. The giant stride was a wonderful contraption. Ropes hung down from a rake wheel mounted on the top of a ten foot pole. Each kid grabbed a rope and away we went. The faster the wheel turned the higher we flew.

Mom let me, Quenton Shuck and Pearl Weiberg out early one afternoon. We sailed like birds on the giant stride, swinging round and round. We went faster and faster. A cracking sound shattered the air. The huge wheel tumbled down. The wheel hit my shoulder, breaking my collar bone. Quenton lay on the ground with blood running out of his hair. We began to cry.

Mom and the other students ran out of the school house. Quenton lay on the ground, bleeding. He had a hole about an inch deep in his head. His parents came and took him to the doctor. He recovered but didn't return to school for two years.

Once I went home to stay all night with Mary and Rose Dolezal who were in the higher grades. We slept in a bed with a goose down feather bed on the springs and another for a cover. We were cuddly warm in our feather beds.

I loved school and learned to read and write and all kinds of wonderful things. We also learned how to be fair when we played.

Mom didn't care if the boys boxed or wrestled as long as they didn't kick or bite. Herb and Theodore Imslun got in a fight. We formed a ring to watch them maul each other. Theodore kicked

Herb in the stomach. Someone ran and told Mom.

Mom broke up the fight and whipped Theodore for kicking. Theodore's mother came to school to chat with Mom. Mom didn't back down. She didn't back down for anybody. Corporal punishment was the way unruly big boys and girls were handled in those days. Ornery students as big as the teacher could make school miserable for timid teachers.

Most parents sided with the teacher. Mom told us if we got spanked in school, she would spank us again when we got home. Dad took us to school on Sunday night and came after us Friday night.

We were happy when spring came after one of the mildest winters in forty years, although a storm in February brought heavy snow. When the snow melted the dirt roads were impassable so we didn't always get home weekends.

That spring George Staley from the Moenville country shot T.C. Wasson. Wasson and his wife came to the house from the creek with a load of wood. Staley wanted to go through a fence by the barn where there was no gate. Wasson objected so Staley shot him and went through the fence. Wasson drove to the barn and unhitched his team while his wife went for help. He wanted to make a will. He died soon after he was shot but not before he had put his horses in the barn.

One cool day, Dad started a fire in the heater and caught the roof on fire. We hurried outside and Mom put us under a blanket while she and Dad doused the fire. We made a tent of the blanket and Baby thought it was great fun to peek out and watch Dad and Mom throwing water on the flames.

In the spring, creeks and rivers ran high. Dams filled with water. In April five inches of rain fell in two weeks, cascading more water into creeks, rivers and ponds. The soil was soaked with life giving water. The cheerful voices of robins, mead-owlarks, horned larks and blue jays mixed with the coarse caw of crows. Golden plovers skimmed above the grass. Wild ducks nested in the marshes.

Grass grew. Calves frolicked in the pastures. Tiny colts ran beside their mothers. Down at the Rogers place, lambs chased each other, bucking and jumping. That was the year Mr. Rogers stepped on a rusty nail and died from lockjaw.

Dad's red sows birthed large litters of tiny red pigs. Our milk cows were brown and roan with two black and white Holsteins. The calves were locked in a pen while the cows grazed on the hillsides. Raised on skim milk, the calves were thin and pot-bellied.

Our hens hatched baby chicks. We helped Mom feed the new arrivals oatmeal and boiled eggs. The mother hens ruffled their feathers and clucked their protests when the chicks ran out-side the small houses Dad built for them. The tiny A frame houses with a divider at the center housed two hens and their families.

Slats across the ends kept the hens inside, but allowed the chicks to go outside. When the chicks began to feather out, the families were allowed to roam free to scratch in the dirt and chase bugs. We liked to watch a chick find a tender morsel, grab it and run with his brothers and sisters hot on his trail. If he was lucky, he got his morsel swallowed before he was caught, if not, he lost part of it.

People far out in the country didn't get around much during winter. Jess and Jiggs Dennis lived a few miles northeast of Uncle Arne's farm. By spring, Jiggs had cabin fever. She longed to talk to someone besides Jess. Their Model T didn't have tires, but Jess cranked the car and drove the five miles across the prairie to Uncle Arne's house anyway.

"I just had to visit somebody," Jiggs said, "and I didn't want to wait any longer for Jess to put tires on the car." Model T's had sturdy wooden spokes and heavy iron rims. Riding on the rim on the soft prairie didn't hurt them a bit.

By 1927 Henry Ford had sold over fifteen million Model T cars and changed the world and probably "lover's lane" forever. Automobiles were faster than horses and buggies and so were the drivers. Horses no longer stampeded in fright at the sight of the smelly, smoking monsters that hogged the roads and roared past in a cloud of choking dust, but they didn't like them.

Aunt Tina and Uncle Charley lived at the Howes place where he worked for Mr. Howes. Aunt Tina often walked to our house to visit. Baby and I walked back and stayed with her and Uncle Charley.

One day we were running barefoot through the ashes where Uncle Charley had burned trash. Baby ran into the ashes and ran out, screaming, a piece of hot melted rubber sticking to her foot. Uncle Charley dunked her foot in water and peeled the rubber loose. We didn't run through the ashes anymore.

We liked to chase each other through the house. We could make a complete circle, going through the kitchen, the living room, the bedroom and through a closet back to the kitchen. Baby chased me around and around and I stepped on a pin. The pin rammed into my foot, hit a bone and bent.

Uncle Charley pulled the pin out of my foot with a pliers and I howled. Aunt Tina poured turpentine on the tiny hole and worried that I would get tetanus, but I didn't.

Once when I opened the door, a snake stuck his tongue out at me from the doorstep. I screamed and Uncle Charley killed the snake.

We learned Mother Goose rhymes and decided to be nursery rhyme characters. Baby was Little Bo Peep, Brother was Jack Be Nimble, Herb was Little Jack Horner. I wanted to be Little Miss Muffet who sat on a tuffet and was afraid of spiders just like me.

Mom and Herb said, "No, you have to be Mary, Mary Quite Contrary. It fits you better."

Aunt Tina and Uncle Charley taught us little ditties that weren't Mother Goose rhymes. Aunt Tina said: "Here I stand as tall as the table. I'll get married as soon as I'm able."

Uncle Charlie said, "Here I stand all ragged and dirty. If the girls come to kiss me, I'll run like a turkey." Then he threw back his head and roared with laughter.

Uncle Charley sometimes got into trouble with his jokes. Two of his nephews from Iowa were visiting one summer. Uncle Charley bragged about being able to shoot like Daniel Boone. Uncle Charley said, "See that guinea over on the hillside. I could shoot her head right off." Her head was barely visible.

The boys didn't believe him. They wanted to see this feat of marksmanship. Uncle Charley pulled up his rifle. He aimed. "Bang!" He shot the head off the guinea. The boys ran in the house and told Aunt Tina. Uncle Charley stayed outside as long as he could. He came in looking foolish with a plucked guinea fowl for supper.

Aunt Tina's living room rug had a rose design. We didn't have a rug. Mom had a kitchen cabinet with shelves for dishes, a flour bin, drawers for cutlery and a storage space for pots and pans. A counter could be pulled out for kneading bread dough or rolling out cookies and cinnamon rolls. Every kitchen had a cabinet. Mom had a full sized buffet with a mirror along the back, too.

For summer cooking, Mom used a three burner kerosene stove. We had kerosene lamps with chimneys to wash and wicks to trim. Those chimneys smoked up and had to be cleaned often.

Calvin Coolidge was President. All was well with the nation, but forbidding clouds were forming on the horizon.

Rain kept falling the summer of 1927, promising a fine crop year. The "Great Flood of 1927" started with a drizzle on May 6. Rain fell gently until May 8 when the sky darkened, the clouds opened up and rain poured. Water sheeted off the hillsides into draws and creeks. Dams flooded and broke, turning draws into raging torrents.

Miles to the north, Plum Creek near Manila was running a small stream. Curt Anderson, who was twelve, heard a roar and saw a gigantic wall of water coming down the creek. Water stretched from break to break, sweeping away any buildings in its path.

The Shoemaker children were playing by the creek when they heard the roar. They saw the wall of water coming and ran for higher ground, leaving their shoes behind. They watched the water roll their chicken house into the flood. The water rolled into Mitchell Creek and on toward Bad River.

The flood tumbled down Mitchell Creek half a mile wide in places. Baby and I were visiting Aunt Tina and Uncle Charley at the Howes ranch.

Uncle Charley put on his rubber boots and waded around in the water on the meadow, checking the depths of the rising water. He stuck an eight foot stick at the edge of the water so he could see how fast the creek was rising. Soon water several feet deep surrounded his stick. We watched him wading through the water and wished he would come out of it.

He came to the house and told Aunt Tina, "We had better go up to Henry and Dena's. The creek is rising fast." The water was an ocean already halfway to the house.

"Do we have time for supper?" Aunt Tina asked. He nodded and she hurried to get supper on the table.

Halfway through the meal, I jumped up. "I'm going to see where the water is." I ran to the door.

"Auntie, Uncle, the water is here." Muddy water washed against the doorstep, sending little tongues of water across the stones. Another few inches and the water would come into the house. "Oh my," Aunt Tina said, "We'll have to leave right away."

They set me and Baby up on the next bench and hurried to put small things on chairs and tables so nothing would get wet. They figured water might flow into the house several inches deep.

Aunt Tina, Baby and I walked to our house. The sun was nearing the western horizon. A rainbow spanned the eastern sky. To the north the flood waters rolled by, carrying trees, logs and small buildings. Dead animals caught in the murderous water floated past.

At our house water raged through the corrals. Blue, Aunt Amanda's saddle horse ran frantically trapped in water up to his knees. He shook his head and nickered. We watched Dad wade into the water and take some corral poles down.

With a snort, Blue dashed through the hole in the fence and ran up the hill to higher ground. He stood regal against the setting sun and looked at the water that had threatened to drown him.

Dad had already let the hogs out so they wouldn't drown. We stood by the house and watched the flood go by. It looked like the ocean was going down Mitchell Creek.

Several miles up Mitchell Creek, the August Peters family were marooned in their log house. Water ran past on all sides. The log sheds with dirt covered roofs were closer to the creek than the house. The corrals and barn had often been flooded when Mitchell Creek ran high.

170

Flood water would tear the woven wire fencing out, but the barn was built into a hillside and had a cement wall to deflect water and protect the barn loft. When flood waters ran high, August and Sylvia had to climb into the loft and pull the harness and saddle out of the stable and take them to higher ground. Nearby was a granary built on stilts. This time water surrounded the house, holding them prisoner inside. They watched the granary float away and wondered if the water would get into their house.

John Peterson came with a team and hay rack from his farm a mile down the creek. Sylvia, Nelson, August and Mrs. Peters were happy to see him. He took them to a flat on the John Larson farm.

August saw a water tank floating away. He swung his lariat, caught the tank by the spout and tied it to a tree. The water didn't get into the house.

At the Bertelson ranch on Bad River, Alvin had gathered fifty head of cattle on the river bottom when water surrounded them. Alvin unsaddled his horse and climbed on the railroad bridge. Carrying his saddle, he walked home.

The horse and cattle went with the river, swimming frantically in the roaring water. Some of the steers didn't come out until they reached Jim Nelson's house two miles down river. None drowned.

Tom Jones called Harry Schofield and told him that Brave Bull Creek was coming down at flood stage. Harry decided to eat supper before taking his family to higher ground. While they were eating, the flood waters rushed past, surrounding their house. Harry waded out and caught his team. He hitched the team to a wagon and drove through the water to the house.

Water ran three feet deep through the doors and windows, in one side and out the other. Mrs. Schofield put the smaller children on the cook stove. Hank was a baby, Myrtle, two and Forest, three. Mike, Martin, Eddie and Joe were all less than twelve. One small boy started to float away. Mrs. Schofield grabbed his suspenders and pulled him back.

Water almost swept the children off the stove before Harry got to the door with the wagon. He loaded his family into it and hauled them to safety. A glorious rainbow spread over the eastern sky as the team waded through the muddy water. Seventeen of Harry Schofield's yearling calves went down the creek and drowned.

Muddy water raged through our corral four days, leaving behind torn fences with flotsam caught in the wires. Sixty red sows came home, walked single file into the corral and died. They had eaten the tiny, but deadly, cockle burr leaves just poking through the soil.

Water ran in the north windows and out the south windows of Aunt Tina's house, washing everything off chairs, tables and beds. The flood waters receded, leaving four inches of sloppy silt on the floor. Somewhere under all that mud was her lovely Persian rug.

Up north at Uncle Arne's farm, water rushed into the dam, filling it so full the water threatened to go over the grade and wash out the dam. Grabbing spades, Uncle Arne, Hallie and Madge dug frantically to get the spillway wide enough to contain the raging water. Water gushed through the widened spillway, carrying with it thousands of bullheads. It tore down the draw past Emil Nemec's house, down a small creek south of Crawford's house, past Doud's house and on to the Highway 14 bridge. The water roared under the bridge and ran on to Bad River twenty miles away.

"Fish went out with the water," Madge said. "Crawfords and Douds saw all that water coming filled with fish and ran to get pans. They feasted for days."

The moisture made the corn pop. You could almost hear the cornstalks grow. Uncle Charley had forty acres of corn and a huge garden fenced with woven wire to keep the rabbits out. When the corn got too high to cultivate, he put his hoe over his shoulder and headed for the corn field. Any weed that dared poke its head up was chopped off at the neck.

When it came to rabbits, Uncle Charley was like Mr. MacGregor in *Peter Rabbit*. He caught a jack rabbit that had sneaked through the fence and was having lunch in his garden. The rabbit got snared in the woven wire and Uncle Charley grabbed his hind legs. I wanted Uncle Charley to let the rabbit go, but he wouldn't.

Dad had a grudge against weeds, too. By the time the corn was too tall for the cultivator, the hot days of July were upon us. Dad had eighty acres of corn on the flat a mile south of the house.

He took Herb, Brother and me to the corn field to attack any remaining weeds. We walked up hill and down dale to the field. Dad carried his hoe and a gallon jug of water wrapped in a wet gunny sack to keep it cool.

"You kids each take a row." He pointed out our rows and strode down his own, whacking weeds. We toiled along behind. Corn leaves rustled in the breeze. Every now and then, Dad reached his hoe into my row and cut a weed.

Herb complained. "You have it easy. Dad helps you." I needed help. I was glad when time came to go home for dinner.

Sometimes Mom and Baby came with us after dinner and a rest that was too short. Pulling weeds was fun at first. We scared jack rabbits from the shade of cornstalks and they hopped away. When the hot sun bores down from a cloudless sky, your throat soon gets parched. Dad strode along, chopping weeds right and left out of two rows. Mom kept up a steady whack, whack with her hoe. I straggled along, wishing for a drink of water.

When you are a little kid, the rustling corn leaves are far above your head. The cornstalks were nearly as tall as Dad. Little breeze gets into that forest of green. You only hear it passing, ruffling the leaves so they seem to whisper to each other. The cockle burrs and sunflowers, missed by the cultivator, have grown into trees with roots that seem to reach to China.

I tugged and pulled at the huge weeds while sweat ran down my face. My cheeks turned red under my wide brimmed straw hat with the red tassels. Dad occasionally reached over and jerked a big weed out with one hand as he went down his rows, whacking weeds with deadly accuracy.

While Herb, Brother and I worked and sweated, Baby played in the soft dirt between the rows. I wished I was little so I didn't have to pull weeds, but I was seven. I had weeds to pull. I thought weeding would be easy, if I had a hoe. Mom let me try her hoe, but the handle was too clumsy.

I gave the hoe back and pulled weeds again, going down the row, wishing for the end so I could have a drink. After what seemed like forever, we got back to our water jug.

Dad took the cork out and held the jug for us to drink. Baby got the first drink, then I got one, and Herb said, 'Don't drink it all. I want some."

I was glad when the sun dropped near the horizon and we went home. Mom got supper while Dad milked the cows and fed the hogs. The boys helped Dad and I set the table.

Hogs didn't have self feeders. They were fed slop of water and barley and had ear corn scattered around in their pen. The pigs fought and squealed, shoving each other as they hogged their share of the delicious slop. The turkeys and chickens slipped around in the hog pen, picking up scattered grain.

That summer we played in the woods, chasing squirrels and cottontails. The cottontails ran into the bush. The squirrels ran up trees and chattered at us, no doubt telling us to go away and mind our own business.

Uncle Walt's dog went with us when we played along the creek. The boys threw him into the water. He swam to the bank, climbed out and shook himself, showering us with water. We learned to swim by watching him.

Dad planted another corn field on the flat east of the house. Mom planted peas, beans, radishes, potatoes, lettuce and beets in a garden at the edge of the corn field. She didn't worry about the rabbits. They didn't eat much anyway.

One day Mom and Dad went to hoe weeds in the garden. Baby and Brother went with them. Herb and I stayed home. A small dam halfway between the house and garage was full of water. A plank ran out to two posts in the water so one could dip water for dish washing and such. Herb and I walked out on the plank. I was holding the cat. She eyed the water suspiciously. "Throw the cat in the water," Herb said. "Let's see if she can swim."

I held the cat over the water, preparing to drop her. She didn't want to swim. She grabbed my wrist and clawed her way up my arm, scratching my wrist. She jumped onto the plank and ran away.

Blood seeped from the scratches. Aunt Tina had told me that if you cut the veins in your wrist all your blood would run out and you would die. The scratch didn't hurt much. It didn't even bleed much, but that scratch scared the living daylights out of me. I screamed and cried and jumped around. Herb tried to calm me. "Don't yell. Mom will get mad."

I didn't care. I was dying. I screamed. I wanted help.

A quarter of a mile away, mom heard my screams and ran home. She looked at my wrist. "Why are you making all this fuss over a little scratch." Disgusted, she went back to the garden. I looked at the scratch on my wrist and thought, I'm not going to die. I was comforted.

The Howes kids had a brown pony that boarded at our place. I liked to ride the pony with Herb's small saddle. One balmy fall day, Mom said we could ride in the forty acre pasture south of the house. I rode the pony and Herb rode Dolly. When I decided I had better go home, Herb said, "Let's ride longer."

"Mom said I could ride a little while and then I had to come home," I said.

"She won't care," Herb said.

We rode up and down the hills. The horses trotted down into a draw. My cinch wasn't tight enough. The saddle turned and I fell into a bunch of cockle burrs. I cried and Herb righted the saddle so I could mount again.

"I'm going home," I said. When we got home, Mom was angry because I had stayed so long. Herb just grinned like a Cheshire cat. She didn't say anything to him.

Our gray tabby had kittens. Baby and I each got one. My kitten was gray with white feet, a white chest and a white face. I called him Tom. Baby's cat was black with white markings. She named him Felix after the cat in the funny paper. Color was the only resemblance Felix bore to the sophisticated feline in the comics.

We loved our cats and dressed them in doll clothes. We could never figure out how to put pants on the cats. We didn't want to cut holes in the pants and cutting off their tails was out of the question.

As Tom and Felix grew to powerful adulthood, they became bitter enemies. This enmity was encouraged by Herb and Brother who shoved the struggling cats nose to nose to promote a fight. Nose contact was against Tom's and Felix's nature. They slapped and growled and tore into each other. Usually Tom ran away first. If left to themselves, the cats simply avoided each other. Tom was bigger, but Felix was quicker. I think Tom was too smart to want his hide torn to amuse two ornery boys.

The boys said, "Felix can lick Tom." If they wanted to really stir the cats up, they put Tom and Felix in a gunny sack and shook them up. Talk about mad cats. The fur flew. Biting and scratching, they rolled on the ground until one tore loose and ran away. I didn't like to have the boys make the cats fight. I didn't like to have them say Tom was a loser either.

One day Herb rode to the house on the most beautiful horse I had every seen. I watched her step proudly up the trail from the barn. She was Morgan and Shetland and stood about fourteen hands.

Dad said, "This pony is for Thelma and Baby when they can handle her."

I wished I could ride the pretty mare, but she was too lively for me. Mom named her Whitefoot because the coal black mare had one white hind foot. Whitefoot was my riding pony and my friend for all my growing years. She was a feisty little mare with a wicked kick for any horse that got close to her hind feet. Whenever she was in a bunch of horses, her flying hoofs quickly cleared a space around her.

Rain storms continued that summer. We liked to watch the lightning and listen to the rumbling thunder. Mom taught us not to be afraid of the black storm clouds rolling in from the west.

Brother, Baby and I stood with Mom and Aunt Tina watching a storm approach one evening. Herb had ridden to the north pasture to get the milk cows. A sudden flash ripped across the sky. Thunder crashed right over our heads. Aunt Tina shook her head. "I don't like lightning. I think we should go in the house."

Mom laughed. "I'm not afraid of lightning. I like to watch a storm."

A brilliant flash of lightning hit an ash tree fifty feet in front of us, tearing out a chunk of bark and leaving a white streak on the tree trunk. Thunder crashed directly above our heads so close it nearly knocked us down. The lightning traveled down the clothesline to the next tree. Mom and Aunt Tina each clasped their hands on top of their head and squatted to the ground. Baby ran in a circle, screaming, "I'm on fire. I'm on fire."

Herb was shutting a gate in the barbed wire fence northwest of the house and felt the shock.

Mom and Aunt Tina stood up, looking foolish. Mom grabbed Baby and said, "Settle down. You didn't get hurt." She inspected Baby's wine colored dress and found a hole the size of a penny burned in the skirt.

Summer drifted into fall and school began again.

Thelma, Julian, Henry Jr. and
Herb in 1924.

Thelma and her doll and buggy at
Aunt Tina's house, 1924.

Summer 1924: Julian and
Thelma in Aunt Tina's buggy
ready to go to town.

Herb, Julian, Thelma and Henry Jr.

179

CHAPTER 13
We Move Again

The fall of 1927, we started school in Midland. We called Brother Henry or Hank. He had failed second grade so he and I were together in second. Herb was in fifth.

Mom had quit teaching and because of this I was reluctant to go to that huge schoolhouse where everything was strange. Herb's teacher was Myrna Blackmore. Mrs. Griffith taught first, second and third grades. She was tall, slender and pretty and strict as an old mother bear. When the school bell rang, we all ran in and were assigned desks. The mothers of first graders brought their children to the first day of school. The mothers all left except Mrs. Berry.

Claude Berry, with his big blue eyes and curly blond hair, sat in his seat, clinging tightly to her hand, begging her not to leave him in this strange place with all the strange people.

When reason would not prevail, Mrs. Griffith escorted Mrs. Berry to the door. Claude clung to her hand, screaming. We all watched with eyes wide as Mrs. Berry gently loosened her hand. Mrs. Griffith held Claude while his mother slipped out the door.

Claude grabbed the door nob. He kicked the door and screamed. Mrs. Griffith held the door shut while his mother tried to reassure him from the other side. Finally his mother left. When

180

Claude tired of kicking the door, Mrs. Griffith lead him to his desk. "Sit down, Claude," she said. Claude slid into the desk and looked around with a sad face. I thought what a big baby he is and felt a little braver.

At recess I stood alone, looking at all the unknown girls, wondering what to do. I knew Verle Funston. She was in my grade. When I was four, I went to Ladies' Aid with Aunt Tina and Verle threw a plum pit and hit me in the eye. I didn't want anything to do with her.

A black-eyed, black-haired girl looked at me and said, "What are you looking at me so funny for?" Then she loped off to the slippery slide. Her name was Helen Pierce, and she became my best friend.

Helen Pierce's folks owned The Bastion Hotel. They had changed the name to The Pierce Hotel. A huge HOTEL sign made of hundreds of tiny light bulbs hung in front of the hotel. You could see that sign for blocks at night.

Helen was an only child. When I stayed with her, we followed the maids Bertha and Martha around as they cleaned rooms. They didn't care if two small girls tagged them from room to room and got in their way.

The third floor was one huge room with nineteen beds. The second floor had a balcony in front. We sat on the balcony in the cool of the evening and watched the cars and wagons go by on Main Street. Midland had two or three other hotels, but the need for them was passing.

One day Helen told me there was no Santa Claus. I was horrified. "There is too a Santa Claus," I said. "He brings us presents."

Helen laughed at my ignorance. "Your parents give you the presents. They just made Santa Claus up to fool kids."

It wasn't news I wanted to hear, but she was older. I thought she probably knew. I felt so bad I went home and told Baby. Baby was only five. She ran into the house crying.

"Mom, Mom," she said. "Thelma said Santa Claus wasn't anybody." Mom scolded me for telling Baby the bad news as if it was my fault there was no Santa Claus.

Several days later, I was standing alone in the hall outside our room. Roy Howes walked over to me. "You're not my girl friend anymore," he said. "I've got a new girl friend now."

I looked into Roy's brown eyes hardly believing what I had heard. I couldn't say a word. I felt deserted, rejected, terrible. Roy looked at me for a moment with a small grin, then he walked into our room as though nothing had happened.

My heart was broken. I slid into my desk, hoping nobody would find out. I was consoled when Richard Huft took a shine to me. Richard was in second grade. His sister Marie had diabetes and was extremely fat. I liked Marie and felt sorry for her because she couldn't have candy or cake or cookies.

Hank and I rode Dolly to school, he in the saddle and I behind him. Herb rode Whitefoot. Dolly was touchy and would kick up if one touched her flanks. I was careful not to let that happen. If we rode bareback, Hank liked to slide back, pushing me so my heels connected with her tender spot. Dolly kicked high. I screamed and the boys laughed.

Aunt Tina and Uncle Charley moved to Midland for the winter. Uncle Charley took his axe and saw and went to the river to cut stove wood and posts. I stayed with them in the winter.

Aunt Tina helped Mrs. Huft with her house work. Mrs. Huft was enormously fat with three chins. Mr. Huft worked on the railroad and looked like a roly-poly bear. Richard was slim like us.

That fall Aunt Amanda and Uncle Walt came back from

Seattle in a new gray Model T coupe with a hard top and windows that rolled up and down. They moved into a house in town. Uncle Walt repaired the State Theater that had been in a fire and built a garage for Lovalds. Mr. Lovald ran The First National Bank.

On Saturday nights, we went to the silent pictures in The Rex Theater. Baby and I liked Fred Thompson and his horse best. In one movie, Fred was locked inside a log cabin in the middle of a forest fire. The flames roared closer. His brave horse kicked the door open. Fred leaped on his horse and raced away just in the nick of time.

Midland built a high water tower west of the schoolhouse. During the winter, the water tower overflowed. Water ran down the north side of the steep schoolhouse hill, coating it with glare ice halfway down. Snow had fallen heavily in December, blocking roads.

All the kids in town gathered at the schoolhouse hill to slide. Herb, Hank and I had Flexible Flyer sleds given to us by Uncle Walt. Twenty or thirty sleds at a time flew down the hill. The year before, Marie Huft sledded down a hill in town and ran into a wagon. Teams and wagons were as common as cars on Midland's streets.

In warm weather, every kid in town played hide and seek in the lumber yard below the schoolhouse, finding hiding places in the lumber.

During the school year, Marie Huft's mother gave birth to a baby girl. The third grade girls drew pictures of a baby on the blackboard and wrote "Marie's Baby" under them. Marie was furious. I drew a picture of a baby and wrote "Marie's Baby" underneath, carefully copying what the other girls wrote. They erased their pictures and ran out to play. I ran after them so fast I forgot to erase my picture. I didn't know there was anything wrong with the picture anyway. Not that is until Mrs. Griffith called me back into the schoolhouse. "Did you draw that picture?" Her voice was stern.

I gulped "Yes."

She informed me that I had done a terrible thing. She spanked me and sent me to my desk for the rest of recess. The spanking didn't hurt. She only swatted me once. I couldn't understand why she was so angry because I didn't erase my dumb old picture.

I didn't even tell Hank and Herb about my spanking. I didn't want Mom to spank me again when I got home. I figured one punishment for one crime was enough. Besides I was mortified. I was glad the other kids didn't know.

We took our lunch to school in black lunch boxes and ate upstairs with Forrest and Alice Buchanan who were in High School.

Car prices were going down. In January Fords were $600.00. The dealer claimed they would go sixty-eight miles an hour. People figured they were speeding right along at thirty miles an hour. In February forty trucks were graveling Highway 14 between Midland and Ft. Pierre. Dozens of horses and mules pulled the grading machinery as they turned Highway 14 into an all weather road.

The spring of 1928, we had to move again because Aunt Amanda and Uncle Walt wanted to move back to their farm.

Grandpa Martin had traded Uncle Arne his farm over by Canning for Uncle Arne's farm north of Midland and $500.00. He let Uncle Arne keep the money because he owed him $500.00. Grandpa sold the farm to Dad. Dad made a down payment and would make payments each year until the farm was paid for. We prepared to move north to the wide and windy prairie while Aunt

Amanda and Uncle Walt moved back to their lovely farm on Mitchell Creek.

Our room gave a going away party for Herb, Hank, me, Bonnie Laymont and David Osbourne. We all felt important and had fun playing games and eating a lunch of apples and cookies. We got a grand send-off to a new world where we didn't want to go. We left Mitchell Creek the first of March 1928.

One day we piled into our Model T which no longer had a top or side curtains because they had blown off in the wind. Dad drove out of Midland on Highway 14 and headed north on the newly graveled orange road. We were going to inspect our new home.

The Model T tooled around sharp curves and up and down steep hills. One curve was named Deadman's Curve after a man who tried to take the square corner too fast and rolled his Pierce Arrow into a pile of junk. Hank's ambition was to own a Pierce Arrow, but when he was old enough to drive one, the company had quit making them.

Fourteen miles north, we went west for two miles past a field and across a scary dam grade that backed up more water than I had ever seen except during the Mitchell Creek flood. The water was teeming with bullheads that made good fishing and a fine meal. It was a wonderful place to swim on hot summer days.

For years I was afraid of the dam grade. In my imagination I watched the car and us either running into the water or sliding and rolling down the steep grade on the other side. There was little danger of doing either. That dam was one of the few large man-made dams in the country. It had been built with scrapers pulled by horses.

We traveled past a woven wire cow yard with a small barn and up a gentle slope. The road ran between a dilapidated corncrib

185

and a fair chicken house with a garage on the north end. Dad stopped the car in front of the house. The buildings were all unpainted, weathered, drab and ugly.

The L shaped house faced east with a partly enclosed porch on the north and east. A one wire telephone line ran south outside our west boundary fence, a hundred yards west of the house. Our place was in Stanley County, but outside the fence was Haakon County.

The front door was open. We scrambled out of the car and ran into the house. A brown bitch and her litter of brown puppies ran around in the house among assorted tin cans and junk. We petted the dogs and would have adopted the whole family, but Mom said, "No, too many dogs." Uncle Arne had taken his wife and seven children, Hallie, Madge, Aline, Gertie, Ted, Arneta and Richard and left his dog and her puppies. Roberta was born after they moved to Canning.

A piano stood against the north wall of the living room. We pumped out many tunes before Uncle Arne came back for it and the dogs. Then Dad bought a player piano, which we played until the mice chewed holes in the bellows and the piano quit working.

A door in the floor opened to a dirt cellar below the living room and kitchen. Thin wallboard bellied in between some studs and out between others, waving around the rooms. A double doorway connected the kitchen and living room. There were two bedrooms on the north and one on the southwest. A summer kitchen was hooked to the east side of the regular kitchen. A cupboard between the rooms could be opened from either side. The house was bigger than Uncle Walt's.

We cleaned up the mess and settled in. Dad made several trips with the wagon, hauling furniture and machinery. The chickens, turkeys and hogs in their crates jostled north across the prairie to their new home.

Mom and Herb saddled Dolly and Whitefoot and drove the sixteen milk cows and the mean Holstein bull to their new surroundings. Another trip brought the horses, including Dad's four work horses: Major, Emmet, Sorrel and Finis. Our saddle horses were Whitefoot, Dolly and old Baldy who didn't work anymore. The rest of the herd were range mares and colts.

Herb broke a chunky, handsome gelding out of Whitefoot to ride that summer. Herb and Hank also broke a bay and white spotted filly belonging to Mom. Mom called her Freckles, and we had two more saddle horses.

Star was black with a white star and a propensity to kick any horse that got close to his back end. Star and Freckles were so lazy, they never moved faster than a walk unless kicked hard or popped on the rear with the reins.

Mom drove the Model T touring car north on the wagon road with Baby and I, our gray mother cat, moving once more, and Felix and Tom. Felix and Tom were in separate boxes so they couldn't fight.

Lake beds full of water sparkled on the prairie. That summer small lakes scattered over the miles of free range outside our west fence and became home to mallards, teal, canvasbacks and mud hens that nested on the prairie and swam in the water. Cranes caught bugs and frogs, and geese stopped on their way north.

Mom said we were moved in "lock, stock and barrel," and so we were. Everything we owned was there except the sheep, which we had given to Aunt Amanda.

I traded my half of Star to Baby for her half of Whitefoot in my first horse trade. I beat the sox off her, but neither of us knew it then. We each wanted a horse of our own. I loved Whitefoot. I wouldn't have sold her for a million dollars.

We moved the stove and table into the kitchen. We used two orange crates for our water bucket and washstand. The orange crates had a shelf for cleaning supplies. They looked nice with a curtain across the front. Some wag said, "The water bucket is always empty and the slop pail is always full," which was more truth than fiction.

Mom had large tin cans that held about a hundred pounds for flour and sugar. Mice couldn't chew through those cans. They could run around and around the can, but their sharp little teeth wouldn't make a dent in it.

Nearly three months of school was left. I dreaded going to another new school. The Liberty School was three and a half miles northeast of our house. Hank and I got on Dolly. Herb mounted Whitefoot. He was the gate opener. We headed bravely for school on a chilly March day.

We rode up hill and down, past Emil Nemec's house almost hidden in a valley to the south, then down a long slope to Crawford's house. A black dog ran out and barked at us. We rode between the house and barn, crossed a small creek, rode past Doud's house and across the school section to the dreaded Liberty School.

A woven wire fence surrounded the square white building and a small red barn. The boy's and girl's toilets flanked the barn. There was a shed for coal and wood and a cistern for drinking water.

We wore high laced boots and overshoes. I wore a bib overall over my dress and hung it in the cloakroom while I was in school. We put our lunch pails there, also. Horses milled around in the school yard and kids played outside. We turned our horses loose in the yard

A tall, slim young man came out and rang the bell. We all

188

went inside. Ralph Jordan, the teacher, assigned us to seats. Everybody stared at us and we stared back. There were eight grades and kids of all sizes from big Donald Burns and Anna Teideman to little kids like me. The Teideman girls had flaming red hair. Anna was like an old mother hen, but Mildred was ornery. She was three years older than I and would just as soon belt me clear into the next county.

The younger students sat on the west side of the room; the older ones on the east. A row of windows let light in on the east side. Blackboards nearly covered the north and west walls. We could watch the traffic go by on Highway 14. One day we watched over a hundred teams of mules go down the road, pulling road grading equipment.

Frances May and Hazel and Lucille Richardson were in my grade. Bernard Burns was in first grade. Herb, Mildred and Willard Burns were in fifth. Glen Crawford, Major Doud and Donald Burns were in sixth and Anna Teideman in eighth.

When we went out for recess, I stood on the front steps, looking forlorn and feeling blue. I didn't know a single person in the new school except my brothers. Millie and Frances ran out of the schoolhouse and stopped to stare at me. I felt like an insect on the end of a pin.

Millie laughed, grabbed Frances by one hand and said, "Let's not play with her." They galloped away, laughing.

I felt even sadder, but Hazel and Lucille were happy to play with me so I felt better. Frances became my best friend at Liberty after she decided she would play with us and find out about the new kid.

Herb and Millie got acquainted fast. She knocked him for a loop before he knew what was coming. Millie tried to knock the daylights out of Herb until he left Liberty. She'd slip up behind

189

him and Wham! A hard shove and she was off to the girl's toilet where no boy dared to follow. Herb had his hands full, keeping from getting knocked on his rear end.

The girls called Millie "Tubby" when we were angry at her. The boys called her "Tub-O-Guts", which is probably why she was always trying to beat them up.

Frances and the Teideman girls and the Burns boys lived north of the school. The Burns boys sometimes rode horses to school and sometimes came with an older brother in their Chevrolet sedan. Frances came in a Model A driven by her dad or her brother Edwin. The Teideman girls rode horses.

Frances was the rich kid in school. She brought the best lunches: sandwiches, cake, an apple or an orange. Her mother packed her a large lunch so she could share with Hazel and Lucille. Their mother had left her family. They lived with their father southeast of the schoolhouse. Hike Richardson was a small, balding, good-natured fellow. Glen Crawford and the Doud children walked to school.

Glen and Major were nice to us pestering little kids. We played circle base and pum, pum pullaway. They could run backwards so fast we couldn't catch them.

Don Burns didn't like little kids, at least not me. He pushed me off the front steps. I fell and jumped up madder than a wet hen. I picked up a clod of frozen dirt and heaved it at his leg. The clod hit him alongside one ear and almost knocked him dizzy. It scared the dickens out of me. Don ran around the schoolhouse, holding his head and never said a word about it. He didn't push me off the steps again.

That spring Uncle Alvin and Uncle Albert got a new F-20 Farmall tractor and sowed their wheat in record time. Dad had to plant his wheat and corn with a team.

190

Anthrax was reported among cattle in Stanley Country. Anthrax became a scourge that killed whole herds of cattle for some ranchers and farmers.

The Roberts family lived a mile and a half south of our place. Their house was better than ours and had the first cement basement I ever saw. Mr. Roberts had about eight hundred acres to farm, a large amount of land for one man to handle with horses and mules. He had a big team of gray mules and a team of horses. He was mean to his horses and soon killed them.

Thomas was two years older than Herb, Irene was Hank's age and Lucille about Baby's age. Their mother was pregnant and so was ours. Whenever anyone called Juliana "Baby", she said, "The baby isn't born yet," so we started calling her Julian.

We visited back and forth with the Roberts family. The kids went to school east of Highway 14. Two miles west of the Roberts place was the Paulson farm. Ione Paulson was my age. Her sister was Julian's age. The land outside our west fence was called free range because most of it had either gone back to banks for defaulted loans or to the county for taxes. Some was owned by absentee owners many miles away.

One day Mr. and Mrs. Kimberlin were fixing the telephone line. She was stooping over in the back of the wagon when the team spooked and ran away. Mrs. Kimberlin fell on her rump. Mr. Kimberlin ran after the team. We stood by our house and laughed. Kimberlins weren't very neighborly.

We pastured our milk cows on the free range during the spring, summer and fall months as did the Roberts family. Herb rode out to get the cows at milking time. Hank didn't like to ride. He rode horseback only to get somewhere. He liked cars better. The rest of us loved horses like Mom did. Dad didn't like horses either.

191

The Midland School, high on the hill, with the water tower to the West. From the schoolhouse we could see the whole town.

CHAPTER 14
Spring Comes to the Prairie

We were always anxious to shed our long winter underwear and lace boots and go barefoot in the soft spring dirt. The chickens and turkeys were glad to see spring arrive, too. When the chicken house door was opened on a balmy spring morning, hens rushed out to scratch in the dirt, take dust baths, look for bugs, and search for places to hide their nests. Roosters strutted and crowed.

Mom warned us not to sit on the ground until the frost was gone or we might catch pneumonia. Although we sat on, rolled in and dug in snow all winter, the bare ground of spring was off limits to our little behinds until the frost had all melted from the ground.

When new green spears poked through the old dry grass, and delicate spring flowers bloomed, Julian and I took off our shoes and went adventuring. We roamed the prairie, picking the tiny yellow violets, (we called them Johnnie jump-ups), the lovely bluebells, and the lily called Star Flower so small the flower would fit on a nickel.

We picked and ate the sweet, dainty white flowers of the Hood phlox. We wanted to eat wild celery like Frances and Mildred did, but Mom said we couldn't eat anything except wild onions and Hood phlox because we might make a mistake and get a poisonous plant like Uncle Charley's father and brother did.

They found what they thought were wild parsnips in the woods. They ate the roots and died. We didn't even dare take a bite of wild celery although Frances and Mildred gobbled wild celery like a cow freshly turned out to pasture.

We ate wild onions until our breath smelled worse than a skunk in a garlic patch. Sometimes we brought handfuls of the pungent herb home from nature's garden. Mom sliced them into the scrambled eggs. Our teachers wouldn't let us eat wild onions. They said we stunk too much.

We gathered beautiful wild bouquets for Mom. She put the flowers in a glass jar on the table.

Julian and I wandered over the east pasture one day. We walked barefoot, picking flowers and dodging the small prairie cactus that hid in the grass.

Julian stepped on a cactus and the sharp spines stuck in her foot. "Hold still," I said. "I'll pull it out."

"No. Don't touch it." She hopped around on one foot until she got nerve enough to let me grab the cactus by one spine and jerk it out. She sat down and pulled out the tiny stickers that were left and we went on.

We hiked for half a mile, eating sweet white flowers. We went down the hill into the draw to walk home. A few steps and we both said, "Ouch!"

We were walking on cockle burrs. Small, brown and prickly, the burrs spread like a carpet over the floor of the draw.

"What are those stickery things," Julian said, standing on one foot and looking for a clear place to set the other foot down.

"Cockle burrs," I said. "We better go back up on the hillside." Squirrels crack cockle burrs and eat the nut inside. I never could see how they chewed the prickly burrs open. We picked our way carefully back up the hill and went home.

We found meadowlark and horned lark nests on the prairie. We admired the tiny eggs, but Mom said we must not touch them. Speckled meadowlark eggs look like miniature turkey eggs.

The prairie was our flower garden. In summer we found lovely purple snake flowers and snow-on-the-mountain. In fall we picked bouquets of bright orange sunflowers and pink and yellow cone flowers. In fall we gathered golden rod also. In spring we

194

looked for the delicate blue bells.

We collected marble sized buffalo beans and took them home. We stuck them together with nails to make pretend horses and cows.

We chased the small striped gophers. The gophers scooted for their dens, dodging through the grass and diving down the hole. Uncle Charley told us we could drown a gopher out by pouring water into the hole. We did want to catch a gopher.

Hank, Julian and I carried buckets of water from the dam and poured the water down a gopher hole. Not a gopher showed his head. I think the gophers sat in their burrows and laughed at the dumb kids as the water ran past. They probably poked their heads up the back entrance and watched us doing all that work.

We watched the dung beetles rolling balls of manure. The female lays eggs in the manure. The large black beetles roll the manure into a perfect ball the size of a marble. We watched one beetle roll over the brown ball, landing on its front feet. Then the other beetle rolled over the ball. Taking their ball to their hiding place, they rolled over and over the ball, falling head over heels. It looked like fun. The brown ball turned gray as dust gathered around it. We never killed the beetles. Mom didn't want us to kill things that did us no harm.

Colorful garter snakes and large bull snakes slithered through the grass. We kept a sharp eye out for rattlesnakes. A rattler will crawl quietly away in the grass, if he can, but if one is coiled and buzzing, watch out. A little Wenger boy was bitten by a rattler and died.

I was interested in the rocks that stuck out of the ground. A rock about three feet square stuck up in the Roberts' pasture. We found a large rock barely sticking out of the ground on the free range.

"I bet there's pirate treasure under that rock," I said to Julian and Hank. I didn't realize that no ship could sail way out here on the prairie.

We put a spade and hoe into the little wagon and went to

195

dig out the treasure. We dug and dug, but the rock was still buried. Hank quit digging. "We can't dig this rock out. Let's go home."

"Let's dig a little more," I said."There might be something under this rock."

We dug more dirt away, but we didn't make much headway. Hank quit again. "I'm tire of digging. I can't dig this rock out of the ground."

I tried to get him to dig more, but he was through. We loaded our tools and went home. I could never get them interested in digging out any more rocks.

The boys helped Dad milk the cows. Dad milked six cows and they each milked five. They hauled the milk cans to the house in Mom's horse cart that had been turned upside down to make a milk cart.

Julian and I were terrified of our mean Holstein bull. We stayed out of his territory. He chased Herb into the barn where Herb hid in the horse manger until the bull got tired of waiting for him to come out and left.

That bull wasn't afraid of man nor beast. Once he caught Dad in the middle of the corral. Dad picked up a fence post and hit the bull's nose. The bull backed off. He left Dad alone after that.

In May Dad hitched Emmet and Major to the lister and planted corn in the east field. With ample rain and warm days, the corn grew fast. The hot days of July came. The cornstalks grew too tall to go under the cultivator axle without breaking.

One hot July morning, Dad pushed his chair back from the table. "Come on, kids. We're going to pull weeds in the corn field today." He went out followed by Herb and Hank.

Julian and I dashed after them, happy that we didn't have to wash dishes. We all wore bib overalls. Hank, Julian and I were barefoot. Herb got a hoe. Dad shouldered the other hoe and we headed for the field.

"Aren't we going to take any water?" I asked

Dad shook his head. "We can drink out of the dam."

We followed Dad and Herb down the hill, past the barn,

across the dam grade and up the long slope to the field. We walked half a mile beside the fence that divided Dad's field from Emil Nemec's, and we were at the dam in the northeast corner.

The lonely cottonwood trees cast green images on the water. Corn glimmered in the sun, waiting for the weeders. We could hear the corn leaves rustling in the breeze.

"I'm thirsty," I said as Dad began pointing out our rows.

"Me, too," Julian said.

"Get a drink before we start then," Dad said.

Several feet of mud surrounded the pond. Herb and Hank walked through the mud, scaring frogs out of their way. They knelt by the water and drank like horses.

Mud squishing between our toes, Julian and I headed for the water. A big frog jumped away and plunked into the pond. On hands and knees, we eyed the water. Dragon flies hovered above the pond. Long legged water bugs skated across the surface.

"Strain the wigglers through your teeth," Dad said, grinning.

We didn't care about the wigglers. They were mostly too small to see. We drank and were ready to weed.

Julian got the row beside Dad. I was next. Some of the sunflowers and cockle burrs were nearly as tall as I was. When Dad saw me or Julian struggling and tugging on a giant weed, he jerked it out for us. Sometimes Hank pulled a weed for me. He liked to show off his muscles.

When we came to the end of those half mile rows, Dad's shirt was wet with sweat and my tongue wanted to stick to the roof of my mouth. We headed back, pulling weeds from more long corn rows. I thought we would never get back to the dam, but we did. We rushed to the pond as thirsty as baby meadowlarks on a hot day.

The sun was our clock. We were tired, but happy when Dad looked at the sun and said, "Time to go home for dinner."

August 10, 1928, Albert Oscar was born in St. John's Hospital in Rapid City. Julian and I stayed with Aunt Amanda and

Uncle Walt while Mom was gone. In those days, the doctor kept a mother flat on her back in the hospital for at least ten days. We waited anxiously for her to come home.

Mom and Albert came back to Midland on the train. Uncle Walt met the train in his Model T. Julian and I were happy to see Mom and our new blue-eyed, blond-haired brother. We called him Buddy. Mrs. Roberts had a brown-eyed baby girl. They named her Marlys.

Uncle Walt gave Buddy a collie pup. Jack went home with us and was loved by the whole family for many years. That was the summer Dr. Minard died, Dr. Verley moved to Midland and the circus came to town.

People for miles around went to the circus. Before the show, the circus wagons paraded through town, pulled by brawny Belgian horses. A lion paced in his cage, glaring at the people on the sidewalks. We loved the elephants in their fancy harness and the pretty ladies dressed in sparkling costumes.

We laughed at the clowns and wanted to sit in the reserved seats where we could see better. Mom said, "Those seats are for people that can afford them." I guess not many people could because those seats stayed empty.

We ate peanuts and marveled at the trapeze performers flitting back and forth on their swings and the high wire walkers high above our heads. We nearly screamed when the pretty lady did the "slide for life", hanging to a piece of leather with her teeth as she slid down a wire from the top of the tent to the bottom.

That circus had the first alligator we ever saw. She had two hundred babies. You could buy a foot long baby alligator for $2.00. Of course, we wanted one, but Mom said, "No."

Tom Roberts said, "We're going to buy a little alligator." I don't think they did. I never saw one at their place.

Mr. Roberts and Tom dug out a coyote den and caged the pups in a double wagon box with boards on top. Herb ran down a coyote pup with his horse on the free range. He tied a bridle rein around the pup's neck and covered the squirming animal with his jacket.

He carried the furious bundle home and tied it to a stake. Mr. Roberts wanted Herb to give him the pup so he could lock it up with his, but Herb refused. One night the pup broke loose and ran away. The Roberts' coyotes gnawed a hole in the wagon box and escaped, too.

Herb was always finding some little critter on the prairie and bringing it home for a pet. He brought home several baby jack rabbits, but they all died.

Ample rain fell that summer, and our house leaked every time a rain storm blew in. Water ran through the holes in the roof and puddled on the floor. We ran for buckets, pans and cans to catch the drip. In the fall Uncle Walt helped Dad put steel roofing on the leaking half of the house. That ended the drips. We had fun sliding down the steel roof until Dad made us quit.

We loved threshing time. The neighbor men and boys came with their teams and hay racks. The women cooked the meal. Our table groaned under the weight of fried chicken, mashed potatoes and gravy, pie and all the other good things.

The hay racks rumbled to the field for their loads. Bundles flew as the men raced to be the first wagon at the thresher. As one wagon was being unloaded, others lined up behind it.

The steam engine puffed smoke, the pulley turned and the long belt hummed. Bundles went into the maw of the thresher. Grain poured into the grain wagon. Straw shot out of the big curved pipe and built a cone shaped stack behind the barn.

We loved to play in the straw stack, jumping in the straw, climbing to the top and sliding down, but Dad stopped us. He needed straw to bed the cows and sows during the winter. He didn't want us to scatter it all over.

Mr. Roberts didn't want kids tearing his straw stack down either. Tom said, "We can slide down the stack if we stay on the side where Dad can't see us." We slid down the Roberts' straw stack on the side away from the house, but we didn't slide down our straw stack.

In the fall, Dad hitched Emmet and Major to the wagon with a high bangboard on one side and drove to the field to pick corn. With the lines tied to the front of the wagon, the team moved down the row, occasionally snatching an ear of corn. Dad picked two rows at a time, the ears hitting the bangboard with a steady rhythm as they dropped into the box. On Saturday Herb and Hank helped him.

That fall Uncle Charley was selling wagon loads of melons in Midland. 1928 was an excellent crop year, but prices were poor. It was a tough year for farmers.

Three packages of shredded wheat cost twenty-five cents, but we couldn't afford it. Aunt Tina bought shredded wheat. I ate some of the little bales at her house and loved it. Apples were a dollar and seventy-five cents per barrel. Dad bought a box or two of apples every fall. We had our apple a day as long as they lasted.

Sporty Chevrolet coupes sold for $755.00. Oaklands were $1337.00 at the Ilg Auto Company on Main Street. Allis Chalmers tractors sold for $1295.00 plus freight from Milwaukee. More people were trading their driving horses for automobiles.

Turkeys were a fair price with toms at thirty-three cents per pound and hens at twenty-nine. Hogs and turkeys bought winter clothing, potatoes, flour, beans, sugar and coal to tide us through the cold season. Yearling steers went to pay on the mortgage.

That winter we got piles of snow and frigid cold. We headed for school in the fall with Ralph Jordan again our teacher. We loved Ralph. Herb and Hank rode Freckles and Star. Julian was in first grade and rode behind me on Whitefoot.

As the gate opener, Herb let us through, then galloped off to school with Hank right behind him. They left us in the dust. Whitefoot could have beaten them easily, but we didn't want to go that fast. Whitefoot trotted along with Julian bouncing on her rump, holding tightly to my waist.

We all rode bareback. Mom's western saddle was too heavy for us to handle and Mom said riding close to the horse was warmer. By the time a winter of bareback riding was over, our horses had a pattern like an English saddle on their backs and sides where our seats and legs had rubbed the hair off.

One of our winter chores was cutting blocks of snow for drinking water and other household use. We cut the blocks of hard snow with a hand saw and stacked them on the porch. Dad put a steel barrel by the heater to melt snow in. The only time Mom had soft water for clothes washing was in winter and in summer when the rain water barrel filled under the eaves.

We used soft water to wash our hair. Pine tar soap shaved into hot water was our shampoo. We washed our hair in the wash dish and rinsed it with vinegar water.

The summer kitchen was also the laundry room, the separator room and the place where we kept our young poultry at night, locked in their cardboard boxes. Dad had a red Beatrice separator, prettier than our neighbor's black DeLavals.

Our wooden washing machine went with us to our new farm. Mom washed clothes on Saturday so we could help. She heated the water in a boiler on the kitchen range. If Dad was in the house, he ran the washer handle. When he wasn't there, Herb, Hank or I got the job.

Mom said, "You have to run the washer for five minutes to get the clothes clean." I thought the five minutes would never end.

Our clothesline was the barbed wire fence west of the house. The barbs held the clothes on the line, unless the wind blew a gale. Then we ran out and chased garments across the prairie. Julian and I hung clothes.

In winter the clothes froze and we brought them in as stiff as boards. They had to hang on lines in the kitchen until they dried. Aunt Tina had a wooden rack for winter clothes drying. Mom used a line strung from a nail on the south wall to one on the north, then to a nail a couple of feet away. Several lines of clothes draped across the kitchen for us to duck under.

Julian and I learned to iron on a wooden ironing board, padded with old sheets with the table and a chair back for legs. We heated three flat irons on the kitchen range and lifted them off the stove with a clamp on wooden handle. Our old Montgomery Ward catalog served as a base for the iron.

Soon the pages were scorched. If the iron was too hot a dress or shirt was scorched, too. Old catalogs were handy. One was kept in the toilet because we had no rolls of toilet paper.

We liked to iron handkerchiefs best. Plenty of them lay rolled up in the ironing basket. Every woman and girl carried a dainty hankie with flowers, butterflies or some other lovely pattern embroidered in the corner. Men carried large white handkerchiefs or blue or red bandannas. We had no tissues to blow our noses on.

Our handkerchiefs became wash cloths when we went to town. Mom or one of our Aunts would say, "You have ice cream on your face. Spit on your hankie, and I'll wipe it off." A spit and a swipe, clean face.

I didn't mind ironing pillow cases, dresser scarves or shirts, but dresses with their endless skirts, puffed sleeves and pleats and gathers were murder. With Mom and three girls in the family, mountains of dresses showed up in the ironing basket.

Since Mom washed clothes for Uncle Albert and Uncle Alvin, there was plenty of ironing to go around. My fussy Uncle Alvin wouldn't wear a wrinkled shirt even for farm work and permanent press hadn't been invented. He said I was "a good little shirt ironer," and I swelled with pride.

I would rather iron clothes than do dishes. I had to do both. I was the dishwasher. Julian was the dryer. I poured water into the dish pan from the tea kettle and went at the job. The dish pan always got a greasy ring around the waterline. So did the wash dish. Detergents didn't exist. A few drops of kerosene would melt the grease ring right out.

In my haste to get the dishes washed, I sometimes left a bit of egg between the tines of a fork or a morsel stuck to a plate. Julian loved to splash those things back into the dish pan. Made me mad. Sometimes I shot them right back into the drip pan.

"Mom, Mom, Thelma won't wash the dishes clean," she'd say, looking at me indignantly.

Julian had eyes like a magnifying glass. She fired a dish back to me if only a tiny speck resided there.

In summer Julian had to wash the separator every day. Washing and scalding the separator with all its disks and pieces was a job I didn't care for.

We waited as long as we could before doing dishes. One day Mom said, "If you got right at it, you could be done in five minutes."

We didn't believe that. We were sure washing and drying all those dishes would take at least an hour. We decided to find out. We tore into the dishes and were through in five minutes. We were amazed.

The lesson didn't take very well. We would rather play a while first. One hot summer day Julian said, "Mom, can we go swimming before we do dishes?"

"We'll do the dishes as soon as we get back," I said.

"All right," Mom said.

We hurried into our red swim suits and ran to the dam. Tippy and Jack ran along as happy to be going swimming as we were.

We splashed in the cool water and jumped off the raft. We ducked under the water. We played like little otters until our skin wrinkled and we sprouted green mustaches from the algae in the water. Finally we had to give up and go back to those awful dishes.

We stopped in the shade of the corncrib to play. The dogs flopped down in the shade to rest. We soon got bored. We had no toys to play with.

"Wish we had our dolls," Julian said.

"So do I." I thought for a minute. "I could crawl in the window and get them." Julian nodded and watched me go.

The window of the northeast bedroom had no screen. The dolls were in our bedroom and the window opened easily.

I ran to the house, raised the window and slipped into the bedroom. I tip-toed across the room to get the dolls. Mom's voice came from the living room and froze me in my tracks.

"Is that you, Thelma?"

I gulped. "Yes." I slunk into the living room. I told her I had come for the dolls.

"If you want to play longer, you have to ask," she said. "You can't sneak behind my back, and you said you would do your dishes as soon as you finished your swim. Get Juliana and get at it." We finished our dish washing and decided not to try to put anything over on Mom again.

Mom taught us to make cakes, pies, cookies and bread. Cutting out cookies with the animal cutters was fun, but I didn't like to cook. Julian enjoyed cooking.

Mom baked six loaves of bread and a huge pan of cinnamon rolls every week. She kneaded the dough in the dish pan and set the pan on the buffet for the dough to rise.

Our screen door was old and dilapidated. The dogs scratched the screen and tore a hole for adventurous chickens to sneak into the house. The chickens wandered around until someone spied them.

With a shout of "Get out of here, you dumb chickens," we tore after the intruders. Squawking, the frantic chickens streaked for the door, wings flapping. Out through the hole, they scrambled.

One hen slipped in, flew up on the buffet and jumped on the bread rising there. Fortunately, a dish towel covered the dough. Mom saw her. She shook her apron.

"Get out of that bread, you silly old hen." With a startled squawk, the hen flew to the floor and ran for the door.

Cobs were thick in front of the chicken house and in the hog pen. Julian and I gathered cobs in a bushel basket for the kitchen range and to start the morning fires. Aunt Tina carried cobs and eggs in her apron. Mrs. Doud burned cow chips in her range. We often saw her and Marjorie gathering cow chips on the prairie.

We turned the crank on the corn sheller to shell corn for the chickens. Mom said laying hens didn't have time to shell their own corn.

Dad or the boys hitched Emmet and Major to the stone boat and hauled barrels of water from the dam for household use. In summer we often hauled drinking water from Crawford's well with the team and wagon.

Mice ran around our house like stampeding horses. The little pests chewed holes in the cupboards and ran over the dishes. Dad nailed tin over the holes and they chewed new ones. Mice nibbled on the butter and chewed on the bread. At night we could hear tiny feet running across the ceiling above our heads. Mom did battle with them with traps. Our cats had a steady job. Mom opened a cupboard drawer and spied a mouse, looking right at her. "Quick, get a cat," she said.

I ran out the door. Tom was snoozing on the porch, the only cat in sight. I grabbed him and ran back into the house.

Mom looked disgusted. "Tom wouldn't catch a mouse, if it ran right under his nose." Tom spied the mouse. He leaped out of my arms and lit in the drawer. He nabbed the mouse and stalked away. Mom was amazed. I loaned Tom to Aunt Tina to catch mice in her house several times.

We stored jars of canned goods--meat, peas, beans--on shelves in the cellar. Dad lugged several sacks of potatoes down the stairs for our winter supply. The cellar had a dirt floor and dirt walls. Sometimes in winter, we played in the cellar, making roads for Hank's toy cars.

During the winter, our cats stayed in the cellar at night. Felix and Tom both wanted to sleep on the top step. As soon as the door was closed, they fought over that spot. One night we put the cats in the cellar. Herb let the door down.

A terrible commotion started, snarling, spitting and growling. The cats bumped against the cellar door. Then we heard "thump, thump, thump," down the stairs.

"Tom is really getting licked this time," Herb said.

I felt sorry for Tom. From the sound, he'd been knocked off the step and rolled all the way to the bottom of the stairs. The next morning when Dad lifted the cellar door, Tom bounded into the living room. We called, but Felix didn't come. Herb and Hank found Felix dead at the bottom of the steps.

Tom lived for many years, lazy, slick and fat. He traveled about the neighborhood for weeks at a time. I worried about him until he returned home.

A small tiger striped tabby was our best house cat. We named her Spitty because she was such a fierce, spitting ball of fur when she was tiny. Spitty never jumped on the table or messed on the floor. She was a mighty mouser, stalking mice like a tiger stalks a deer. She kept the mouse population in fair control and supplied us with kittens.

Mice weren't our only pests. Our house had bedbugs. They came out of the cracks in the walls and made homes in the creases of our mattresses.

A bedbug grows to about house-fly size only flat. At night bedbugs run out of cracks and creases and swarm over people. They suck blood like vampires. We slept through bedbug attacks, but Mom and Dad didn't. Mom threw the covers back and bedbugs ran in every direction. She was horrified.

There was no spray to kill them. Mom swabbed the cracks in the bedroom walls and the mattress creases with kerosene every day and finally got rid of the blood suckers.

CHAPTER 15

Winter

Dad tore down some ramshackle buildings and built a cow barn with stanchions on the north end of the horse barn. He built a board fence on the north side of the corral from the horse barn to the south end of the corral. He stacked hay along the north fence.

He didn't have money to buy shingles for the barn roof or batts for the cracks between the boards. The wind howled through the cracks. Snow blew into the barn. Rain dripped through the roof. The horses and cows were ready for winter.

Every fall Mom sent an order to Montgomery Ward for winter clothing: long handled underwear, high lace boots, over-shoes, long stockings, coats, boot pants for Herb and Hank. We all wore four buckle overshoes. My cap had ear flaps that fastened under my chin. Uncle Walt gave Herb and Hank leather aviator caps that snapped under the chin. We wore scarves and mittens.

Thus bundled up, we mounted our horses and headed for school. On bitter cold days, our feet got so cold our legs felt like fence posts when we slid off the horse and hit the frozen ground. One cold day when the wind blew from the northeast, I froze one ear. My ear stuck out stiff and white. Ralph Jordan held a handful of snow against it to keep it from thawing out too fast.

Some days the school room never got warm. The teacher came early and built the fire, but the room was so cold we could see our breath. We wore our coats and clustered our desks in a half circle around the furnace. We didn't get much studying done those days.

When blizzard winds screeched around the corners and moaned under the eaves, we pulled the quilts over our heads and slept with a warm flat iron wrapped in a cloth at the foot of our bed. By morning the iron felt like a block of ice.

Snow swirled through the cracks in the north bedroom wall, leaving tiny drifts across the quilts where Julian and I slept. Herb and Hank slept in the south bedroom where the snow didn't sift in. Mom, Dad and Buddy slept in the living room. Each bed had a long flannel sheet that doubled over at the foot so we couldn't get our feet out in the cold

While we slept, the fire in the stove burned out. The water in the water bucket cracked and popped and froze solid. In the morning Dad built the fires, and we all rushed into the living room to dress by the heater.

With a blizzard on, we couldn't go to school so Mom sent us into the north bedroom to "wear off steam" when we got too rollicky. Hank, Julian and I each put a hand on a small table and ran around the table until we were exhausted. Then we panted back to the warm living room.

Sometimes we clamped one roller skate to our shoe and chased each other around the kitchen table, into the living room, around in a circle and back around the table.

In the afternoon, we begged Mom to let us go outside and see what the blizzard was like. She said, "Bundle up good and don't leave the house. You would get lost in a second and couldn't find your way back."

We bundled up in scarves, caps, coats, mittens and over-shoes and went out the door. Jack got up from his warm bed on the porch and followed us. He looked at us like he thought we were crazy, but he had to be sure the dumb kids got back in the house. We could see nothing but a sifting white wall.

The wind and snow nearly took our breath away. We worked our way along the east side of the house. The barn was out of sight. The chicken house had vanished.

We stood on the south side of the house, out of the wind,

and tried to see into the choking white mass that got in our noses and eyes and hid the hills. Soon we battled our way back to the front door. Jack sighed and went back to his bed. We went inside to the welcome heat and took turns sweeping the snow off each other.

Down in the barn, the cows shivered while snow blew through the cracks and coated their bodies with white. Star, Freckles and Whitefoot stood in the shelter of the board fence. When they got cold, they ran and bucked around the pen, then stopped to stand, tails to the fence while sifting snow settled on their backs.

If Dad could see his way, he went to the barn and fed the livestock. Mom worried about him because there was no rope from our house to the barn and the distance was far. He would come back, looking like a snowman.

After the blizzard died, we had to wipe the snow off our horse's back before jumping on board unless we wanted wet rear ends. In winter we took our bridles to the house at night so the bit would be warm. An icy bit will freeze to the horse's mouth and tongue and take off some hide. I held the bit in my hand to keep it warm as I ran to the barn.

One blizzard howled out of the northwest and caught us at school. Swirling snow filled the air. We could barely see the barn. Ralph wouldn't let anyone go until someone came for them. We had no food. Parents came for children until only Martins, Crawfords and Douds were left.

Two wagons appeared out of the snow. Mr. Crawford and Mr. Doud drove up to the schoolhouse. Herb and Hank went with Glen in the Crawford wagon. Julian and I climbed into Doud's wagon and snuggled under quilts with Marjorie. Major stood with his father as we headed south across the school section to Douds.

We stayed the night at Douds while the wind piled snow into huge drifts outside. With no phone, our parents had no way of knowing where we were until we got home the next day.

Mom warned us to take our heavy coats when we went to

school in fall and spring. She said, "A beautiful morning can turn nasty by afternoon."

We got tired of wearing those heavy coats. One balmy March morning, we headed for school, wearing light jackets. My black velvet jacket reached to my waist and had an open front. The day turned blustery just like Mom said.

Julian and I headed home. As Whitefoot loped across the prairie, the northwest wind nearly tore my lovely jacket off my back. I tried to hold it shut with one hand and hang onto the reins with the other, but the wind kept yanking the jacket away. Julian clung to me. I was chilled to the bone when we got home. I didn't forget my coat again.

We kept gallon syrup buckets under our beds for pee buckets. Aunt Tina had a white chamber pail with a lid, but Mom's chamber pail had long ago gotten full of holes. She couldn't afford another.

On frigid winter nights when the water froze solid in the water bucket and ice in the wash dish rose into a hump, the pee buckets froze, too. Julian and I were pee bucket emptiers.

One morning Julian grabbed a bucket and ran down the hill. I followed. She emptied her bucket and turned back just as I let mine fly. The whole bucketful slopped on her. She was madder than any wet hen I ever saw.

She ran to the house. "Mom, Mom, Thelma threw pee all over me." Mom scolded me. I didn't mean to hit her. I felt sorry for her. She was mad at me nearly all day.

Going to the privy in the winter was an adventure. The farm didn't have a toilet so Dad scrounged boards and built one. He didn't have enough boards for a roof. You could look at the sky while you sat in the two holer. The privy wasn't bad in summer, but in winter snow settled several inches deep on the seat.

We ran down in the early morning, sat on the snow and got cold rear ends. Mom scolded us. "Brush the snow off before you sit down. You sit on the snow and melt it. When I go down the snow has turned to ice and I can't brush it off."

When blizzards roared and fuel was low, we couldn't keep the kitchen and living room both warm so Dad hung a quilt in the wide doorway. We spent the day in the kitchen with the fire roaring in the range and a pot of beans bubbling on the back of the stove.

When our coal and wood supplies got dangerously low, Dad hitched up the team and headed south. Wearing his horsehide coat that reached to his ankles, he stood in the wagon, back to the wind, as the horses trotted down the trail. The cold thirty mile trip to Midland and back took two days.

He bought coal, flour, sugar and beans. He stayed the night at Uncle Walt's house, loaded a few logs from the creek and came home. Herb helped him saw the wood into chunks with the crosscut saw.

On bitter cold days, we pulled our chairs in a circle as close to the heater as possible and sat reading or coloring and shivering. The choice place was to stand behind the heater which turned red in spots. If one had a good location by the stove and left the chair to get a book or toy, somebody might grab the chair. Mom made a rule that if one left a chair to get something, someone else couldn't grab the chair. If one left to play, the chair was considered vacant and up for grabs.

I went after a book. Herb took my chair. I came back and said, "Mom, Herb took my chair and won't get off."

"She left," Herb said, grinning.

"I did not. I just went after a book. I was coming right back. Get off my chair, or I'll knock your block off."

"Give the chair back, Herbert," Mom said. I sat down, giving him an indignant glare and opened my book.

Winter brought the Christmas program at school as we celebrated the birth of Jesus. We practiced our pieces, plays and songs. We decorated the Christmas tree and clipped candles to its branches. We drew names. Ralph said not to spend more than a quarter on a present.

Dad took us to town to do our Christmas shopping. As if

by magic, an aisle in C.E. Murray's Store was taken over by toys. We loved wishing through this aisle, looking at the dolls, the red cast iron Model T cars, the wind-up toys, the games and sleds. We finally made our selections.

Wearing his long horse hide coat, Dad hitched Emmet and Major to the wagon and took us to the school program. Snuggled under quilts, we sat on the hay in the bottom of the wagon and listened to the wagon wheels squeaking in the snow. Millions of stars, bright, cold and faraway, twinkled overhead.

The whole neighborhood crowded into the schoolhouse for our program. Our stage was the back of the schoolhouse with sheets strung on wires for curtains. We spoke our pieces, performed our plays and sang the beautiful Christmas songs: Away In A Manger, Oh Little Town Of Bethlehem, It Came Upon A Midnight Clear and the rollicking Jingle Bells.

Gifts were opened. Each child got a sack of candy from the school district. Everybody got popcorn balls. After the festivities were over, we headed home to Mom and Buddy for two weeks Christmas vacation.

We helped Mom make Christmas cookies. We cut out camels, ponies, dogs, stars and Christmas trees and ate cookie dough scraps. Mom made Norwegian cookies called fattigman's bockles (fatman's buckles) that were delicious and always she fried the round white lefsa on top of the kitchen range. We loved lefsa spread with butter and jelly and rolled into a cylinder.

Christmas morning we rose early to open our presents stacked around the tree. We found dominoes and checkers, dolls and jackknives. Hank got a red cast iron Model T coupe. He loved cars. We got balls to bounce and tops to spin. Uncle Walt and Aunt Amanda gave us each a pair of ice skates. Our stockings were filled with candy and nuts. We were soon cracking nuts with hammers, pliers and nutcrackers until nut shells littered the kitchen floor.

After breakfast we bundled up and rode the mile and a half to the Roberts' home for dinner. Snow squeaked under the horses' hoofs. The day was clear and cold. Even the sun looked cold. Dad carried Buddy wrapped in a quilt. I kept warm behind Dad and Julian behind Mom. Herb and Hank rode Whitefoot.

When we rode through the gate, a short distance from the Roberts' house, Buddy got one hand uncovered. His hand got so cold that he had fingerbites and cried. Fingerbites make you jump around and wring your hands. Mom soaked our hands in cold water until the sting went away.

We were anxious to try our new skates. We ran to the dam, clamped skates to our boots and tightened the clamps with the key. We fastened leather straps around our ankles and toes and wobbled off across the ice. We skated around on the dam and listened to the ice crack like a rifle shot. We learned to skim over the ice, avoiding the bumps and cracks.

Sometimes Glen or the Roberts' kids skated with us. We spent many happy hours on the ice, coasting down the hills on our sleds.

That winter Buddy learned to walk. Dad held him up on the table, and Buddy ran like a little race horse around and around the table. When he was six months old, he was walking alone. Mrs. Crawford was amazed to see tiny Buddy in his little white gown walking all over the house.

January of 1929 brought deep snow. Our horses floundered through belly deep drifts, breaking trails to school and home, trails that drifted shut again whenever the wind blew. We missed a lot of school because of stormy weather and were late more than we were on time. We were happy to see spring come.

Snow melted. Water ran down the draws into our dam. Ducks, cranes and geese flew north. The lake beds on the free range filled with water.

At school the boys played marbles. They played for keeps so the games were exciting. Herb and Hank used steel ball bearings for shooters until the other boys outlawed steel marbles. Too many glass marbles were broken.

Dad planted corn and wheat in the east field and sixty acres of flax in the fields north and south of the house. He was going to give the flax to Grandpa for the farm.

Grandpa had said, "Plow the land around the house and plant flax, Henry. Flax will grow good on sod. I vill take the flax for the farm. You can pay for the farm in one year."

Dad hitched up Major and Emmet and walked up and down hills that never should have felt the bite of a plow. He walked, sweating in the heat and shivering in the cold, up and down those endless furrows.

The horses pulled the plow, the disk, the drag and the planter. Months later lovely blue flax flowers covered the field, but the flax didn't yield well. The price was poor. The flax was nearly worthless. Dad still owed Grandpa money, money that he didn't have.

Sometimes our Model T stopped dead without warning. Dad would take the coil out, roll a few inches of tinfoil off and put it back. Spark flowed and the motor roared again.

Mom drove the Model T touring car to town to sell cream and eggs and buy groceries one day. She let Herb drive home. Julian, Hank and I sat in the back. Buddy sat on Mom's lap.

Herb steered proudly up the road and ran into the ditch. The car careened across the ditch and up an embankment, tipped up on two wheels, then settled back. Mom drove the rest of the way home.

Herb was good at thinking up schemes that got everybody in trouble. That's probably not what he had in mind, but that is often what happened.

He offered to teach me to drive the Model T touring car when I was nine. He forgot to ask Mom if he could. The car was parked east of the house in front of a pile of boards. Herb cranked the Model T. By some miracle, the motor started without backfiring and breaking his arm. I sat behind the steering wheel, clutching it tightly. Herb climbed in beside me. "Put her in low," Herb said, forgetting to tell me which was the low pedal. I looked straight ahead, stepped on reverse and backed up into the wood

214

pile. Fortunately, the motor died. That ended my automobile driving for about seven years.

I wasn't beyond making my own blunders. A blue roan cow fell down in the dam one morning. She was weak and couldn't get up or hold her head out of water. Dad waded into the dam and put a halter on the cow. He tied her head to a post so she wouldn't drown. He came to the house to eat breakfast before hitching the team and pulling her out of the dam.

Mom told me to go to the hen house and get the eggs. Dad said, "Run down to the dam and see if that cow has her head above water."

I ran to the dam. The cow's head was under water. I ran to the hen house, gathered the eggs and ran back to the house. "The cow's head is under water," I said. Dad bolted for the door and ran to the dam, but he was too late. The blue cow was dead.

"You should have pulled the rope tighter and lifted the cow's head out of water," Dad said. "Then you should have come to the house and told me. Then you should have gathered the eggs."

Sometimes orders are confusing. Mom sent Hank and me to the dam to carry water to the hogs one hot July day. Dad was in the field. Herb was down at Bertelsons, learning to drive their new tractor. The hog pen was home to about ninety half grown pigs and ten sows.

"How much water are we supposed to give them?" Hank asked.

"Just leave the tank full," Mom said, logically.

We took a large bucket and headed for the corner of the hog pen about fifty feet from the dam. Dad had wired the handle of a wash tub to a corner post for a watering tank.

We waded through mud into the water and filled the bucket. Carrying the heavy pail between us, we lugged the water to the fence and dumped it into the tub. The pigs heard water splash and ran from every direction. They crowded together, squealing and pushing. The hogs emptied the tub before we got back with another bucket of water.

We dumped in more water. The squealing pigs slurped and crowded and pushed, all trying to drink at the same time. The pigs drank, and we lugged water. We ran to the dam, back to the tub, again and again and again. Our steps grew slower. The sun bore down. Not a cloud in the sky. A meadowlark sat on a post and sang. Pigs rooted one another out of the way. Every time we came with a bucket of water, we found the tub empty and squealing pigs looking for more water. We poured another bucket of water into the tub and wiped our sweating faces. We watched the water rapidly disappearing down red pig necks.

"We ain't never gonna get this tank full," Hank said. "They drink the water faster than we can carry it. You get in the pen and chase the pigs away. I'll fill the tank."

I climbed into the pen and picked up a stick about half the size of a baseball bat. Shouting and waving my club, I kept the thirsty pigs at bay while Hank lugged water. After five or six trips, the tub was full clear to the rim. I climbed out of the pen and we ran. Nearly every farmer raised hogs. Dad's herd of red Duroc sows lived in a ten acre hog pasture. When pigs were born during freezing weather, Dad brought the litter of velvety piglets to the house. He put them in a box on the oven door of the kitchen range to get warm. We held the little squealers before Dad took them back to their mothers.

Those red sows were extremely protective of their babies. Dad built a flat topped hog house for one fierce sow. The sow bore a litter of twelve pigs. Dad thought she had too many babies. Another sow had too few. Dad decided to steal a couple of squealers from the fierce mama and give them to the other one.

The hog house roof was low. Dad crawled inside and tried to steal a couple of pigs while they were nursing. The sow roared up, snorting and threatened to tear his leg off. Dad grabbed a board and held it in front of himself and pushed three hundred pounds of furious mother pig back while she grabbed pieces out of the board trying to get him. Dad streaked for the hog pen fence and dived over.

The sow trotted back go her house, grunting and shaking her head in satisfaction. She paused in the doorway to give him a look that said, "If you don't mind your own business and leave my babies alone, you'll wish you had." Then she swaggered into her house.

Dad scratched his head and thought about the problem. He hit on a plan. Taking a bucket of corn, he called the sow over the hill while her babies slept in a little pile in the hog house. The sow was hungry. She trotted after him. He poured the corn on the ground, and she began to eat.

Dad slipped back to the hog house while the sow gobbled corn. He crawled into the hog house, grabbed a pair of piglets, turned and crawled toward the door. The pigs squealed, long and loud. Dad crawled faster, a screaming baby pig in each hand. The angry sow met him in the doorway. Dad dropped the pigs and grabbed a board that was laying on the floor of the hog house.

Using the board for a shield, he pushed the furious sow backward while she gnashed pieces out of the board. He crawled out the door and sprinted for the fence with the mother hog snorting at his heels. Dust flew along with Dad over the fence.

The sow ran back to her brood and counted them. She still had twelve babies. She lay down, grunting with pleasure and let her babies nurse. She raised twelve healthy pigs.

The dam was our favorite place to play in summer. Herb and Hank built a raft. Julian and I would take the raft into breast high water and dive off. We paddled around, staying in shallow water.

Jack went swimming with us. We learned to swim by watching him paddle around in the water. We spent hours in the dam on hot summer afternoons, swimming, ducking under the water, ducking each other under the water.

We took Buddy wading while Mom sat on the bank. Hanging onto our hands, he ran with us into the water. Jack ran into the water, grabbed Buddy's diaper and tried to drag him back to Mom.

Rain fell in good supply that spring and summer with an abundance of rain in July. Dad filled his corncrib with big ears of yellow corn.

Grandpa Martin came, driving an old team down the road from the east one day. Jackie Behrens, Aunt Helen's older son, sat on the wagon seat beside Grandpa. Grandpa came for his flax, but there was no flax. He stayed for a while, then hitched his team and headed for Uncle Arne's place. He left Jackie with us. He had driven all the way from Sioux Falls. Now he was going to Canning.

Jackie stayed for several months and went to school with us. Mom treated him like she did us. She heard Herb tell Jackie, "When Mom spanks you, cry real loud and she'll quit sooner." Jackie had been in so many different homes, he hardly knew how to cry anymore. He had been with Aunt Gina for a while, then Grandpa brought him to us. He came and took Jackie away again although we wanted him to stay. This time Grandpa left Jackie with Uncle Arne.

Later Grandpa put Jackie and Richard in the boy's orphanage at Boystown, Nebraska. Aunt Bird paid the bill of $60.00 per month. They stayed in Boystown until they were sixteen, then left to be on their own. I didn't see Jackie again for over sixty years.

Uncle Arne and his family had settled in on their farm over by Canning. They were neighbors to Grandpa Martin's brothers Ole and Gilbert Martin. Gertie often rode past Uncle Gulick's dugout house when she went after her father's work horses. Sometimes she stopped to talk to Uncle Gulick. He always wanted her to eat.

Gertie said Uncle Gulick was a nice old man, but he wore his clothes until they fell apart without ever washing them. His house was the messiest place she ever saw.

Once he made pancakes for her. He set a plate of pancakes on the table. "Sit down, Gertie. Eat."

Gertie sat down and picked up her fork. She didn't want to eat because his house was so dirty and the chickens got on the table. She didn't want to hurt his feelings, so she tried to choke down some pancakes. When Uncle Gulick wasn't looking, she stuffed pancakes into the back pockets of her overalls. When she mounted her pony, she sat on the pancakes. She rode away from the house and threw the soggy pancakes to the striped gophers scurrying about in the grass. When Uncle Arne got pneumonia and died in 1929, his family moved to Pierre.

Uncle Charley farmed his homestead and supplied us with all the melons we could eat. He sold wagon loads of melons in Midland again. In September Uncle Charley and Aunt Tina rented the McHenry farm about five miles northwest of Midland on shares. McHenrys went back east, leaving a fine herd of milk cows, chickens, a smart cat and an ancient Franklin automobile.

Aunt Tina loved that tiger striped cat. He caught mice and never messed in the house. He did on one occasion use her chamber pail when he was desperate after being left in the house when they went to town.

The McHenry farm was a model of efficiency. A well with a windmill was hooked up to ditches so the garden could be irrigated. They had fenced a grove of trees that contained wild plums, chokecherries and currents. Aunt Tina could pick fruit in her own back yard. We were fascinated with the gas jet lights that lighted the house bright as day.

Aunt Tina and Uncle Charley were allowed to use the Franklin touring car with its rubber bulb horn and brake on the left hand running board. The Franklin was a summer car with neither top nor curtains to keep out the rain and cold. The problem was that neither of them could drive a car. Aunt Tina asked Uncle Alvin to teach her to drive. He showed her the fundamentals-- which lever to shove forward, what was low, brake and high. He drove her to the field west of his house, let her take a few turns around the field and left her to learn on her own.

Aunt Tina drove around and around the field until she knew every gear and how to use it. She was ready to drive to Midland and she did. She became an excellent driver just as she had been an excellent horse woman. Uncle Charley never learned to drive well. He usually drove to Midland in the wagon. I rode with him once, and we had dinner at Maggie McKim's Restaurant on Main Street.

Aunt Tina soon wanted a car of her own, newer than the Franklin. They bought a gray Model T coupe from Bill Elrod. Aunt Tina taught Uncle Charley how to drive, but he had trouble getting the machine to stop for gates. Aunt Tina said, "Now when we get to that gate, Charley, step on the brake pedal. The car will stop."

"All right." Uncle Charley steered grimly toward the gate. He stepped on the low pedal and ran right through it. Aunt Tina turned the key off and the car stopped with the gate draped over the hood. Uncle Charley shook his head. "The car don't stop when I step on the brake. I don't understand it. It stops for you."

"You didn't step on the brake, Charley. You stepped on the low. The brake is on the right. The low is on the left and reverse is in the middle." She was exasperated, but she never lost her temper or her patience.

At the McHenry place Uncle Charley was doing exactly what he hated to do, milking cows. He hired Raymond Christianson to help with the chores. Aunt Tina would gladly have milked cows, but Uncle Charley didn't like to sit under a cow with a bucket and coax milk into it.

He wasn't lazy though. He loved to hoe and pull weeds in his garden and corn field. When they lived on the Walton place, he walked four miles to McHenrys, picked turkeys all day and walked home at night, up and down the hills, straight as the crow flies.

CHAPTER 16

The Great Depression

On March 4, 1929, Herbert Hoover was inaugurated 31st President of The United States. I proudly wore a Hoover and Curtis button to school and voted for Hoover in our mock election because my parents were Republican.

The Stock Market crashed on Black Thursday, October 24, 1929. Some men watched their fortunes disappear into the mist and committed suicide. Most Americans tightened their belts and looked for a better future. The better future was a long time coming.

Farmers grew desperate over the low prices for their cattle and crops. On Black Tuesday, the Market fell even farther, heralding The Great Depression.

Banks began to close, a trend that continued into the 1930's. My father and mother lost the money they had in The Midland State Bank when it closed forever. My brothers and sisters and I lost our small savings accounts. We still had some coins in our Red Book Banks. Sometimes we shook the coins out and counted the dimes, nickels and pennies. Dad shook all the money out of our banks and bought food with it.

So with Herbert Hoover began The Great Depression or as some called it "Hoover Days." The Great Depression was to change my father's politics forever. Not so my mother. She remained a Republican all of her life. She believed, and rightly so, that Herbert Hoover was an honorable and honest man and loved his country. The depression was not his fault.

Hard times dealt a triple blow to farmers and ranchers in western South Dakota. They fought dry weather and grasshoppers as well as low prices. Some people even blamed Hoover for the drought and grasshoppers.

Since prohibition was the law of the land, bootleggers made whiskey to sell and anybody that wanted beer brewed it at home. Uncle Albert aged his brew in the closet. Jack Oviatt kept his beer under the bed.

One Sunday afternoon, Don offered to show us his Dad's beer and give everybody a drink. We crawled under the bed in his parent's bedroom. The bottles were lined up neatly against the wall.

Don opened a bottle and offered everybody a sip. Aunt Tina had told me about the evils of liquor. When the bottle came to me, I hit Don's hand and knocked the beer bottle to the floor. Don was upset because I spilled his Dad's beer.

In December of 1929, the new Legion Hall was dedicated in Midland. We were excited about the new theater and the "talkies" as we called the movies. The hall was used for dances, basketball, school plays, traveling entertainment and funerals. No longer would the Midland basketball players have to practice outside, wearing gloves and overshoes.

Christmas of 1929 stands out in my mind. Mom had said, "We don't have any money to buy presents this year," so we weren't expecting any gifts. We were waiting for a new baby. So was the Roberts' family.

We didn't even have a Christmas tree until the teacher gave us the tree from school. We put the tree in the living room and hung our lovely decorations on the branches. We clipped the candles in their delicate bird holders and lit them. Buddy looked at the beautiful sight and clapped his hands with delight.

We were disappointed because we wouldn't get any presents, but we hung our stockings in the wide doorway anyhow. The next morning, we were up early to see if anything had magically appeared in our stockings.

Julian and I slept in the living room. We couldn't believe our eyes. A doll peeped out of each stocking. Herb's and Hank's stockings had mittens in them. Julian looked at me, her eyes wide. "There is, too, a Santa Claus," she said.

I thought she must be right. We took the dolls out of our stockings and dumped the contents on the bed. We found oranges, nuts, Christmas candy and a dime. Buddy got a silver dollar and a little wagon that Dad had made out of a cheese box.

Julian and I hugged our dolls. Mom said, "Aunt Amanda and Uncle Walt gave you the dolls and mittens." That explained the Santa Claus business. Juliana and I loved our dolls with their molded hair and cute dresses. We took them outside and forgot them on the ground. Rain came and softened the clay. The wet clay stunk, and the poor dolls were ruined.

We ate peanut brittle and cracked nuts with hammers, pliers and nut crackers. Soon nut shells were scattered about, but Mom didn't care. The kitchen was full of the delicious smell of roasting turkey and apple pies. Our aunts and uncles came for dinner.

Aunt Amanda stayed and on December 30, they sent Herb, Hank, Julian and me to the Roberts' home. Dr. Verley delivered Annetta Jean on December 30, 1929. Buddy called her Missy because Aunt Amanda had said, "Isn't she a cute little miss?

The Missy soon changed to Mickey. Mickey she remained. Buddy loved his baby sister. He would hold out his arms and say, "Put her right there."

"Sit on the bed and you can hold her," Mom would say. Buddy sat on the bed, holding his tiny sister as she looked at him with her big blue eyes.

Dad had no money to pay Dr. Verley, but he had butchered the fierce Holstein bull. He gave half of the meat to Dr. Verley in trade. Dr. Verley had a maternity ward in his home. Dad laughed and said, "Doc is going to feed that tough old bull to the pregnant women in his hospital."

We had to eat that tough old bull, too. I think they ground

him into hamburger. Mom put up many jars of meat in the fall and winter. Dad butchered hogs. Bertelsons butchered a cow. We took turns turning the handle on the grinder and watching the long strands of meat come out. Mom mixed pork and beef and made patties. The patties were fried in large frying pans on the wood range and stored in crocks.

The meat was delicious. Dad kept a quarter of beef in the cold north bedroom which was our freezer. When Mom wanted to fry steak, Dad sawed off a chunk of frozen meat. When warm weather came, Dad cut the meat up and Mom canned it in a boiler on our kitchen range.

Mom canned chicken, peas, beans and corn. We picked wild plums, chokecherries and buffalo berries to make jams, jellies and sauces. Our cellar was loaded with canned goods when winter came. Storing all that food kept us from being hungry during The Great Depression.

We picked wild fruit on Mitchell Creek and Bad River. Mom planned to pick chokecherries on the Bob Gray place six miles north of our farm. The Bob Gray place was a deserted road-house where the infamous Kennecke murders took place during homestead days.

Mom told Mrs. Roberts we were going there to pick chokecherries on Saturday. When we got to the patch, we found few berries. Mrs. Roberts said they went there and picked buckets of berries.

Dad had the same kind of luck with the hay he was going to cut. He told T.W. (Talton) Roberts that he was going to cut hay on the free range west of our house. "I'm going to start cutting tomorrow."

Dad hitched Emmet and Major to the mower and drove to the hay field. T.W. was going around and around Dad's chosen haying spot, his big gray mules pulling the mower as the tall grass fell before his sickle. He had driven two miles to cut hay in Dad's back yard. Dad shook his head and found another place to mow.

The Roberts' family came from Illinois. They didn't talk

like we did. They said, "You 'uns" and "We-uns" instead of you and we. Mrs. Roberts had a baby girl that summer named Cleta.

During the long winter evenings, Dad entertained us with his violin and the dogs howled from the porch. He could play all the old tunes and any new ones that anyone would whistle for him. He played for dances all over the country. When Crawfords came to visit, Dad played the violin and Mr. Crawford chorded on the piano. At Crawfords he chorded on the organ. Dad could play the harmonica, too, and so could Herb. The rest of us weren't as musically inclined.

Hank and I played mumblety peg with his jackknife. You opened the short blade clear open and the long blade halfway. You stuck the long blade into the floor, flipped the knife into the air and the blade it landed on determined the score. The first person to get five hundred won the game.

One day Dad lost his glass eye. He came in the house and looked in the felt case. No glass eye. "Have you kids been playing with my glass eye?"

We all denied his accusations. He grumbled around, sure one of us had taken it. He sat down by the table and jumped up like a wasp had stung his behind. He reached into his hip pocket. "There's my damn eye," he said, holding it up for us to see.

Mom was an expert seamstress. Her treadle sewing machine hummed as she made dresses for the girls and herself. She cut dresses for us from her old dresses and from dresses that Aunt Tina and Aunt Amanda gave her. Flour came in sacks of flowered gingham and mothers made dresses and underwear for their little girls from the pretty fabric.

Julian and I learned to make neat patches on the knees and seats of all the overalls in the house. We patched all the heels and toes of worn socks also. We all hoped this depression wouldn't last and that next year would be better. It wasn't. The depression, like a giant dog, was shaking the life out of our world.

The beginning of the "dirty thirties" was upon the country by the end of summer. Ample rain fell in July. Corn and wheat fields were lush until the rain quit like someone had shut off a giant faucet. Temperatures soared, and even the deep holes in the creeks evaporated away in the searing heat.

Horses from the open range streamed to their watering holes only to find the holes dry. The animals died, piling up until the carcasses of dead horses clogged the drinking places. Some range horses watered every other day, running forty miles to Bad River for a drink, then back to their range.

Crawford's well got so low that Glen saddled his horse and drove their livestock to our dam for water. He swam with us, then drove them home again.

Prices were headed toward the bottom. During the 1930's a farmer south of Midland sold two hundred head of cattle for $15.00 a head. Wheat was sixteen cents per bushel, then dropped to five cents and then three. Eggs were six cents per dozen in Midland and getting cheaper.

Mom said, "We might as well throw them over the hill."

We did throw rotten eggs left from an incubator hatch down the hill south of the house. Rotten eggs made a delightful pop on impact, but if one exploded in your hand, you were showered with a stinking mess.

We got a car that summer. Whitefoot's second colt was named Snip. Herb broke him to ride. Uncle Alvin bought a new Model A Ford coupe, making a down payment with his World War I pension loan. Due to poor crops and poorer prices, he couldn't pay for the car. He dealt the Ford to Uncle Walt.

Uncle Walt traded his Model T to Dad for Snip and a bay colt. We were happy. We had a way to get to town besides the team and wagon again. We rode in the trunk, using a stick to brace the lid open. The ride was dusty and noisy, but we didn't mind. If the road was bumpy, someone hung onto the stick to keep the lid from bouncing down on our heads. Mickey and Buddy rode in front with Mom and Dad.

Aunt Amanda wouldn't have to crank the Model T anymore. One day she was going to crank it up and go to town. She

226

told Julian to step on the brake when the car started.

Aunt Amanda jerked up on the crank. The motor roared. Julian stepped on the low. Pushing against the car, Aunt Amanda shouted, "No, no, step on the brake." Julian shifted her foot to the brake pedal and stopped the car. She painted the brake pedal red so she wouldn't make that mistake again.

In Midland the first colored movie shown at the new Legion Hall was Hit The Deck with Gene Kelly. Dad found enough money to take us so we piled into the Model T and went to town.

Gutzon Borglum and his crew were carving George Washington, Abraham Lincoln, Thomas Jefferson and Theodore Roosevelt on Mount Rushmore in the Black Hills.

The drought was being felt in South Dakota. The alfalfa was poor. The wild fruit dried on the bushes. Hordes of grasshoppers were preparing to eat what little vegetation there was.

Trucks large enough to handle substantial loads were coming into the country. Roy Blackmore drove the White Eagle gasoline truck from Midland to farms with tractors. He bucketed the gasoline out of his tank in a five gallon bucket and poured it into the farmer's barrels.

In spite of the dry weather and grasshoppers some wheat made from twelve to fifteen bushels of shriveled wheat per acre. According to The Midland Mail, the price of wheat was the lowest since 1654 in Liverpool, England.

Grasshoppers were so thick on the highways that they clogged car radiators, making the cars boil. The highways were greasy with smashed grasshoppers.

County fairs were called off. There was nothing to exhibit. Some farmers were so hard up they couldn't pay the taxes on their land. The counties took the farms for taxes. Dad owed both the loan company and Grandpa.

Julian and I loved to visit Aunt Tina and Uncle Charley and play in the red barn. The roof didn't leak and no holes marred the sides. We played in the grove of trees and drank from the well.

Uncle Charley's irrigated melon patch was loaded with melons.

We went to visit them one day with Mom in our Model T. When we were ready to go home, Aunt Tina and Uncle Charley decided to drive to Midland. Julian and I went with Uncle Charley in their car. Mom, Aunt Tina, Buddy and Mickey followed.

The cars tooled down the hills and across the small creek and pulled onto the highway. As we turned toward Midland, Julian and I looked back. "Here they come," I said. "Don't let them pass us, Uncle." Uncle Charley stepped on the gas. The car roared down the road about thirty miles an hour. Julian and I watched out the back window and told him if they were gaining.

Uncle Charley poured on the gas. The Model T seemed to fly. When we got to Midland, Aunt Tina said, "My goodness, you went fast. We couldn't keep up with you." We looked at Uncle and grinned.

By chicken canning time in August, rain fell, helping the limping corn crop. Still the moisture was too little, too late. Ears were small. Farmers were cutting corn for fodder and Russian thistles for hay. Prairie hay was too short to cut.

Herb and Hank went with Dad to haul stickery Russian thistle hay. They tramped the hay into the hay rack as Dad pitched it on. Their legs were red with thistle scratches by the time the first load came to the barn. Mom dug out two pairs of World War I canvas leggings to protect their legs.

Thistles made poor feed. Molasses made them more nutritious if one could afford it. Even thistles beat an empty pitchfork. Farmers were beginning to feed cottonseed cake to cattle. The cake came in huge chunks as hard as coal. If a cow got too much, she would go blind.

That year Midland had twenty-two substantial businesses, four of them general stores that sold groceries and dry goods such as overalls, pants, shoes, anything to wear or sew. Murray's Store carried the latest fashions, but few people could afford to buy them.

We were never hungry during the depression. Hungry perhaps for a different kind of food, but no stomach clutching hunger like some people suffered. We would have liked more apples and oranges. A banana was manna from heaven. Grapefruit was non-existent at our house, but Aunt Tina and Aunt Amanda served them.

We had plenty of beans, rice, sugar, flour, potatoes and meat, although Mom did ration meat. In order to have a second piece, we had to eat the fat from the first piece. (They hadn't discovered that fat was bad for you yet.) Since I hated fat, I seldom ate a second piece of meat. When our meat store was low, Mom made a rule that we could only have two pieces of meat.

We lived by that rule, but one day Bernard and Willard Burns came home to stay overnight with Herb and Hank. Julian was afraid they wouldn't know the rule. If they took more than two pieces somebody would come up short. We sat down for supper, and Julian said, loudly, "Mom, we each get just two pieces of meat, don't we?" Julian got her point across, but Mom looked like she would have liked to crawl in a crack.

Mom canned peas, corn and string beans when we had a garden, but in the thirties if a plant poked its head through the dry ground, it withered or got gobbled up by a hungry grasshopper.

We had plenty of eggs to eat except during the winter when the temperature dropped so low the hens froze their combs. A hen with a frozen comb sits around with an aching head and refuses to lay eggs. During the deep cold, the poor chickens huddled in the coop while the water froze in their drinking pan. When the weather warmed toward spring, Dad found eggs frozen solid.

Snow fell deep during the winter of 1930-31. A hungry coyote caught a rabbit only to have an eagle contest him for his prey. The eagle dived down and beat the coyote with his powerful wings and clawed him with his sharp talons. The coyote dropped the rabbit and nabbed the eagle's throat. That ended the fight. The coyote dined on rabbit and eagle.

Mays bought a spanking new Model A Ford Sedan just

before Christmas so Frances rode to school in style. Ford roadsters had gone to a new low of $430.00 FOB Detroit. The Doud and Crawford boys drove slick blue racing cars. The cars had one seat and no top and were built like a stubby cigar. We thought they were wonderful. Just before Christmas, Major rolled the Doud racer into a pile of tin. Fortunately, he didn't get hurt.

February brought a thaw, sending water down creeks into Bad River. Water ran down the draws into our almost dry dam. A blizzard in April brought more welcome moisture and made farmers happy, but the depression was tightening its screws.

Prices dropped like there was no bottom. Cream hit a new low of sixteen cents per pound of butterfat. At three cents a dozen, eggs weren't worth hauling to town. Wheat, corn and barley brought three to five cents per bushel. Dad brought baskets of big beautiful ears of golden corn to the house for fuel. I watched those ears of corn go into the heater and thought what a shame to burn food. Chickens weren't worth hauling to town either.

Dad bartered our worthless chickens to the magazine salesmen who came through the country with chicken crates on the fenders of their Model A's. Dad traded the old hens and roosters for The Country Gentlemen, The Dakota Farmer, The Farmer and The Farmer's Wife. We got The Saturday Evening Post from Uncle Albert. Dad subscribed to The Mitchell Republic so we had a daily paper, too.

Whenever the monthly magazines came, we gathered around Mom's chair after supper and she read the latest story installment to us. We heard the western stories by Zane Grey, hot off the pen of the famous author. We loved the stories about Peter Rabbit and his friends. She read thrilling stories from The Bible, too. We heard about Baby Jesus, David and Goliath, and Daniel in the lion's den.

We shelled corn for the chickens while Mom read to us. I liked to pop the kernels off an ear with my thumb.

We looked forward to spring because Aunt Tina and Uncle Charley were going to move to the Calhoun place. Uncle Charley was tired of milking cows again. He still farmed his homestead and that summer walked ten miles south, hoed in his corn field all day and walked home in the evening.

Calhoun had refused to rent his farm to Roberts again so Uncle Alvin and Uncle Albert rented it. They had rented and fenced a two by three mile chunk of the free range west of our house.

The Roberts' family moved to his father's homestead which was a hop and a skip across a couple of draws south of our farm. The Roberts' kids would be going to our school. Their house was tiny with a kitchen, living room and bedroom downstairs and a tiny room in the attic where Tom and Mrs. Roberts' brother Urval slept.

CHAPTER 17
Grandpa

When spring came, Uncle Alvin moved about three hundred Hereford cows into the big pasture. Our milk cows grazed there as did the Roberts' milk cows. Mr. Roberts didn't ask if he could pasture his cows in the Bertelson pasture, he just turned them out and dared anyone to do anything about it.

Mr. Roberts was hard on horses. His draft animals all died except his jack mule. He bought a bay horse to go with the mule so he had a team again. His farm ground had been cut from five hundred acres to around a hundred so he got by with one team.

We were happy when Aunt Tina and Uncle Charley moved to the Calhoun place. Uncle Charley milked one cow and planted a large garden with a melon patch northwest of the house.

Many an afternoon, we walked down the trail to visit Aunt Tina and Uncle Charley. Sometimes she walked to our house to visit. Often on a lovely afternoon, we would see Aunt Tina and Uncle Charley coming from the south, she riding bareback on Red, Uncle Charley leading the old workhorse.

I spent a lot of time at Aunt Tina's house. Aunt Tina taught me to sew on her treadle machine. My feet pedaled so fast that I sewed my finger as well as a dress for my doll. During school, I would walk down on Friday night, stay the weekend and walk home on Sunday. If cows were grazing along the fence, I crawled under the wire and walked far out in the field so the bulls wouldn't see me. Actually, the bulls would rather eat grass than chase a small girl through the corn field.

232

In the summer, I rode Whitefoot to her house and stayed a week at a time. I often rode the big pasture with Uncle Albert in his Model T roadster with no top. An epidemic of blackleg was killing calves. Every day we checked those that might be sick and dying. Many died before ranchers began to vaccinate for the dread disease.

As we bounced over the prairie, I tried to swat the flies that landed on my pants leg, but they were too fast for me. When we found a dead calf, Uncle Albert rubbed the calf's shoulder.

"He died of blackleg all right," he'd say. "His hide crackles like a piece of paper."

Uncle Albert wasn't a big man anymore when I knew him. He limped along with one stiff leg. When he sat on a chair, the stiff leg stretched out in front of him. He teased us and gave us coins to spend. I loved him, but Julian was afraid of him. He scared her with his wild stories and teasing. I knew him as a gentle man who let me go with him in his Model T.

At family gatherings, Uncle Albert entertained us with stories. He was full of tales about ghosts and strange happenings. We knew there were no ghosts because Mom told us, but that didn't stop us from being delightfully scared. After dinner, we all gathered around the kitchen table to listen to Uncle Albert's stories. "I was playing poker with some men in a hayloft back in Iowa," he said. "The cards were all dealt when one fellow dropped a card. The card fell through a crack in the floor."

The man looked a his cards and shook his head. "I wish I had that card back. I'd take it from the devil himself." To everybody's horror, a large, hairy hand reached through the crack and handed the man his card. Of course, we believed every word.

Once mysterious footsteps were heard in a church at night. Anyone who went past the church at midnight heard the steps. One man looked through a window and saw something white disappear behind the pulpit. People said the church was haunted.

A group of men gathered at the church at midnight, determined to find out what was going on. Tap, tap, tap, footsteps came toward the door.

A burly man said, "I'm not afraid of any ghost. I'm going inside and see what's there." He had a blanket in his hands. He opened the door. A white thing tripped toward him. The men stood outside, frozen with fear. The big man jumped inside the door and dropped his blanket over the white thing. He carried it outside, set it down and removed the blanket. A sheep ran away.

Uncle Albert's story about "The Coffin In The Basement" had us shivering in our chairs.

A group of men sat around a table during a wake. The body was in the basement. They lit a lamp and talked until midnight when someone said they should go downstairs and check on the coffin. Nobody wanted to go down into the dark basement. One man laughed. "You're a bunch of cowards. I'm not afraid. I could go down there and drive a nail in that coffin."

"Here's a nail and a hammer," someone said. "Go down and nail this nail into the coffin, if you're so brave."

The man took the hammer and nail and a lamp and went down the stairs. He set the lamp on the coffin. The men heard the whack of the hammer pounding the nail into the coffin. Then they heard a thud and silence. They waited, but their friend didn't return. Someone looked down the stairs. "Hey, are you all right?" Nobody answered.

They went slowly down the steps. They found their friend lying by the coffin with his coat tail nailed to its lid. When he turned to go and felt the tug, he fell dead. I didn't get over being scared in the dark until I was forty years old.

Bertelson's range cattle streamed in to our dam to drink and stayed in the water, soaking their feet for several hours each day. Millions of flies swarmed off the cows and flew to our house. They dived into the milk buckets and drowned in the skim milk when Dad separated.

Waving two dish towels in the air, Mom chased flies out of the house. Clouds of them flew toward the braced open screen door and onto the porch. She never got them all shooed away, but she thinned them out so we could eat without being bothered by them diving into our food. We wore out many fly swatters.

Mom hung sticky fly paper ribbons from the ceiling in the kitchen. Those sticky ribbons would wind in your hair, if you didn't duck when you went under them.

Sometimes Mom sprayed flies with a hand sprayer. She covered everything with dish towels that she didn't want unconscious flies to fall into and pumped the air full of fly poison. We all went outside for a few minutes while flies dropped on the table and floors. Then Mom dashed in, swept up the flies and dumped them into the stove before they revived and took up the attack again.

Being only a few months over a year apart, Buddy and Mickey were in diapers at the same time. When they were supposed to be learning what the pot and the outdoor biffy were for, they spent a lot of time running around with bare butts.

Wet pants were discarded wherever they happened to be when they got wet. Sometimes they went to the pot on the kitchen or living room floor. Julian had the kitchen and I had the living room to clean up, if they had an on-purpose accident. If a cat did his job on the floor, we could rub his nose in the mess and throw him outside. Mom wouldn't let us do that with Buddy and Mickey. They had us at their mercy.

Mom sent me or Julian to catch whoever shed a pants and took off with the bottom half bare. Once Buddy headed outside, shedding his pants on the porch as he ran. Grabbing a clean pants, I tore after him. I caught him in the Model T touring car. He sat behind the wheel, making motor noises as he drove lickety split over an imaginary prairie. "You have to put your pants on," I said.

"No." Buddy shook his head, his bare bottom bouncing on the seat. I hauled him out of the car kicking like a steer at branding time. He struggled and screamed while I forced him into his clean pants. He went back to driving wherever he was going.

Around the first of July, when heat waves shimmered along the horizon and meadowlarks sat on the fences, tongues hanging out, Uncle Alvin declared it was branding time. He started the round-up before the sun came up so as to get the cattle corraled before the day heated up.

I didn't like to rise before day light, but I wanted to help so I rolled out of bed, bridled Whitefoot and galloped after the herd. Whitefoot loved to chase cattle. Uncle Alvin laughed when she turned after a cow so fast I was left sitting in the air. I landed on the ground, got up, swung on her back and sent her after the dusty cattle. Uncle Alvin said, "She can turn on a dime and leave you some change."

We gathered cattle from the big pasture and drove them to the corrals on the Calhoun place. The Calhoun place had the only set of wooden corrals in the country. Tom and T.W. brought the Roberts' herd. Owen Lohn came with his cattle from four miles south. Joe Illian brought his small bunch from two miles west, and the McCready cattle came from the east.

Mr. Roberts was vaccinating cows for anthrax and stuck a needle through his hand. He was sure he would get the disease.

"You won't get anthrax," Uncle Alvin said. "You just vaccinated yourself." Mr. Roberts was scared. He hurried across the dam grade, rushed into the house and soaked his hand in iodine water. He didn't get it but a rancher over west did and died.

We enjoyed having the Roberts' kids so close too our place. We swam together in summer and skated in winter.

Our parents didn't get along as well. They barely spoke to each other and then only if they couldn't get out of it. Trouble came when Grandpa Martin came to stay with us. Mr. Roberts wanted to buy our farm from Grandpa.

Grandpa was eighty years old, a tall, spare man with a huge mustache. Grandpa would pour cream in his coffee, then pour coffee into the saucer, blow on it to cool the drink and suck the coffee out of the saucer. The cream left a white rim on his mustache.

Grandpa loved to read. He would say, "Get me a book, Telma. Get one with a little romance in it." Romance was easy to find. Mom's bookcase was filled with books by Zane Grey, Harold Belle Wright, B.M. Bower, and Edgar Rice Burroughs. I would get Grandpa a romance and he would happily settle down to read. I think he liked *Chip Of The Flying U* as much as I did.

When Grandpa wasn't reading, he played solitaire. He invented a new game where he dealt all the cards face up and moved them from pile to pile. Hank and I thought Grandpa cheated now and then.

One day Grandpa had every card out where he could play except one. That card was buried under a pile where it would be impossible to get at. Grandpa shuffled his cards, over and over while Hank and I watched. Hank said, "You're beat, Grandpa. You can't get that card out."

"Oh, yah," Grandpa said. "I vill get it ."

Hank watched Grandpa like a hawk watches a mouse in the grass. Then we got distracted for a second. When we looked back, the buried card was out of the pile. Grandpa was finishing his game.

"Grandpa, you cheated," Hank said.

"Oh, no." Grandpa gathered his cards to start a new game. "I beat old Sol."

When we went to town, Grandpa stayed home. T.W. Roberts watched our car leave, then walked down across the draws to visit Grandpa. He told Grandpa he would buy our farm. Grandpa needed the money to pay on a farm he had bought near Sioux Falls. He didn't know that Mr. Roberts didn't have any money either so he sold the farm to him.

Before winter Grandpa went back to Sioux Falls to live with Aunt Sophia. We never saw him again. Grandpa wrote Dad a letter, saying that he had sold the farm to Roberts and he wanted us to leave by September 1.

Mom told us that we might have to move away. We couldn't understand why Grandpa wanted us to leave. Dad wrote Grandpa a letter that said Grandpa owed Dad $1500.00 for improvements to the farm, plowing and building the cow barn.

Grandpa said Dad owed him for the buildings he had torn down and for the corn that had been left in the corncrib. At three cents per bushel, the corn was worth about $3.00.

We stayed on the farm. We had no place to go. Mr. Roberts told Dad he would give us until the first of October to leave. Dad said, "I'm not going."

"I'll get the sheriff and put you off," Mr. Roberts said.

Dad was angry. "If I leave, I'll beat the tar out of you first." The neighbors warned Dad that T.W. Roberts carried a twenty-two pistol in his pocket for such an emergency.

Mr. Roberts told the neighbors we were moving away. One Saturday night after we had gone to bed, Mom looked out the window and saw a string of car lights approaching from the north. "Quick, get up and dress," she said. "People are coming."

We hurried into clean clothes. Julian and I picked up the things scattered around the house and stuffed them into our closet.

Mom lit all the lamps and we waited for the surprise party to arrive. Cars parked beside the house. People poured through the door. Women brought cake and sandwiches. Dad played the violin. Mr. Crawford played the piano. The neighbors gave us a rousing going away party. The Roberts family came and partied with everybody else, but we didn't leave.

Grandpa and Mr. Roberts took Dad to court to make us move. Mom and Dad went to Ft. Pierre to fight for their right to stay on the farm. Months later Judge Hughes had not handed down a decision. Dad went to Ft Pierre and asked him, "Have you reached a decision on our case?"

"Are you still living there?" Judge Hughes asked.

Dad said, "Yes."

"Well, stay there," the judge said. So we did. Years later Dad paid off the mortgage to the loan company and owned the farm. He bought land until he had a considerable acreage.

We didn't know what to think about Grandpa. He wanted to be good to us, but he tried to move us off our farm. I felt bad because I thought Grandpa was a mean old man. My cousin Gertie said they loved Grandpa. He bought them candy and did odd jobs for their mother when he visited them.

She made me feel better about Grandpa. He was an old man without money, trying to get what was owed to him, only there wasn't any to get. Grandpa was bitter. He said his children got all of his money. Now he needed money and couldn't get any.

The depression was bearing down. Some wag wrote this Twenty Third Psalm Of The Depression. *"Hoover is my shepherd, I am in want. He maketh me to lie down on park benches, bum breakfasts and put off dinners and suppers. He leadeth me through great need. He restoreth my doubt in the Republican Party. He leadeth me in paths of destruction, I do fear evil, for thou art against me. They prepareth a reduction in my wages before me in the presence of mine enemies. Thou anointest my income with taxes and my expense account runneth over my income. Surely unemployment, and poverty will follow me all the days of the administration, and I will dwell in a rented house forever."*

CHAPTER 18
Poultry Talk

In 1931 the grasshoppers got thick. The Midland Mail was loaded with advice about killing grasshoppers, but the hordes of hoppers chomped on. Farmers could get poison laced bran from the Government. The mash was to be scattered in the fields to kill the hungry insects. The mash would kill any cow or horse that ate it, too.

Grasshoppers furnished food for our poultry. Nearly every farmer kept fifteen or twenty turkey hens and a strutting turkey gobbler. Dressed turkeys brought a good price even during the depression.

Turkeys, chickens, ducks, geese, even guineas, we raised them all. Anyone driving into our yard was met by an awful racket. Guineas were the watchdogs of the farm. If they spotted a coyote or a hawk, they ran, squawking for shelter, thus warning the rest of the poultry of danger.

In the fall when people stood outside talking, geese, young and old, gobbled and honked, trying to drown out the humans. If someone laughed, a cacophony of animal sounds erupted. Turkeys and geese seemed to enjoy the conversation.

In the spring the turkey gobbler strutted around in front of his admiring ladies as if he owned the whole farm. We kept an eagle eye on the turkey hens because they stole their nests away. Mom wanted the first fifteen eggs from each hen to set under chicken hens or in the incubator. After Mom got the eggs she wanted, the turkey hens were allowed to hatch a brood.

240

Finding a turkey hen's nest was never easy. Turkeys can't be kept in the chicken house with the chickens. They'll get sick and die. Turkeys want to be out in the air like their wild brothers and sisters. In winter the turkeys roosted on top of the barn or chicken house. Lined up, facing the wind, heads tucked under a wing, they went to sleep. They were tough birds. They sat through the blizzards of winter and the heat of summer. Sometimes, if a blizzard lasted too long, some of the turkeys got a mouth full of snow. The snow froze and stopped their air so they died.

Since turkey hens lived outside, we couldn't lock them up to get the first eggs. We had to find their nests. Turkey hens never go straight to their nests. They wander around, catching bugs, looking as if they hadn't a thing on their minds. If a turkey hen spotted someone following her, she meandered around until the watcher gave up and went away. She might hide her nest beside a fence post, under a pile of boards or in the weeds. Turkey hens hollowed out a spot, lined it with feathers and grass and laid their eggs.

If Mom saw a turkey hen sneaking away, she said, "There goes a turkey hen. Quick, run out and see if you can find her nest." Somebody ran out to trail the turkey hen. She meandered about, picking up bugs and seeds, looking as though she had nothing better to do than find something to eat. She stopped often to stretch her long neck and swivel her head about, looking for any Martin kid who might be on her trail.

We tried to be smarter than the turkey hens, but those old hens laughed and said to themselves, "You silly Martin kids can't outsmart me." If we saw a turkey hen looking at us, we stood as still as a post, trying to fool her. Sometimes we found a nest, more by accident than by trailing. Mom and Dad usually found the nests.

We took the turkey eggs and substituted three or four hen eggs to fool the hen so she would continue to lay in the nest. If we took all of the eggs, she would find another hiding place. Turkey hens can't count, and they can't tell the difference between their eggs and a chicken egg. Their object is to fill the nest with fifteen or more eggs and set on them until the little peepers come out.

Mom had two kerosene heated incubators. One held a hundred hen eggs, the other held a hundred and fifty. Turkey eggs are bigger than hen eggs so Mom couldn't hatch as many of them. When hatching time drew near, we hovered around the incubator door, waiting for the little cheepers to pop out of the eggs.

When someone shouted, "I see one that's pipped," we crowded around to watch the crack get larger until the shell split and a tiny wet chick tumbled out. Soon the glass door was crowded with fluffy chicks, hopping about, cheeping for food.

The boys donated their bedroom for a brooder house. Mom removed the furniture and put papers over the floor. We filled the steel feeders with starting mash and placed them around the room. The waterers were canning jars tipped over on a tray. Mom put the chicks in a box and dumped them on the floor. She let us each hold a chick, telling us to be careful and not squeeze it.

We scattered oatmeal and bits of hard boiled egg on the floor and watched the chicks scramble after the food., The chicks gobbled oatmeal and egg bits until their little gullets looked like they had swallowed a marble. They chased one another about the room, stealing food and running with it.

We laughed as the chicks scrambled and fought over pieces of egg. Soon they were gobbling mash out of the feeders. At night we put the chicks in cardboard boxes so they wouldn't pile on top of each other and smother.

The chicks lived in the bedroom until the weather outside warmed up. Soon the chicks began to sprout feathers. Some of them got bare behinds and were extremely homely before they feathered out. By the time the chicks were ready to live outside during the day, the newspapers were scratched to bits and the room was a terrible mess. We got busy with mops and water and cleaned the bedroom.

Herb and Hank built a pen for the chicks outside and we moved them out into the sun. If rain clouds threatened, we ran out and gathered the chicks into boxes and brought them into the house.

Even fully feathered, half grown chicks can't stand a pouring rain. If they are left soaking wet, they may die. When a rainstorm came up, Julian and I ran out to chase half grown chicks. Soaked chickens soon stand shivering, unable to move. They probably wished they had stood still in the first place. We put the shivering chicks in boxes and brought them into the house. If a fire burned in the kitchen range, we set the boxes on the oven door. The cold wet birds got warm and dry and the kitchen smelled of wet chickens. When the clouds had passed, we took the chicks outside to chase bugs again.

Small turkeys are harder to care for than chickens. They are also dumber which makes them pretty stupid. Mom always set some turkey eggs under chicken hens. The hens hatched chickens, turkeys, ducks and geese. They accepted anything that came out of an egg. I don't think they would have taken an alligator or a turtle.

I wonder how the chicken hen kept the huge goose eggs under control. They had a harder time keeping track of the goslings and ducklings. Those little buggers liked to play in the water and go for a swim which nearly drove the mother hen crazy.

The turkey hens hatched around fifteen poults. The poults grew fine with their mothers unless the hen took them out in wet grass when they were small. If a baby turkey gets too much dew, he will curl up and die. Morning dew was scarce in the thirties.

With grasshoppers so plentiful, raising turkeys didn't cost much. The half grown turkeys gobbled hoppers until their crops looked like they had swallowed a baseball. Then they sat in the shade and waited for their crops to empty and their gizzards to grind up the grasshoppers. In the fall, Dad fattened the young turkeys on corn and wheat.

When they were ready for market, sometime before Thanksgiving, Mr. Crawford helped Dad pick off the feathers. Dad returned the favor. We all picked pinfeathers after supper, a job I did not relish.

The young chickens hung around the house because that is where they were fed when they were small. They roosted on the porch or flew up on the car; wherever they could find a perch. All that poultry hanging around made a mess on the porch.

When time came for the young chickens to roost in the chicken house, we slipped up on them in the dark after they had gone to roost. Dad would catch a chicken by the legs and hand it to one of us until we each had from two to four chickens. Two chickens dangling by the legs in one hand was a little heavy for Julian and me, but we struggled to the chicken house with them. The dumb chickens roosted right back there the next night and the next. After a week of carrying obtuse chickens to their new home, most of them got smart and stayed.

Ducks are an unconscious lot. The ducks lived in the chicken house during the winter and at night. They preferred to live on the dam, but if we wanted any duck eggs, we had to lock the ducks up at night. Otherwise they laid their eggs in the dam until they built a nest.

Julian, Hank and I went to the dam about sundown and threw rocks at the ducks to herd them off the pond. Julian and I ran along one side of the dam and Hank along the other. When the ducks got to the widest part, some wise old duck always tried to break back and lead the flock to the middle of the pond.

Hank threw rocks, splashing water in front of the run-aways. Quacking indignantly, the ducks turned and swam into the narrow west end of the dam and we had them. They swam ashore and waddled out of the water.

Jack and Tippy helped us herd the ducks to the hen house, quacking their protests all the way. We locked them up for the night. The next morning we let them out and gathered five or six eggs from the hen house floor. The ducks waddled off to the dam.

We set the duck eggs under chicken hens in the corncrib. We had moved the setting hen from the chicken house to the corn-crib during the night and locked her in a box. After a few days, the hen accepted the box for her new nest.

A hen had to set twenty-eight days on duck eggs and thirty-one days on goose eggs. The hens couldn't tell time. They sat on the eggs, waiting patiently for something to pop out.

When their downy babies appeared, the mother hen became protective, fluffing her wings at us and pecking any hand that reached under her to see how many babies had hatched.

Buddy and Mickey loved to hold the chicks. Sometimes Mom let them play with a couple of chicks, if they were careful not to squeeze them. Mom never let us abuse little animals.

Geese are a lot smarter than ducks. We got our start in geese from the Roberts' family. Mom bought a setting of goose eggs and set them under a chicken hen. The hen set for thirty-one long days, but nothing happened. Mom carefully broke an egg. The egg was rotten. So were all the other eggs. Mrs. Roberts told Mom, "Geese are funny." They had three hens and a gander. "Our gander will only mate with two of the hens." That explained why we didn't get any goslings from those eggs. Mom bought the outcast goose hen and a gander and we began to raise geese.

Those geese gave us an education in the ways of geese. When a mother goose makes a nest, she doesn't intend for anyone or anything to steal her future babies. Father Goose is just as fiercely protective as Mother Goose is. Most geese prefer one mate so a gander, a goose and goslings make a family.

Approach the nest when Mother Goose is in residence, and she will tear out of the nest with both wings flapping, hissing like a snake. The gander is usually close by to help her chase away intruders. He guards the nest while she eats and drinks.

We learned to walk carefully around a goose nest. One goose hen made a nest in a coil of woven wire by the hen house. Julian and I took a bucket and tried to steal a few of her eggs.

Mother Goose hissed at us and stretched her neck in a menacing fashion. Father Goose came running, hissing and flapping his powerful wings.

"Get out of here, you dumb Martin kids," he hissed. A hefty gander, beating at you with his wings, can turn your legs black and blue. He'll grab a hunk of flesh and twist while trying to break your arms and legs with his hard wings. We ran fast with him on our heels.

We waited until Father Goose went to the dam for a drink. I picked up a stick and tried to chase Mother Goose off the nest. Hissing, she stretched her long neck and grabbed the stick. Hank came to help. "I'll get her. I'm not afraid of an old goose." He grabbed her neck and pulled her off the nest. We snatched a few eggs and ran for the house with the angry mother goose chasing us.

Geese are excellent parents. They care for orphans better than some people do and certainly better than a turkey or chicken hen does. A turkey or chicken hen will run a hungry little intruder off and try to peck him to death in the bargain. Geese adopt orphans.

Little green goslings are as cute and innocent as they can be, but half grown goslings are as homely and awkward as an animal can get. Mother and Father Goose take wonderful care of their babies. Bother the goslings and you'll have the mother and father both flying at you. We had a lot of respect for geese parents.

Geese wander about, talking to each other and their children. When they grow to adulthood, a gaggle of geese can be terribly noisy. They squawk loudly at every noise they hear, especially people talking. A group of geese strolling past seems to be trying to get into the conversation

We raised a lone gander that stayed on the porch with the dogs. He grew up thinking he was a dog. When the dogs ran, barking at an approaching car, he waddled as fast as his short legs would go after them. He tried to eat with the dogs to Jack's annoyance. The gander finally found the dam and joined the other geese.

One summer we raised a bum lamb. The lamb thought he was a dog, too. He ran with the dogs to bark at cars. He could run as fast as the dogs could, but he never learned to bark.

As soon as the fryers were big enough to eat, we had fried chicken for Sunday dinner. Chicken, mashed potatoes and new peas from the garden made a delicious meal. We tried to raise peas, snap beans, radishes, lettuce, swiss chard and potatoes. The potatoes usually weren't much bigger than marbles.

Some years we raised enough peas and beans to can twenty-five or thirty quarts. Shelling all those peas was a big job. We tried every way we could think of to make pea shelling easier and faster. A bushel basket of peas takes a lot of shelling. I sat and shelled peas until my fingers ached and my back did, too. So did Julian.

Then Mom read in a farm magazine that if you put pea pods in boiling water, the peas would shoot out the end of the pod. You could shell peas even faster by running the hot pods through the wash machine wringer.

Shelling peas with the wringer sounded like a fine idea, but running soft pea pods through the hand wringer on our old wooden washer didn't work very well. I put pea pods into the wringer while Julian turned the crank. Peas squashed and green pea juice ran down my arms. A few times the wringer nearly got my fingers. We quit that method. We sat down and ran the warm pods between thumb and forefinger and peas shot out of the pod and into the kettle. We shelled peas and Mom packed the jars. She boiled the peas for three hours in the wash boiler on our kerosene stove.

We stored our precious peas in the cellar. In some houses, people had to watch out for rattlesnakes in their cellar. Mrs. Stone who lived southeast of our place went into her cellar one day and heard a buzzing noise. She thought a jar lid had loosened and the contents was fizzing out of the jar. She reached for the jar and heard the buzz again. A rattlesnake was coiled around the jar, keeping cool. She tore out of the basement and got her husband to kill the snake.

The fall of 1931, Herb started high school in Midland. He stayed with Uncle Albert and rode horseback or walked the two miles to town. Herb loved music. He was in the orchestra and chorus. He was also on the honor roll. Hank, Julian and I rode off to Liberty.

CHAPTER 19
School Days, Good Old Golden Rule Days

Merle Simpson greeted us at Liberty the fall of 1931. Merle was a small lady, shorter than the students in seventh and eighth grades. She was a good teacher and we liked her. She let us call her Merle.

The Roberts' kids started going to Liberty that fall. We often met them at the Crawford place and rode to school with them. Irene and Lucille rode Diamond. Tom rode his tall bay stallion Tony, named after Tom Mix's horse. Tony was a pretty horse with a blaze face and white socks.

One morning Julian and I and the Roberts' girls were riding a quarter of a mile behind Hank and Tom when we saw smoke ahead. We galloped to the spot and found a tiny fire spreading in the buffalo grass. We jumped off our horses and beat the fire out. Then we rode to school and told Hank and Tom we knew they had been smoking because they set fire to the grass and they better be careful where they threw their matches. They looked foolish.

Verlyn Hagan and Olivia Dennis from north of school started the year after Julian did. They each had a batch of younger brothers and sisters so a new Hagan or Dennis showed up in school every year or so.

Gloria Saucerman and Marjorie Doud were three years behind Julian in school. Marjorie walked to school. We often gave her a ride home. She was bossy and thought she could make us take her almost to her house. If she got too bossy, we made her walk the last half mile. That made her angry and tickled us. Gloria lived south on Highway 14. Her father brought her to school, but she walked home.

Monday, Wednesday and Friday, we rode a mile south on Highway 14 to pick up our mail. We let Marjorie and Gloria ride to the mailbox with us. Whitefoot didn't care as long as nobody kicked her in the flanks. If she got kicked, her hind feet flew into the air as she tried to buck us off.

One day we rode down the steep grader ditch beside the road. Marjorie screamed for us to quit. I guided Whitefoot up the grade again. Marjorie screamed. I pushed back as Whitefoot scrambled up the bank. Marjorie hung fast to Julian. Julian clutched me around the waist. Gloria hung on to Marjorie. I pushed, and they slipped back. Marjorie screamed, "Quit. We'll fall off."

Leaning back, I headed Whitefoot up the bank. Gloria slipped off Whitefoot's rump, pulling Marjorie with her. Marjorie clung to Julian as tightly as a burr. Julian clung to me, and we all spilled into the ditch. Whitefoot turned around and looked at us. Marjorie bawled like a calf. Gloria jumped up. Julian and I laughed and got back on Whitefoot. Still howling, Marjorie said, "I'm not going to ride with you."

"Okay," I said. "Walk home then."

Gloria climbed on behind Julian. We started down the road. "Wait, I want on," Marjorie screamed, running after us. We helped her on the horse and rode to the mailbox. Gloria got off and went down the road. We let Marjorie, still angry, off at her turn-off.

Whitefoot loved to race. She never let another horse get ahead of her. We raced Irene and Lucille across the school section with Whitefoot showing Diamond her heels. One afternoon Hank and Tom caught up with us. Tom grinned. "I'll bet Tony can beat Whitefoot," he said.

"I'll bet he can't," I said.

Tony pranced and danced beside Whitefoot. Whitefoot laid her ears back and pulled at the bit. "I'll race you to Crawford's gate," Tom said.

"Okay." I loosened the reins and kicked Whitefoot's sides. She leaped into a gallop. Ears back, she tore down the wagon trail, her flying hoofs kicking dirt in Tony's face. Tom and Tony ate our dust all the way to the gate. I pulled Whitefoot up to wait for Irene and Lucille. Tom looked disgusted. He and Hank galloped toward Crawfords.

Whitefoot and Star would shy at almost anything. They jumped wildly sideways at a piece of paper, a jack rabbit, a bird flying under their nose, a culvert in the road. Every time we rode over the culvert in the road north of Douds, they shied. They leaped to the left, saw the other end of the culvert and leaped back. I usually took Whitefoot over the culvert at a walk and she only rolled her eyes. Hank put Star into a gallop and headed for the culvert full speed. Star leaped left, then twisted right and sped on down the road.

One afternoon Julian and I were hurrying home after school. Whitefoot trotted between the house and barn at Crawfords and around the chicken house. As we turned the corner, a gray cat dashed from beside the chicken house and ran under Whitefoot's nose. Whitefoot leaped in the air, dodged to the side and left us sitting on air. We hit the hard ground with a thump. Whitefoot stopped and looked at us like she wondered what we were doing. She never ran away and left us. I swung on her back and rode to the fence. Julian climbed on the fence, slipped on Whitefoot's back, and we went home.

Whitefoot was deathly afraid of barbed wire. Barbed wire was scattered here and there on the prairie from homestead fences. If Whitefoot ran into it, she went wild, bucking and running until she was clear of the cutting barbs. She ran into a piece of barbed wire west of Crawfords one afternoon. She leaped high and lit bucking. Julian and I sailed over her head. Hank caught Whitefoot. She was still terrified with about ten feet of wire caught in her tail.

Hank couldn't pull the wire out of her tail, so he helped me and Julian on Star and he rode Whitefoot. She pranced and danced all the way home. When we told Mom and Dad about our wild ride, Julian couldn't remember anything that had happened. Mom said she was "knocked out on her feet."

We learned to watch out for Whitefoot's wicked heels. Mom said, "Never lead another horse behind Whitefoot. You might get kicked by accident." Herb forgot and got kicked in the head. Hank led Whitefoot through the small wooden gate by the barn. Herb came behind with Freckles. As Herb stepped through the gate, Whitefoot let fly with both hind feet. One foot caught Herb in the middle of the forehead.

Dad brought Herb to the house with blood streaming down his face. He had a gash across his forehead from his hair line to his eyebrows. Dad cranked the Model T and took Herb to Midland to Dr. Verley. Dr. Verley had no anesthetic. He took twenty-one stitches to close the wound while Herb gritted his teeth. "He's a brave boy," Dr. Verley said as he poked forty-two holes in Herb's forehead.

I tied Whitefoot in the barn at Aunt Tina's house one afternoon. Uncle Alvin came from the field with a load of corn. He unhitched his team and brought them to the barn. As he opened the door and sent them to their stalls, the team walked single file behind Whitefoot. She lashed out with her deadly hoofs. Uncle Alvin said, "She got both of them in the belly before they got past."

Whitefoot would race anything with legs or wheels. I raced George Doud in his Model A roadster and he had to speed up to thirty-five miles an hour to get past her.

Spring came after a long hard winter. The kidnapping of the Lindbergh baby on March 1, 1932 shocked the nation. We watched every paper for news about him.

With spring the baseball teams began to practice. We watched the Bunker boys play Midland, Hayes, Ottumwa and Southeast Midland. Herb and Hank didn't play.

In school one day, we decided to have a wedding. Verlyn was madly in love with Julian. He thought a wedding was a grand idea if he could be the groom and Julian the bride. Julian demurred, but we talked her into it.

We picked a bride's bouquet of wild flowers. Hank was the preacher. We held the wedding in the woodshed which was nearly empty of coal and kindling. Hank stood in front with a book for a pretend Bible. Julian held the flowers. Verlyn stood beside her, looking happy. The rest of us were the wedding guests. Hank went through the ceremony and pronounced them man and wife.

Verlyn thought "the wedding" was such a good game that he wanted to marry Julian again the next day and the next and the next. Julian got tired of weddings. Verlyn persisted and Hank talked her into getting married one more time. Then she rebelled and we had no more weddings.

We often played in the woodshed among the broken desks. One day someone moved a board. A mouse ran across the floor. Mildred jumped on a desk and screamed, "Help, there's a mouse." We stared at her in amazement. If we could have caught the mouse, we could have chased mighty Millie all over the school yard.

Verlyn was a spinner of wild tales. A car went past the school house at recess. Upright rods on each fender had cross pieces, pointing forward. "See that car, Gloria," Verlyn said. "It has guns on the fender and the men are going to your house and shoot your dad."

Gloria went into hysterics. She ran in circles, screaming. We tried to calm her down. We told her the story wasn't true. We said Verlyn was fooling. She kept screaming. Ralph Jordan tried to reason with her. She wouldn't listen to him either. He took her home in his car. She was still screaming as he drove through the gate.

Sometimes we stuck pins through our shoes and pricked the kid in the seat in front of us. We thought it hilarious to watch the person nearly jump out of his seat. The teacher didn't think it was funny.

When our school work was finished, we were allowed to read books from the several book cases. I read every reader, every history book and the complete Compton's Encyclopedia from cover to cover.

In January and February, snow storms whipped across the country, blocking roads. Star and Whitefoot struggled through belly deep snow drifts, but we missed a lot of school that long hard winter. The mail didn't go through for weeks at a time.

CHAPTER 20
Grasshoppers and Wind

Anthrax was a severe threat to cattle that summer. Farmers and ranchers vaccinated their cattle, but some ranchers lost a big part of their herd anyway. Uncle Alvin and Uncle Albert lost a few cows and Uncle Charley burned the carcasses.

With Herb gone, I became a full time cow milker. I milked four cows before going to school and four when I came home at night. I didn't mind because when I was on milking duty, I didn't have to wash the supper dishes.

During warm weather, we squirted milk on our hands to make them slide easier down the cow's teats. Milking was a breeze unless one got a hard milker. We had two hard milkers that Dad milked. If he wasn't home, Hank and I each milked one. We struggled to get a pin sized stream of milk from those fat brockle faced cows.

By the time cold weather came, milk ran off the ends of our fingers and almost made icicles. Dad said "You have to milk with dry hands now or the cow's teats will freeze." Milking dry took some getting used to. If Dad was hauling hay or working late, Hank and I had to milk all of the cows.

In summer flies swarmed into the barn and made milking a miserable chore. The cows kicked and switched their tails constantly. Keeping the bucket right side up was a fight. Sometimes a cow would kick at the flies on her belly and stick her dirty foot in the bucket. That wasn't so bad, if the bucket wasn't full of milk. One cow would kick at the flies and swing her foot out, knocking me, milk stool and bucket over backwards. I think she did it on purpose. She always acted innocent like she wondered what I was doing, sitting in the gutter with milk spilled all over me. "Don't sit so close," Dad said. "Watch out for her hind feet. She'll spill your milk." She already had.

I sat so close to the cow that my head touched her, and the little red mites crawled off the cow into my hair. The mites didn't like human blood. They climbed right back off as soon as I left the barn. They fled in disgust and looked for another cow, or died in "no man's land" before they found one.

Cows would swat at the flies on their bony rumps with a long tail and wrap the brush around my head, catching me across the eyes. In the fall, cockle burrs in the brush made that tail a formidable weapon. One cow was bob-tailed. When she hit me along side of the head with her stub tail it was like getting hit on the head with a club.

I tied one cow's tail to her leg with some strands of tail hair. She worked with her tail until she got the knot loose and wham! she whacked me again.

The barn cats loved warm milk. They would sit a few feet away, watching the milk stream into the bucket with longing eyes. I had fun, shooting a stream of milk at a cat. The cat caught the milk in its mouth. They ran over and milk ran down their chest, but they came back for more.

Julian had no desire to learn to milk. She stayed in the house and baked cakes and helped get supper.

Herb was gone most of the summer so I got the job of rounding up the milk cows every evening. I bridled Whitefoot and loped across the prairie with Jack and Tippy running beside the horse.

Tippy was a small tan terrier with white face and belly. Millie brought her to school and gave her to us when she was a tiny puppy not much larger than a kitten. We all loved her. We gave her to Mickey, but she slept with me and Julian.

As I rode the pasture, the dogs chased jack rabbits that

raced away, then jumped high and looked back to see how close the silly dogs were. I watched hawks circling high overhead, searching for gophers, mice and snakes. I saw a hawk dive, grab a snake and fly high in the air. He dropped the snake and followed the writhing body to the ground. Grabbing the dead snake in his sharp talons, he flew away.

Mom told us that in summer, cows head into the wind to blow the flies away. In the heat of the day, cows stood belly deep in the dam to cool off and fight flies. When the afternoon cooled, they spread out to graze again.

Sometimes our milk cows got scattered among several bunches of range cattle. I'd start six or seven cows toward home, then go off and find the rest. I might miss the whole herd in a draw the first time over, or the milked cows hid among the Herefords. I never went home without the cows. We needed the cream and they needed to be milked.

Sometimes I met the cows coming home because their bags were tight with milk and they wanted relief. The cows acted innocent like they weren't hiding the first time I passed.

One day I loped Whitefoot all over the pasture, looking for the cows. Tippy ran beside her with her tongue hanging out, panting. Her short legs were barely keeping up.

"Want a ride, Tippy?" I leaned down, grabbed her collar and lifted her on the horse. She sat in front of me and rested. After that Tippy rode in front of me until she accidently scratched Whitefoot's neck. Whitefoot leaped sideways. I dropped Tippy and clamped my legs around Whitefoot. She wouldn't let Tippy ride anymore.

From the time Buddy was three years old, he rode with me every chance he got. He rode behind me on Whitefoot when I went after the cows. One day Mickey said, "Can I go, too?"

"Ask Mom," I said. She ran into the house and soon returned ready to go. I helped her on in front of me. We went after the milk cows. By the time we found the cows and headed home, Buddy was asleep with his head leaning against my back and

Mickey was sleeping in front of me.

Often Mom, Julian, Buddy, Mickey and I rode to visit Aunt Tina. Mickey sat on Freckles behind Mom. She grabbed the saddle strings and bounced along like a little monkey when she was a tiny girl.

Whenever we rode or walked, we were alert for rattlesnakes. When we adventured at home, Jack and Tippy spotted any rattler that lurked in the vicinity. Jack took care of Mickey and Buddy. He would have given his life for them or any of us. We always killed any rattlesnakes we ran into.

Julian and I were visiting Oviatts when they lived west of our place. Waneta, Don, Jackie, Julian and I had been playing barefoot in the creek. We ran out of the creek and headed for the house. I was in the lead, running fast. I thought I kicked a rope. It flew over my head and lit in front of Don. Waneta hollered, "Look out. You kicked a rattlesnake." We killed the snake and took the rattle to the house to show their mother.

"Rattlesnakes won't die and quit wiggling until the sun goes down," Waneta said.

"Not even if you cut their head off?" I asked. She shook her head. I believed her, but we didn't stay to see.

Luella Rank, Ida Oviatt, and Bruneta (Brownie) Sturdevant were sisters and second cousins of our mother on Grandma Bertelson's side. We visited back and forth with them. Ranks lived on a farm eleven miles north of ours in the Moenville country. Bruneta Sturdevant lived in Midland where she and her husband operated The Sturdevant Drug Store. They had four children: Buddy, Helen, Audrey and Joan.

Waneta Oviatt was Herb's age. Ramona Rank was Hank's age. Then there was Thurman, Barbara and Junior Rank and Donald, Jackie, Dottie, Lois and Karol Ann Oviatt.

Herb decided that I was either Don's or Thurman's girlfriend, depending on which family was visiting that Sunday. He held my arms so I couldn't hit and said, "Kiss her, Don," or Thurman.

"Okay," Don said, giving me a peck on the cheek. Herb turned me loose and I lit into Don and whipped him while Herb laughed.

I hated Don and Thurman. They didn't like me either. The dislike lasted into the teen years. They would dance with Julian, but not with me. Maybe they were afraid of my fierce scowl. I wanted to dance with them, but they wouldn't ask, and I didn't know how to make peace. Junior and Jackie weren't afraid of me. They whirled me about on the dance floor when they barely reached my shoulder.

Uncle Charley was still the watermelon king. He took a five gallon bucket in each hand and trudged to the dam for water to pour on his melon vines. He rested by the north window in the living room and drank a glass of cool water from the cistern.

The water in the cistern stayed cold all summer because Uncle Charley shoveled the cistern full of snow in the winter. The snow didn't all melt until July.

Uncle Charley managed to raise some watermelons. We ate our fill every time we visited them that fall.

Uncle Charley was still trying to conquer the Model T. Uncle Alvin decided he wouldn't ride with Uncle Charley anymore. "He just freezes to the wheel and runs into things," Uncle Alvin said.

Uncle Charley was approaching the back end of the hay rack and forgot to step on the break. He froze to the steering wheel and smashed into the back end of the rack. He was driving to the barn and misjudged the turn onto the dam grade. The car headed for the water. Uncle Charley jammed on the low pedal and drove into the water.

In June we went to the Midland Lutheran Ladies' Aid picnic at Steien's grove. For twenty-five cents we got our fill of delicious salads, meats, pies and ice cream.

We wandered along Mitchell Creek which was dry, crossing the creak on a huge cottonwood log. Little Clayton Nelson fell off the log and lit in the rocky creek bed eight feet below. He did-

258

n't even cry.

Buddy and Mickey were big enough to ride Star and Freckles. They would coax me to get the horses for them so they could ride around the house. Buddy carried a hair brush to pop Star on the rump and make the fat pony trot.

Farmers were desperate. Eggs were worthless, and cream was cheap. Grasshoppers were eating the corn. Crops were poor at best and worth almost nothing. Some grain was shocked. Some farmers were using the new combines that harvested the crops in the field. Millions of grasshoppers hopped and gobbled through field and garden. Some farmers tried to poison the hoppers with a new fungus poison, but there were too many grasshoppers.

Farmers couldn't get much for their livestock at auction. A horse sold for seventy-five cents. Milk cows brought from two to seven dollars each. A farm wagon went for seventy-five cents. Banks were forcing farmers to sell even though they couldn't get anything for their livestock.

One woman tried to keep the bank from selling cows by wrapping her arms around the gate post of the corral to keep the men from opening the gate. They dragged her away and drove the cattle from the pen. The men were going to take a mule, but the bank rep said, "You can't take the mule. It isn't on the mortgage." The farmer was left with one mule and no cattle.

In Iowa farmers banded together and bought a neighbor's cattle and machinery for five and ten cents per item, his land for five cents an acre. When the auction was over, they gave the property back to the farmer. That stopped forecloser sales in that neighborhood.

Mom earned a few dollars each fall by feeding the cowboy crews driving cattle to Midland for shipment to Chicago and Sioux City. The cattle trail ran past outside our west gate. Large herds of Hereford cattle moved to market from the ranches in the Moenville country. George Neif and Julius Roseth drove cattle on the market trail for many years. They paid Mom a few welcome dollars for feeding the crew. We liked to watch the herds travel along the fence.

The cattle waded into our dam to drink and bedded down in the Bertelson pasture west of our house. When the herd was finished grazing and bedded down for the night, the cowboys went to bed. They were up early before the cattle started to graze. If the cowboys weren't there when the cattle got up, they headed for home. The cowboys ate breakfast and headed their herds south ever alert to keep the Bertelson cattle from mixing with their herd.

We studied the Montgomery Ward catalog and wished for this toy and that until we wore the catalog out. Hank wished for cars. Julian and I wished for dolls and bicycles. Mom said, "We'll get that when our ship comes in." I thought a ship would really come some day.

I really wanted a bicycle. Mom said I could trade my horse for a bike, but I didn't want one that bad. Hank traded some ducks to George Doud for a blue bicycle. I was so desperate that I traded ducks for a blue bicycle frame. I put twelve inch iron wheels on the bike, but the contraption wouldn't roll down the hill properly.

Sometimes Hank let me ride his bike. He said, "Don't ride it down the hill," meaning the slope west of the house. I took his bike for a spin and headed west along the trail. I looked down the steep hill. Hank would whiz down that hill. I thought I could do the same.

In a reckless moment, I headed down the hill. The biked picked up speed. The wheels turned faster and faster. My feet lost the pedals. The bike crashed, throwing me over the handle bars. I picked myself up out of the dust.

My wrist was sprained. Hank was coming. The bike had a sprung front wheel. He didn't say anything, just sadly pushed his bike back to the house.

Mom gave us lectures on many subjects. We would sit around the kitchen table and listen to her words of wisdom. During the depression, she often talked about how to succeed in life. "You have to grab opportunity by the forelock," she said.

Julian looked serious for a moment, then said, "And Daddy

grabbed it by the tail." Poor Dad. The weather and ignorance of the country had knocked him for a loop. The depression, draught and grasshoppers were trying to add the knock-out punch.

The American economy hit rock bottom. In July 1932, President Hoover signed the Relief and Reconstruction Act which allowed The Federal Government to loan money for public works and relief. Wages declined. Banks were closing. Unemployment reached a new high.

In Germany Adolph Hitler assumed the office of Chancellor on the invitation of President Von Hindenberg who regarded Hitler as the best alternative to the chaos threatening Germany. It was a mistake that would cost the world dearly.

President Hoover started the WPA dam building program. Farmers hitched their teams and built dams. Dad hitched his team to the wagon and went to Hayes sixteen miles northeast of our place. Walking behind teams pulling plows, slips and scrapers, farmers built a dam that backed water for several miles up a small creek and became a favorite fishing spot. Dad stayed at Hayes all week and earned $30.00 per month.

As Hank, Julian and I rode to school one morning, we wondered if there would be enough money so we could go to the movies again. We didn't worry about clothing or food. We had food and clothes. That money must have been a relief for our parents. Mom and Dad never worried us with the desperation of their financial situation. We thought being poor quite normal. Most of our neighbors didn't have any money either.

Lillian Scott, a pretty blond neighbor, was our teacher. Lillian read books to us before school. We brought the Tarzan books. The kids loved them, but when Lillian started through the romantic parts, her face turned pink and she said, "We'll skip this part." We always missed the romantic parts of the Zane Gray books, too.

We had to memorize poetry. We learned the beautiful poems of Longfellow, Riley, Holmes and other great American poets. My favorite was Longfellow's "Psalm Of Life." I still remember part of it.

> *"Life is real, life is earnest,*
> *and the grave was not its goal.*
> *For dust thou art, to dust returneth*
> *was not spoken of the soul"*

Julian liked Longfellow's "Inch Cliff Rock" especially the last part:

> *"Sir Ralph, the rover, tore his hair*
> *and cursed himself in his despair."*

Sir Ralph was a pirate and had destroyed the light on the Inch Cliff Rock so ships would go aground on the rocks and he could plunder them. A storm forced his ship onto the rocks and the ship came apart on The Inch Cliff Rock. Served him right.

One poem was about a little girl trying to learn her multiplication tables. She could never remember the answer to six times nine. Her mother suggested that she call her doll Mary Ann, "Fifty-Four" until she remembered. The little girl didn't like calling "such a perfectly lovely doll, such a perfectly horrible name," but she did and learned the combination. Then came school. She said and "Sakes alive, I answered Mary Ann."

Hank had to recite this poem and he said with a grin, "I hated to call such a perfectly horrible doll, such a perfectly lovely name." Even the teacher smiled.

Some mornings we sang before classes began. On Friday afternoon, we had drawing lessons and spelling bees.

Franklin Delano Roosevelt was inaugurated 32nd President of The United States on March 4, 1933. He said, "Let me assert my firm belief that the only thing we have to fear is fear itself." The words were borrowed from Henry David Thoreau, but they were what the country needed to hear. People began to hope again.

The first part of 1933 was mild. Uncle Walt worked on a

house for George Purcell. A heavy wet snow in March stopped the mail carriers for several days and stranded motorists on the highway between Midland and Hayes.

The warm weather and moisture brought the wild flowers.

Lillian let us go outside the school yard and pick flowers. During the noon hour, we chased over the prairie, hunting flowers. One day we headed west, following a flowery trail. We went farther and farther, picking bluebells and Johnny Jump-ups. We came to the vacant Richardson house over a mile west of the school house.

Someone said, "We better go back to school." We went back faster than we went away, but not fast enough. We were an hour late for school. Lillian's blue eyes shot fire as we slipped into our seats.

"You will not play outside the school yard anymore," she said.

The Midland Cooperative Marketing Association bought J.C. Russell's Store and moved their merchandise to the new building. The Cream Station stayed where it was.

The Midland Mail said that Mrs. J.A. Peters had a runaway with her team and wagon and ran into the train in Midland. Mrs. Peters was not hurt.

In May Buddy came down with pneumonia. He was desperately ill. Dad called Dr. Verley. "The child has worms," Dr. Verley said and left some worm medicine. Buddy's lungs rattled with every breath he took. He would feel better in the morning and be delirious by afternoon. He had a raging fever and hallucinated about baby chicks. He told Mom there were chickens in his underwear.

"There aren't any chicks in your underwear, Buddy," Mom said.

"Yes, there are," Buddy said. "Take them away."

"Where are they?" Mom asked.

"Right there." Buddy showed her. "Take them away."

Mom pretended to pick chickens out of his clothing and his

bed until he was satisfied that they were all gone.

Buddy's fever raged on. We were afraid he would die. Mom did everything that she knew to do for him, but he only got worse. Mom and Dad were desperate. Mrs. Doud and Mrs. Crawford came to see how Buddy was getting along.

He lay on his bed, face flushed, lungs rattling. "Do you have any wool cloths and mustard?" Mrs. Doud asked. Mom gave her some squares of wool cloth and the mustard. Mrs. Doud put a mustard plaster on Buddy's chest. That night his fever broke, and he began to improve. Mrs. Doud saved his life.

Dad bought Mom a new gasoline powered washing machine. The new Maytag was put in the summer kitchen with the exhaust running out through a convenient hole in a south window.

You had to tramp hard on the pedal several times to start the wonderful machine, but it roared and chugged and churned the water like a dream. Even the wringer turned by motor power. The wringer swung around from rinse tub to rinse tub. It would even reverse, but you had to watch your fingers. That wringer gobbled fingers as quickly as it gobbled clothes.

The wringer grabbed Mom's fingers and ran her hand halfway through before she hit the reverse and ran them back out. That hurt. Buddy was helping her, dipping clothes out of the rinse tub, getting in her way. The hungry wringer grabbed his hand and swallowed it clear to the elbow. He howled and Mom hit the release. The wringer popped open.

Spring started with good moisture. Grazing land rented for four to eight cents an acre. Corn grew tall, the leaves whispering in the slightest breeze. Grain crops were lush. Green grass covered the hills and valleys like a carpet. Dad was happy. Then the hungry grasshoppers came.

They came in great clouds. Mom said, "Look up. You can see them. Grasshoppers are coming by the millions."

Flying high in the sunshine, they looked like tiny silver planes. Grasshoppers settled so thick on the sides of our house there wasn't space for another grasshopper to light. Hoppers covered the shady side of every post and ate big holes in them.

Black amber cane fields were safe because grasshoppers don't like cane. Dad would harvest cane for the livestock, but the grasshoppers ate corn fields into the ground, stripped gardens and cut wheat heads off to fall on the ground.

One farmer, so the story went, came in from the field and tied his team to a post while he went to the house for dinner. When he came back, the grasshoppers had eaten his team and were pitching horse shoes for the harness.

CHAPTER 21
Wind and Dust

Uncle Charley planted forty acres of corn south of the house on the Calhoun place. The corn was about five feet tall when the grasshoppers flew in. Every day he hitched old Red and Gray to his cultivator with a sheet rigged like giant wings on each side and drove to the field to do battle with the hoppers.

He drove up and down his corn rows, chasing grasshoppers out of his field. He kept the hoppers hopping so much in the daytime that they didn't have time to gobble much corn, but they chomped merrily through the night. One could hear millions of jaws grinding steadily down the rows. The corn didn't have a chance.

In the end, Uncle Charley had corn stalks standing like tiny fence posts....no leaves, no ears, no tassels, just bare stalks. It was enough to break a farmer's heart, but instead of crying, they made jokes.

Turkeys went crazy. They didn't know which grasshopper to chase next. The Bunker Bubbles column in The Midland Mail said, "Grasshoppers great and small have stalled the turkeys one and all."

Edgar Joy combined a large wheat acreage for Uncle Alvin and Uncle Albert. They were lucky to get three to five bushels per acre after the grasshoppers got through with the crop. Joys raised two thousand turkeys. Those birds cleared a few hoppers off their place.

Bunker wasn't beat yet. According to Bunker Bubbles,

266

"We're not licked. Don't you cry. There'll be a shower by and by. Dams will fill, water holes, too; then you and I won't be so blue."

A pounding rain ran thirteen feet of water in the dam on the Burns' farm. Our dam was deep, as was the one at the Calhoun place. We had plenty of water, but the grasshoppers were eating everything in their path.

The hungry hoppers chomped away over field and meadow and into the woods and the yards in town. They ate the bark and leaves and chewed tender branches, leaving nothing but a stump.

The grasshoppers weren't satisfied with eating everything we had outside, they hopped into the house, perched on the window curtains and ate holes in them.

Buddy and Mickey came into the house, clutching a grasshopper in each hand. Buddy gave me two large hoppers. "Tie these grasshoppers together," he said. "We want to play they're horses."

I tied the grasshoppers together with about twelve inches of string. Buddy prodded his team and they hopped along. Mickey's team was one big hopper and one small one. Every time she started her team, the big one jumped and dragged the little one through the air behind him.

A farmer on Bad River had a beautiful alfalfa crop growing, purple blossoms nodding in every breeze. He came into the house one evening and told his wife, "Tomorrow, we'll cut the alfalfa." The next morning, the field was as bare as a sidewalk. Grasshoppers had eaten every plant.

We often ate wheat, whole or ground, for breakfast. We ground wheat in a small red mill. Grinding wheat or corn was a daily summer chore, making food for us and the poultry. I ran bushels of grain through the little red mill.

When Buddy was small, he couldn't pronounce "l". He tried to explain to Mickey what the red mill was. He touched the mill and said, "Miah."

Mickey could pronounce her "l's", but she heard what he

said. "It's a miah."

Buddy said, "No, not a miah, a miah."

Mickey said, "Miah," sounding hopeful.

"No, not a miah, a miah." Buddy was about to jump in the air and scream.

I said, "It's a mill, Mickey."

"Oh," she said, "A mill."

"Yah," Buddy said. "It's a miah." That was settled.

Buddy had a temper. He climbed into the big rocker in the summer kitchen one day. He rocked harder and harder. The chair tipped far up on the front of the rockers, then far to the back. Buddy laughed and rocked harder. The chair tipped forward and crashed, spilling Buddy on the floor. He jumped up madder than a fighting rooster. "Kick the dumb chair," Julian said.

Buddy lit into the chair and kicked it with both feet. Mom said, "Don't teach him to kick things when he's mad. He has to learn to control his temper, not make it worse."

Saturday was market day. We climbed into the Model T and went to town to trade our cream and eggs for groceries. Midland was crowded with people. We went to the movie which cost a dollar for a family. Movies always drew large crowds.

Tom Berry, the cowboy governor, was in the governor's chair in Pierre. A Democrat governor didn't change much.

Paul Prairie Chicken, an aged Indian who lived along Bad River, predicted the greatest flood in history in July. He moved to the top of the high bluffs to keep from floating away. The flood didn't come. People wished it had.

We had our share of wind storms that summer. One June storm came up toward evening. High winds chased black clouds out of the west. A bunch of young turkeys on the Roberts' farm had gone to roost on the hay rack south of the barn. T.W. and Lucille rushed to the barn to hold the hay rack down.

T.W. grabbed one end of the rack. Lucille grabbed the other. They held the rack down with all their strength while the turkeys clung to their precarious perch. The wind howled and tore at them.

A sudden strong gust tore the rack from Lucille's grasp. T.W. held on. The wind lifted the rack, flipping it over. T.W. shot through the air, flew for about fifty feet, lit on a small barn and bounced to the ground. He got a bad scalp wound, facial cuts and two fractured vertebra. Lucille wasn't hurt. The turkeys blew around and found shelter elsewhere. Dr. Verley came to take care of T.W.'s wounds. T.W. recovered and attended the July 4th celebration at Midland.

Midland's celebration was a huge success with nearly three thousand people crowding the streets. Firecrackers popped and cap guns banged. My ears rang for days after the celebration. There was a horse shoe pitching contest for men. Midland lost the baseball game to Kadoka. There were footraces for all ages. Julian and I lined up with the girls. The runners shot down the track. Four girls ran ahead of me. Frances won, as usual.

I complained because I never won. Mom said, "If you run out to the gate west of the house every day you can win." Every day I sped to the gate and back. When The Farmer's Picnic came in August, I was ready. I lined up with the other girls, eager as a race horse. When the starter said, "Go!" I leaped forward and I never looked back. I ran like an antelope with a wolf on its tail. I came in first and won three dollars. Frances couldn't believe I beat her.

Grasshoppers kept coming by the millions. Turkeys, ducks, chickens and geese couldn't keep up with them. Even The Government couldn't stop the plague.

Grasshoppers weren't the only pests. Black and gray blister beetles and Colorado potato bugs were chomping on our garden, too. We had no effective poison for them. Mom sent us into the garden with cans of kerosene. We walked up and down the rows, picking off beetles and potato bugs and dropping the buggers into the can. It was an operation in futility. If we had managed to pick off every bug in the garden, the grasshoppers would have eaten every spear anyway. They left the gardens like the fields, bare.

The Nash Coffee Company had a contest in which they gave a small red wagon to the kids that brought the most Nash coffee cans to The Midland Co-op. We gathered Nash cans from our folks and from our Aunts and Uncles, all heavy coffee drinkers. We won the wagon for Buddy and Mickey.

In late summer, The Government came out with wheat allotments that would give wheat farmers payments.

A long dry spell ended with a good rain the first part of August, too late for grain, but welcome for cane fields. Farmers were beginning to hope, but the grasshoppers saw to it that there was nothing to sell.

Pork and beans were ten cents a can, a boneless picnic ham was ten cents a pound at Murray's Store. We couldn't afford such luxuries. We raised our own ham and cooked our own beans. Aunt Tina bought pork and beans. I thought they were so delicious that I persuaded her, against her better judgement, to open two cans for supper. I said, "I'll eat what's left."

With only Uncle Charley, Aunt Tina, Uncle Alvin and me to eat them and plenty of other food, too, there were too many beans. Aunt Tina had to stop me from keeping my promise for fear I would explode.

Farmers hoped for better prices, but when you can buy a pork roast for ten cents a pound and beef steak for fifteen, the animals are extremely cheap on the hoof.

The Federal Government jumped in with a hog buying plan designed to keep prices from dropping and maybe jack them up a bit. The Government would buy four million pigs at six to nine cents a pound. One million sows to farrow within three weeks would be bought at market price plus $4.00 per head. Packers would butcher the hogs and sell the meat at the General Relief Administration at cost. The pork would not be permitted to compete on the open market.

The Government sent the meat back to us as moldy ham and bacon. Mom washed off the mold and we ate the meat.

The Government offered relief to people unable to support

270

themselves. They said, "All people whose earnings last year have been affected by dry weather, hot winds, grasshoppers, etc., and have no other means of support." That included most people in western South Dakota.

Besides moldy ham and bacon, The Government gave us beans and rice. Rice with raisins and cream is delicious.

The Haakon County Relief Agency published this warning: "No alcohol is to be purchased if you expect help. No going to dances or shows, card rooms or any place of amusement where a fee is charged. Operating automobiles, the use of radios or telephones and expenditure of money for permanent waves or hair treatment by members of families on relief is also barred." Mostly people didn't pay any attention to the rules. Everybody got relief anyway. Dad got a monthly check of about $19.00 from The Government.

The Midland Mail poked fun at the depression with this ditty: "Twenty-five cents for a chicken; one dollar for a shoat; a horse and cow thrown in to boot, the farmer is still the goat."

I guess The Government thought people should walk thirty or forty miles to town. Dad could carry a ten gallon can of cream and Mom and the kids would bring up the rear with the egg crates, or they could hitch the team to the wagon and spend a couple of happy days going to market. Washington wasn't any smarter then, than it is now.

The NRA blue eagle with claws appeared in store windows across the nation wherever merchants had agreed to pay a minimum wage for a set number of work hours. Thus the forty hour week was born.

As if the grasshoppers and dry weather weren't enough, some days the wind blew so hard we couldn't see the sun for dust.

In August Aunt Amanda and Uncle Walt took Julian and me to the Black Hills. We climbed into the trunk of the Model A with a stick to prop the lid open and away we went.

Rapid City was the biggest city we had ever seen, a beautiful city spread along the valley with the mountains to the west.

Haze hung over the mountains. Rapid City has since reached out and swallowed farms and climbed mountains.

We headed south to Uncle Walt's rustic cabin halfway up a mountain in Custer State Park. The roads were mainly gravel. Dust billowed out behind the car. Facing backward, we saw where we'd been instead of where we were going and had a wonderful time. We marveled at the beauty of the pine clad mountains. We climbed boulders and waded in a mountain stream. We had never seen a brook before. We followed the clear cold stream as it rippled over the rocks and came upon two boys also wading in the water.

We recognized our old friend Roy Howes. He introduced us to Harold Norby. Harold's father was superintendent of schools at Midland. They had cabins nearby. "Want to see a cave we found?" Roy asked.

We did. The boys led us along the brook, into the woods and up a mountain to a cave entrance. Timbers used by Indians many years earlier were still in place along the roof. We followed the boys into a small room. "Indians hung meat on those timbers," Harold said.

We were impressed. We imagined a group of Indians sitting around a fire in the cave. We took turns crawling inside a tunnel, but it was pitch dark ahead. We decided to get a flashlight and come back to explore the tunnel, but we had to travel on before we had a chance to really explore.

Uncle Walt drove up a winding gravel road to Mount Rushmore. Mr. Borglum showed us his model of Washington, Lincoln, Jefferson and Roosevelt that he was going to carve on the mountain. We watched the workmen suspended in swings from the top of the mountain as they chiseled and blasted rock away.

In Hot Springs, we swam in the warm water of the Evans Plunge. We traveled the Needles Highway and marveled at the granite formations. We visited Pete Jacobson and went fishing in a brook. Uncle Walt caught a small trout.

I took his rod and went fishing. I whipped the rod back and snapped it forward to send the fly onto the shining water. The line tangled in a tree behind me. That ended my trout fishing, and I spent an hour untangling the line. We hated to have our grand vacation end.

1933 badly bent Uncle Alvin and Uncle Albert. They were deeply in debt. Most farmers were in debt or at best flat broke, although some people were said to have money buried.

Dad's cattle were mortgaged so he sold the yearlings in the fall. They weren't worth much, but neither was corn or wheat. Buyers offered five to seven cents for live poultry. There was never much money to pay on the mortgage.

Dams in the Manila country northwest of our place got so low they bogged cattle. Jack Oviatt found a homestead in a rancher's pasture southwest of Midland. Jack built a board shack covered with tar paper with no wallboard on the inside. He delivered Lois there with no doctor to help. Later he traded his homestead for a farm north of town, then like a lot of others, he gave up on South Dakota and moved to Oregon.

A horse buyer came through the country, buying mares to ship south and raise mules. He paid a good price, $25.00 each. Dad sold every mare from the wild bunch that the buyer would take. I was upset when my filly from Mom's Florrie was in the bunch. I went into the summer kitchen, hid behind a cot and cried. I couldn't bear to part with the filly even though she was wild and full of life. The horse buyer said, "That filly isn't even worth the $25.00 I'm giving for her."

"I'll give you back your money," Dad said. "Leave her here."

The buyer said, "No, no, we're taking them all." They did. The mares were delivered to the railroad yards in Midland and were soon on a train headed for the south, nickering Dixie at the top of their lungs. It was probably just as well. That high spirited filly would have been too much horse for me anyway.

On hot summer afternoons, we swam in the dams and cooled off. We were visiting Aunt Tina one afternoon and Essie Curtis came over to swim with us. Julian and I sneaked around, ducking each other under the water.

Julian slipped up behind Essie and shoved her under the water. Essie surfaced, Julian shoved her under again. She came up, blowing like a whale. We thought it was hilarious. Sputtering, Essie said, "I can't stand to get water in my ears."

"How do you wash your ears then?" smart Julian asked.

Essie told Uncle Alvin that we ducked her. He complained to Mom. Mom thought it was funny because Julian was five years younger and about half as big as Essie. Essie wasn't used to rough housing like we were, but we liked her.

I often stopped to play with Essie when I rode after Aunt Tina's mail. The McCready farm had a windbreak of trees on the north and west, unusual on our treeless prairie. We climbed the trees and played Tarzan and the apes. I was Tarzan and Essie was the ape.

When Essie was in first grade, she attended The Prairie Queen school several miles southwest of the McCready farm. One day she ran to the toilet back of the school house. She heard a rattlesnake buzzing down in the hole. Frightened, she hesitated, but she had to go. She climbed up and sat down above the rattler.

The McCready house was a strange contraption built of homestead shacks fastened together into one large house. Some of the shacks had nearly flat roofs, some had gable roofs. All were covered with tar paper.

Mrs. McCready's house was neat and homey with braided rugs on the floor and colorful hooked rugs on the backs of rockers. She died in 1933.

Essie and I were loping our horses along the south side of a field when we saw a rattlesnake coiled in the path. I jumped off and landed on the rattler. I tramped the snake to death with my boot heel. Essie told Aunt Tina and Uncle Charley, "She jumped right in the middle of that snake and killed it." They said that was a foolish thing to do. They were right. I didn't think a rattler could bite through my boots. I was wrong. My guardian angel must have been watching over a dumb kid.

274

In September the First National Bank said business was improving. Maybe. You could buy weiners for twelve cents a pound, if you had twelve cents. Dad bought apples from Don and Homer Burns who trucked them in from elsewhere. School started again, making us both sad and happy.

Julian and I went off to Liberty, riding bareback on Whitefoot. We no longer needed a fence or a boost to mount. I grabbed a handful of mane, swung on Whitefoot's back and stuck a foot out. Julian grabbed my hand, stepped on my foot and landed behind me.

Julian mounted by grabbing the mane, stepping on the bone hump at the top of the horse's leg and climbing aboard. We could ride like Indians. I could ride at a gallop, sitting sideways like Aunt Tina did when she was a girl. I could pick a handkerchief from the ground or jump off my horse at full gallop.

On a bright September day, we headed across the prairie for school. Grasshoppers jumped out of the short, brown grass. When we topped the ridge west of Crawford's house, we could see the school house, shining white in the distance.

CHAPTER 22
Millie and Irene

Herb went off to Midland for his Junior year, staying with Uncle Albert again. Herb was a lot like Uncle Albert. They both ran around until noon with their shoe laces untied.

I was in eighth grade, Hank and Julian in seventh. School was hard for Hank. He was far sighted and didn't have glasses. The words blurred, making reading his lessons extremely difficult.

Our teacher was Constance Wiseman, a beautiful young lady with dark hair and brown eyes. She was our first teacher at Liberty who was not called by her first name. We called her Miss Wiseman.

By the time the frost would have been on the pumpkins if dry weather and grasshoppers had let us raise any, the young turkeys were getting fat. Young gobblers strutted, wings dragging the ground, tails fanned as we gathered cobs for the cook stove. Gobbling filled the air. The louder we talked, the louder they gobbled.

Coyotes killed fifty of Hike Richardson's turkeys. Hike ran in bad luck. Turkey rustlers were abroad, too. Some farmers moved beds outside close to the turkey perches. Turkeys perch on hay racks, corrals and the top of buildings. Turkeys will sit on the perch and wait to be grabbed. They stretch their necks and sound alarmed, but since they can't see in the dark, a stealthy thief could get the whole crop, if he could reach them.

We worried about our turkeys, but nobody came and tried to steal them. Fat dressed turkeys brought about $2.25. We needed

276

that money to buy clothes and winter supplies.

On November 11, a terrible dust storm swept across the prairie. The storm was a foretaste of the black blizzards that would blanket the midwest in choking dust from Texas to North Dakota. Kansas dirt drifted as far east as New Jersey. Some days the dust was so thick we couldn't see the sun. Cars went down the roads with lights on. People wet cloths and put them on window sills to keep out the dust. Still dirt sifted in, covering beds, tables and chairs.

Dad bought a Zenith radio from Oscar's Service Station. The Government had forbidden us the pleasure of a radio, but nobody paid attention to the silly rule. We loved the plays and comics on the radio.

I was dragged kicking and screaming into the teen years. Most kids can't wait to grow up. I couldn't see any advantage in it. I didn't think grown-ups had such a good deal.

When I was thirteen, Dad decided I should learn to dance. By that time I had quit hiding in the bedroom with the little kids and sat on the plank benches along the wall with the ladies and girls. Dad coaxed me onto the dance floor, and I swear, I had two left feet. I stumbled after him a few steps. "I'll lead, you just follow," he said. "Don't watch your feet just keep time to the music."

What time? I could hardly keep track of my feet let alone the music, but I learned. Dad taught me to polka, waltz and two step. I learned to square dance and loved it.

Dances were held in homes around the neighborhood. We had several at our house every year. We danced with anyone who asked us from grandfathers to our little brothers. Country dances lasted until four in the morning. In summer daylight was coming by the time we started home.

Getting ready to go took half the afternoon. Mom heated the curling iron in a lamp and wound my dark brown hair around it. "Is that too hot?" she'd ask and back off a bit if it was. She curled my hair and her own and the kitchen smelled of burned hair. Julian had curls without the iron.

Julian and I shined and polished everyone's shoes and cleaned and pressed pants for Dad and the boys.

Dad bought a banjo from Cousin Hallie and gave it to Herb. Herb played his banjo every night and nearly drove Uncle Alvin crazy with his foot tapping. Herb and Dad played for dances. We had music at our house nearly every evening.

I danced with the Crawford, Doud and Burns boys. We glided silently around the rough floors of farm houses because I could never think of anything to say.

I was never the Belle Of The Ball like my mother was. I was more of a wall flower. Julian could talk the ear off a wooden Indian. The boys lined up three deep to dance with her. She chattered and kidded them, and they had a grand time. I wished I had her gift of gab. I would have had more fun.

Going to dances in winter was an adventure. Our cars had no heaters. If a window was broken, a piece of cardboard was put in its place. We carried quilts and snuggled under them to keep warm. We bundled up in heavy coats, overshoes, mittens and caps. The driver had to scrape a small peek hole in the frost on the windshield so he could see the road. When we got to our destination, the quilts went over the radiator to keep the block from freezing. Sometime during the evening, men went out and started their cars to warm them up.

Miss Wiseman wouldn't go outside and play with us. Many a noon her fiance stopped to visit her. Naturally she stayed in the school house and talked to him instead of keeping track of the shenanigans going on outside.

When the Roberts' kids came to school at Liberty, Tom fell for cute petite Frances. If we played baseball and Frances caught the ball, she ran behind the barn, the ball clutched in her hand. Tom ran after her to get the ball. Irene and Millie ran away with the ball, too. They liked to have the boys come and take the ball away from them. Julian and I were frustrated. We wanted to play baseball and those girls wanted to play a different kind of game.

One day Frances ran behind the barn when the horses

were chasing around the yard. Tom's stud grabbed her arm and dragged her about ten feet. He left a nasty bite mark on her arm.

That was the winter that Julian and I did battle with Irene and Millie. Irene and Millie were buddies. Frances, Julian and I were "on the other side of the fence."

We quarreled with Irene and Millie when we played games at noon and recess. Millie refused to be caught when we played circle base. We had to be on guard or she might give us a hard shove and run away. She couldn't knock me around anymore so she picked on Julian. That was a mistake.

Millie teased Julian. Julian dived at Millie, grabbed a fat leg and hung on. I ran around the coal shed to check on Julian and found her clamped to Millie's leg. I scowled fiercely at Millie. "You better not hit her," I said. Millie smiled and tried gently to remove Julian from her leg, but Julian was like a bull dog. She wouldn't let go. Millie dragged her around until the bell rang.

We all ran for the school house. I dashed into the hall and bumped into Millie. She wrapped a brawny arm around my neck from behind and Irene doubled up her fists and punched me. Julian tore into Irene, both fists flying. Miss Wiseman rushed out to see what was causing all the commotion. She broke up the fight and gave us a lecture about getting along with fellow students.

When recess came, Frances, Julian and I refused to play with Millie and Irene. The other kids sided with us. We didn't let them play circle base with us. They tried to get in the game, but no one would catch them. The whole affair would probably have been forgotten if Millie and Irene hadn't told the teacher.

Miss Wiseman marched us into the schoolhouse. Millie and Irene giggled as we shuffled to our desks. Miss Wiseman looked stern. "You children have to play together," she said. "You can't leave anyone out."

We spent the rest of recess sitting in our desks, looking at each other. Next recess we still didn't let Irene and Millie play. They tattled, and we all spent another recess in our desks. Irene and Millie decided staying in school with the rest of us wasn't any fun so they went off and played by themselves for the rest of the school year.

Millie tried to get even with me by teasing Whitefoot. Millie would sneak up and tickle Whitefoot's flanks. Whitefoot's ears would snap back and she would kick. "Quit teasing my horse before somebody gets kicked," I said. Millie laughed at me.

She pestered Whitefoot until she nearly got kicked. I knew that sooner or later someone would be hit by a flying hoof. I went to the school house and discussed the problem with Miss Wiseman. Miss Wiseman was disgusted. "I can hardly control what other children do to your horse," she said.

"Okay," I said. "I'll do it myself."

"No, no," she shook her head. "I'll talk to her." I guess she did because Millie quit tormenting Whitefoot.

Miss Wiseman tried to make arithmetic more interesting with a game. We each cut a small car out of construction paper. She ran strings across the top of the blackboard. We each put a car on a string. Your car moved ahead according to the correct problems. First car across won.

I got in trouble with Miss Wiseman when she told us to figure how much paper would be required to paper a room.

She said, "Take the width times the height time the length and you will have the answer.

I dared to disagree. "That will give you the cubic feet," I said. "You have to find the square footage of each wall and the ceiling to find out how much paper you need."

Miss Wiseman shook her head. I worked the problem my way. The other kids worked it her way. She counted my problem wrong. I often wondered if she knew I was right, but wouldn't give in to a smart aleck kid.

Another dry year was shaping up. A couple of fine rains in May boosted the grass and started the crops on their way. The Midland Co-op was paying sixty-two cents for wheat, a long ways above three cents. Prices were going up. We hoped prosperity was on its way.

280

Then the south wind blew, bringing great clouds of Texas, Oklahoma, Kansas and Colorado dust, which blew into our house and settled thick on floors and furniture. Drifts piled up on front of our house. The Russian thistles tumbled across the prairie and stuck in the barbed wire fences. The fence between our field and Emil Nemec's field was buried under dirt as fine as sand. Crops were blown out of the ground.

In Eastern South Dakota where more land had been plowed, shelter belts and corrals filled with dirt. Day turned to night. People drove with car lights on in the middle of the day. Machinery left in fields was buried. Dust blew as far east as the Atlantic Ocean again.

Summer heat opened cracks two inches wide in the ground. Uncle Alvin dropped a large crescent wrench in a crack when he was working on machinery in the wheat field. The wrench went so far into the ground that he couldn't see it. He never got his wrench back.

Plagues of grasshoppers swarmed over the land. Turkeys and chickens nearly went crazy, chasing hoppers. Even the ducks and geese chased grasshoppers.

The Government sent everybody a calf to eat. I thought we should raise the little bugger, but Mom said, "No, we're supposed to eat it." And eat it we did. I would have hid it over a hill, but The Government made you give back the ears to prove you ate it.

Clouds came up and people looked hopefully for rain, but no rain fell. The clouds drifted east to the corn fields of Iowa. Dark clouds in July brought five inches of rain that filled dams.

Julian and I ran out and gathered our half drowned chicks and put them in the summer kitchen. They huddled in miserable groups and stunk up the room.

One Sunday afternoon, Julian and I walked to the Roberts' farm to play with Irene and Lucille. Paulsons were there. We played Ante Over over the granary. Ione, Velda and I played against Irene, Julian and Lucille. The ball came over the granary. Ione caught it. "You sneak around that side," she said, pointing north. "I'll got the other way and catch them when they come around."

When they saw me, they ran screaming right into Ione. Lucille began to cry. "Ione hit me in the stomach." She doubled over, clutching her stomach.

Irene slugged Ione and the fight was on. Julian and I stood, staring at the silly spectacle. The parents rushed outside.

Lucille was crying. Ione and Irene were fighting. "Ione hit Lucille," Irene said and punched Ione in the face. Ione hit back.

Mr. Roberts and Mrs. Paulson began yelling at each other. Mrs. Roberts and Mr. Paulson watched them. Mrs. Paulson said, "Come outside the fence and Emil will whip you."

Mr. Paulson was over six feet tall and all muscle. Mr. Roberts stood about five feet six. He grabbed a four foot length of steel pipe that was laying on the ground. He raised the pipe above his head and slammed it down toward Mr. Paulson's head. Mr. Paulson ducked and the pipe crashed against his shoulder. He never moved. He just looked at Mr. Roberts with a slight smile on his face.

Julian and I ran for home. We dived under the fence, ran down the next draw and up the hill. We hit the screen door and burst into our house.

"What on earth is wrong with you?" Mom asked.

"Mr. Roberts is trying to kill Mr. Paulson," Julian said, gasping for breath.

"What?"

"He is," I said. "He hit him with a piece of pipe." We told her the story.

The next day the sheriff came and asked us about the fight. Mrs. Paulson wanted Mr. Roberts put under peace bond. I don't think they were friends anymore.

The rain in July brightened the grass and crops for a while. Still the incessant wind howled and screamed across the land, tearing at the grass roots and uncovering arrowheads that had lain buried for a thousand years.

282

The Midland Co-op offered ninety-six cents a bushel for wheat, but there was no wheat to sell. Farmers seemed to shrivel up with their crops. More farm families were "throwing up their tails" and leaving, heading west. Gaunt men walked the highways, seeking work that wasn't there. Hoboes hung around the railroad tracks, catching rides on the freight cars. Sometimes entire families rode the rails, searching for a place to get food and housing.

We were never that desperate. We always had food and a warm house to live in, except at night when the fire went out.

Another fall came and I looked High School in the face.

CHAPTER 23
High School, Here I Come

Julian and Hank in eighth grade and Buddy in first rode off to Liberty the fall of 1934. I hated to leave the safety of Liberty, but I had graduated. I thought I might stay home, but Mom said I had to go to High School.

She took me to Ben's Barber Shop for what she thought was a fashionable haircut that cost twenty-five cents. Ben invited me to sit in his barber chair, cranked it up to the proper height, took his huge shears and ruined my long brown hair. Hair fell in great gobs to the floor. He snipped and clipped and shingled up the back. He cut bangs in the front and left about enough hair to cover my ears on the sides.

Ben smiled and handed me a mirror. "How do you like it?"

Mom said my hair was lovely. I looked in the mirror. I was horrified. My neck looked three feet long. I looked like a giraffe or an ostrich with a topknot. I hated my haircut.

Frances and I headed for Midland High School. My feet wanted to go the other way. She was excited about this new adventure. I stayed with Aunt Amanda and Uncle Walt. Frances got a batching room upstairs in the Pete Elrod home in the center of town.

Uncle Walt took me to school, let me out and drove away. I looked at the town spread over the flat below the school house. A herd of strange people milled around in front of the building. Older students laughed and talked. Freshmen looked bewildered. I took a deep breath and joined the herd going up the steps.

284

The Freshmen trotted upstairs with the older students. Eighteen Freshmen settled along the east side of the assembly room. A long row of windows filled most of the east and west walls of the large room. Herb sat on the far west with the Seniors. Juniors and Sophomores filled the space between.

Frowning, I studied the room of about sixty students. I spotted Harold Norby, our friend from the Black Hills trip. Roy and Mona Howes had moved to Rapid City. My friends from Grade School were all gone. I knew Sara Lee Kessler and Verle Funston from second grade in Midland.

Ida and Verna Ocheltree looked lovely with the same hair style as mine. Ida was in my class. Most of the girls curled their hair and wore it above the collar. The boys combed their short hair back and slicked it down with plenty of Brillentine hair oil.

I towered above most of the boys and all of the girls in my class like a pine tree in a forest of elms. I was the tallest girl in school and such a bean pole that Mom thought I was sick. She took me to Pierre to see Dr. Riggs. The good doctor laughed and said, "There's nothing wrong with her. She's just long and thin like a railroad track."

Mainly we Freshies were a timid lot among the more sophisticated older students, but not Orville Bentley, Conrad Sandal and Paul Sandbo from the Moenville country. After several years out of school, they came to Midland to further their education. They weren't afraid of anybody, not even the teachers.

I was the homeliest, shyest girl in school. Herb told Mom boys didn't dare talk to me. He said, "If they even look her way, she scowls so fierce, she scares them half to death."

By the time school started, the South Dakota Rural Credit had sold 53,646 acres of mortgaged land west of the Missouri River for thirty-three cents per acre. They had a lot left that nobody wanted even for thirty-three cents. If prosperity was on the way, it was mighty slow. One man sold eight ducks for ninety cents, a shade over eleven cents a piece. He should have eaten them.

The Federal Government gave notice that no cattle could be shipped from Haakon County until further notice. The Government continued to buy cattle in South Dakota throughout the summer. They paid $20.00 per head, shot the cattle and buried the carcasses. Dad didn't sell any cows. We milked ours.

In Iowa the Government bought thousands of baby pigs and slaughtered them to reduce hog numbers. While meat was buried, hungry people roamed the nation.

Farmers were trying to put up thistle hay, and the wind was blowing the tumble weeds away. Thistles raced across the prairie to lodge in fences and stop the sifting, drifting dirt. A little hay had grown on Bad River bottoms and escaped the grasshoppers. Uncle Alvin and Uncle Albert were hauling hay and wheat straw from the Linder ranch up the river. Dad bought cottonseed cake for our cows.

When the time came for the cattle to head for the shelter of the Bad River breaks, Uncle Alvin opened the south gate of the summer pasture and let them out. The herd headed south, rested overnight at Steiens and went on to Bad River.

That fall Midland established dormitories for country students in two houses north of Main. Mrs. Munn and Mrs. Gulbranson were the dorm cooks and matrons for the girls.

The dorms were crowded with fifteen boys in one and fifteen girls in the other. The girls shared two bedrooms and the hallway upstairs with no bathroom upstairs or down. Running to the outdoor biffy on a cold and windy morning was most uncomfortable, but everybody had to do it.

Staying in the dorms cost $4.16 per month, except for students with families on relief. The Government paid $3.36 per month for them. The Government donated two carloads of wood and fourteen tons of coal to keep the pot bellied stoves going. The Government wanted to be sure the students got enough to eat so they donated six beeves and three pigs to supply meat for the table and a milk cow to furnish milk.

George Fish, an old man living on the east side of town

286

near Mitchell Creek, donated the use of his milk cow in return for keeping her all winter. The cow's stayed in George's pasture and Charley Illian, dorm janitor, milked them.

I slept on a cot in Aunt Amanda's living room. Uncle Walt took me to school in the car when he was carpentering and during winter. Otherwise I rode Blue and stabled him in the Douglas barn a quarter of a mile west of the school house. On warm spring and fall days, I often walked the four miles to school and home.

The town students hiked down the hill and home for dinner. I carried my lunch and ate in the basement with Herb and the other country kids.

While we timid Freshmen were trying to get used to a new school, the Sophomores were trying to scare us with the coming initiation. On a sunny Monday after school, Midland High's students and teachers headed for the park on the banks of Mitchell Creek. The Sophomores climbed into a farm wagon and ordered ten Freshies to pull them to the park.

Like well trained Belgian horses, Orville, Conrad and Paul took their places at the tongue. The Shetland ponies of the class pushed. The girls followed the creaking wagon to the park. The prancing horses stopped on the flat among the trees. Surrounded by the older students, we waited for the next move.

Frances won a boxing match against rugged Conrad Sandal. They played a few more dirty tricks and then we played games, roasted weiners and ate salad and pickles.

The boys had to wear their shirts and ties backward for a week. The girls wore men's socks and garters and no powder, rouge or lipstick. For four days we obeyed the Government rule against cosmetics.

Girls wore mid-calf dresses or wool skirts and blouses or sweaters. We wore bobby socks or knee length silk stockings. The boys wore dress pants and shirts with their neckties neatly tied.

I had only two or three outfits. When I wore a pale blue lacy blouse to school, a girl said, "Mona Howes wore that blouse last year."

287

I felt like hiding under my desk. I wished I could throw the lovely blouse in the trash, but I needed it. I bravely wore it many times.

I will never forget my first school dance. The Senior Class gave the first school party, the Freshmen the last. Uncle Walt and Aunt Amanda brought me to the party, then went to play Rook with Reverend and Mrs. Olson.

The boys pushed the desks out of the east grade school room and we had a dance floor. Teachers came to chaperone. Somebody wound the phonograph and put on a record. Soft music filled the room. Wearing a big grin, Willard Burns came and asked me to dance. We circled the dance floor with the other dancers, and I couldn't think of a word to say. He never asked me to dance again. Frances talked and laughed and had a wonderful time. How I envied her.

Herb was right. I scared the boys. They scared me, too. Besides a horrible haircut, I had pimples. I tried to eat yeast cakes to cure my pimples, but I couldn't stand the bitter taste. Good thing. I might have swelled up like a loaf of bread.

When the basketball season started that winter, Uncle Walt asked me if I wanted to play basketball. I had never had a basketball in my hand, but I was eager to play. After supper he took me to practice and I fell in love with the game.

We played half court, six girls to a team, three on each court and no crossing the center line. Coach Sletvold told me he would make me into a great guard. He taught me to pass the ball, pivot, and guard. Girls weren't allowed to dribble the ball. One step, one bounce and throw the ball. At five feet eight, I was the tallest girl on the floor. Coach put me on the first six with his Junior and Senior girls and told me to guard the center.

We were excited about our first game. We played before the boys. The Auditorium filled with people. We suited up in our tiny room while Belvidere suited up in theirs. The Belvidere girls, in green, marched onto the floor. Coach Sletvold sent me out with Midland's team. We ran onto the floor, dressed in our red and white uniforms.

The centers jumped. Belvidere captured the ball. Girls ran all around me. The ball sizzled past me. I froze to the floor. Coach looked alarmed. I was in a daze. Belvidere made a basket. Coach called time out and removed me from the game.

Sad and embarrassed, I slumped down beside him. He wasn't angry. He said, "Don't pay any attention to the people. Just go out and play. Take the ball away from them. Don't let those girls bluff you." He sent me back and I never got stage fright again. Belvidere trounced us 38 to 4. We beat the Okaton girls several times, but we never got close to Belvidere.

When the weather was fit, Uncle Walt cranked the Model A and took Aunt Amanda and me to the home games. We cheered the boys, both in victory and in defeat. That year brought mostly victory. Midland was conference champs.

Religious education was taught by Reverend Olson and Father O'Dowd. Reverend Olson gave each of us a tiny Book Of John, the Book of Love. My favorite Bible verse was John 3:16 "For God So Loved The World That He Gave His Only Begotten Son That Whoever Believes In Him Shall Not Perish, But Have Ever lasting Life."

This wonderful minister taught us about God's great love and the saving grace of Jesus Christ. He reinforced the teachings of our mother and Aunt Tina and Aunt Amanda who lived their faith.

Herb and I went home for two weeks Christmas vacation. I found tiny ceramic boy and girl statues in Murray's store for a dime each so I bought ten. My Christmas shopping was done. I gave a girl to Frances. She gave me a red initial pin. The weather was nice enough so our aunts and uncles came for Christmas dinner. I gave each of them a doll, too. I still have two dolls.

Snow storms and heavy rains in April settled the dust and made farmers smile. Wheat and corn would have ample moisture for a good start.

Uncle Walt was carpentering on an apartment in The First

National Bank building. The bank and an apartment were on the first floor. The Midland Mail publishing office occupied the basement. The Northwestern Bell Telephone Company office shared the second floor with several apartments. Operator Gladys Ravenscroft hooked up callers, told people the time and sent the weather report out on all the lines. After school I sometimes played baseball with a bunch of grade school boys.

A rolling cloud of dust boiled out of the south the end of April. The relentless wind blew the wheat fields of Kansas into a great choking cloud of dust. Once more wind carried Kansas soil all the way to the Atlantic Ocean. The black blizzard blew fine dirt into our houses to settle on tables, chairs, windowsills, beds, and floors. Everything was covered with dust. Noon turned almost as dark as midnight and cars crept down the roads with their lights on.

By the middle of May most small grain was planted. Dad hitched the team to the lister and planted corn. School was drawing to a close. I was exempt from semester tests in one subject, Herb in all five. Frances was exempt in two subjects and said, "What's wrong with you? You're smarter than I am." Maybe she was wrong.

On their Skip Day the Seniors picked up Mona Howes in Rapid City and toured The Black Hills for three days. Herb graduated in a class of fifteen with the motto, "Tonight we launch, where shall we anchor?", a fitting motto for a group of young people with little prospects for work and a small chance for a further education.

We were happy when school closed for the summer.

CHAPTER 24
1935

On a June afternoon black clouds rolled out of the west. "There's a storm coming," Mom said. "Run out and get the chickens and turkeys." Julian and I grabbed boxes and ran outside to gather the young poultry. The young chickens and turkeys ranged close to the house yet, roaming around in the weeds, catching bugs and grasshoppers.

We tore after them. The foolish chickens hid in the weeds. We snatched them up and stuffed them into the boxes as lightning ripped across the sky. Thunder boomed and crashed. Big rain drops splashed on the dry ground, kicking up puffs of dust.

We dumped our boxes of chicks in the separator room and ran out again. Rain poured down. Bedraggled, wet chickens and turkeys huddled in the weeds. Their feathers clumped together, showing patches of cold pink skin. They couldn't run anymore. I think they were happy to see us.

We carried boxes of shivering chickens and turkeys to the house. Then we ran out and put the baby ducks and geese inside. By the time we finished, we were as wet as the poultry.

We stood at the window and watched the storm with Buddy and Mickey. Water sheeted off the hill sides and into the draw south of the house. It ran down the draw, carrying dried grass stems, bugs and grasshoppers into the dam.

When the storm was over, we opened the door and chased the poultry outside. The hens ventured out of the hen house again. Weeds and grass were bright and clean in the sunshine. Small ducks and geese played in tiny puddles.

We took Buddy and Mickey outside to wade in the mud and water as a glorious rainbow spanned the eastern sky. Mud squished between our toes as we waded in the water running down the draw.

Creeks ran bank full into Bad River. Water holes were full once more. Crops were looking good and this rain would give them a boost.

Julian, Essie and I decided Bunker should have a girl's softball team. Midland and Southeast Midland each had a team, so why not Bunker? Jolly old Mr. Winters agreed to be our manager.

We needed balls, bats, a catcher's mitt and a first baseman's glove. Nobody else wore gloves. But we didn't have any money. We only had a ball and bat. "Where are we going to get money to buy equipment?" ever-practical Essie asked.

After some thought, Julian said, "We can have a benefit dance at our place."

"Yeah," I said.

"That's a good idea," Essie said, "but we need more girls to make a team."

"We'll ask Irene and Lucille and Frances. Maybe Mildred will play, too. That's seven," I said. "We only need two more."

Mom said we could have the dance at our house. Dad and Herb agreed to donate the music on violin and banjo. We could hardly wait for the great night to arrive.

Neighbors and friends from miles around crowded our house. Foot stomping melodies brought dancers to the floor. At midnight people ate cake and sandwiches and drank coffee from tin cans.

Essie passed a hat for donations. She was the only one with nerve enough to do it. She made a nice speech, thanking the musicians for the music and everyone for donations to our softball team. Julian and I followed Essie into the bedroom to count our loot. The bed was full of sleeping children.

We counted our hoard of nickles, dimes and quarters. We

had over $5.00. We were elated. We could buy all the equipment we needed. Essie put the money in her purse and stuck the purse in a dresser drawer. We went back to dancing.

Later Essie checked her purse. The purse was empty. Our money was gone. Jackie Oviatt was playing in the bedroom. Essie accused Jackie of stealing our money.

"I didn't take your money," Jackie said and told his father.

Big Jack was madder than a wasp in a bottle. He gathered his family and went home. Mom scolded us for accusing anyone of stealing our money. Essie cried. I don't know who got our money, but we never saw it again.

The next afternoon, we caught our horses and rode to the Bunker ball diamond for our first practice. We carried our ball and bat. We sat on the prairie in the hot sun, waiting while our ponies cropped grass. Mr. Winters didn't show up and neither did any other girls. We rode home feeling deflated.

Several days later, Mom said she saw Mr. Winters in town. He said he drove to the Bunker Diamond and didn't find anyone there. That was the end of the Bunker Girls Softball Team.

Dad traded some range horses to Bill Elrod for a Model T coupe for Hank. Julian and I didn't have to ride in the trunk anymore. We rode with Hank when we went to town.

I learned to drive the Model T and Hank let me take his car to go to visit Aunt Tina. The Model T putted down the trail for a quarter of a mile and stopped dead. I got out and cranked. The motor didn't even sputter. I turned the choke and pulled it out like I had seen Hank do. I got out and cranked. Nothing. I turned the choke and cranked. I cranked until my arm was sore. I gave up and went to find Hank.

Hank was a whiz with cars. He loved to tinker and fix. He knew everything about that Model T. He inspected the choke and looked disgusted. "You got this choke turned so many times, it's flooded. You're only supposed to turn it half a turn."

He started winding the choke back. After thirteen turns, the choke was back to normal. He spun the crank and the motor roared to life. I went to Aunt Tina's house.

Whitefoot dropped a dark colored foal that spring. Mom named the tiny filly Darkie. I played with Darkie, scratching her rump until she craned her neck back and tried to scratch her rump with her teeth.

Buddy loved to ride Whitefoot with me. One day we headed for Aunt Tina's house with Buddy sitting behind me on the saddle skirt, asking questions about everything he saw.

"What's that bird sitting on the fence?" he asked, pointing at a meadowlark perched on the barbed wire.

"A meadowlark," I said.

"What's he sitting on the fence for?"

"He's tired."

"How do you know?" By that time I was out of answers, but Buddy never ran out of questions.

We celebrated the Fourth of July in Hayes, the oasis in the desert between Midland and Ft. Pierre. Dusty Highway 14 split Hayes right down the middle. Hopkins General Store did a good business in fireworks.

The Fourth was a blistering day. The M&M Tent Shows were in town and allowed people to shelter from the sun in the huge show tent. We shot fire crackers, watched The Tent Show and gathered with the crowd to watch Eddie Burrus ride a bucking bronco in a corral of cars. I thought he was a fine rider. Mom said he pulled leather, which meant he grabbed the saddle horn.

I decided to break a horse to ride. I ran a trim black filly that Mr. Crawford had given to Buddy into the corral on the Calhoun place. I chased her into the chute and put a halter on her. She eyed me suspiciously, but she wasn't wild. Uncle Charley came to help me break her to lead.

We grabbed the lead rope, opened the gate and braced our feet. She stepped through the gate and ran to the end of the rope. Uncle Charley was like a rock. She whipped around the end of the rope. She tried to pull away, stirring up some dust. She tugged until she got tired. She looked at us, feet braced. I pulled on the rope. "Come on," I said.

She leaned back and refused to budge. "Pull her sideways," Uncle Charley said.

I jerked her off balance one way and then the other. Each time she set her feet and hauled back.

"I'll get behind her and scare her," Uncle Charley said. He shooed the mare until she understood what she was supposed to do. She followed me about the pen. Now all I had to do was ride her.

Uncle Alvin showed me how to Scotch hobble her, tying one hind foot to her neck so she stood on three legs. I waved a gunny sack around her until she didn't even flinch when the sack snapped around her head. I was feeling like a real cowboy. I was ready to take a ride. Uncle Alvin grasped the halter and held the filly still while I swung on her bare back.

She was rooted to the spot. I kicked her ribs. She stood like a wooden horse. I drummed my heels against her sides. She grunted. I looked at Uncle Alvin and shook my head. How could I break a horse if she wouldn't move?

Suddenly she ducked her head and kicked high. I slid to her neck. Her back end went down and her front end went up. I slid back to her rump. She crow hopped across the corral with me bouncing on her back like sack of potatoes. Uncle Alvin stood back and laughed.

I stayed aboard until she quit bucking. I had conquered my first bronc. I rode her around some, but she was pigeon-toed and would never make a good saddle horse. I turned her back in the pasture. She raised a dapple gray filly for Buddy.

Buddy and Mickey never tired of riding. After supper I often carried the saddles to the house and saddled the sewing machine and the piano stool. Buddy climbed aboard the sewing machine and Mickey mounted the piano stool. They galloped across an imaginary prairie after imaginary cows until bedtime.

July ushered in a blistering heat wave. Temperatures soared to 108 degrees. Grass began to dry, but wheat yields were fair, meaning about ten bushels to the acre. Anthrax was still killing cattle. Dad vaccinated our cows, but one day we came home from town and found a brockle faced brown cow dead in the corral.

We decided Mr. Roberts had brought a cupful of cane down and poisoned our cow, a ridiculous assumption. The cow was mine. Dad had given each of us a cow. I don't know why. He had to sell the calves and give the money to the bank. I suppose he hoped that someday he would be paid up.

Grandpa Martin died of a heart attack at Aunt Ida's house in Sioux Falls. Dad took the train to Sioux Falls for the funeral. He came home, driving a Willis Knight sedan, his share of the inheritance. The Willis Knight was the fanciest car we had ever seen. The navy blue car had a plush navy blue interior, seven lights on the inside and a clock on the dash. We loved that car. No more riding in the trunk of a Model T.

That fall the ranges were in good condition over most of western South Dakota. People hoped the drought was broken.

Mickey and Buddy rode off to Liberty School, taught by the famous frontier school teacher, Miss Corey.

Julian and I went to stay with Aunt Amanda and Uncle Walt for another High School year. We tried to get Hank to go to High School, but he said he was through with school. Uncle Alvin and Uncle Albert sent Herb to The School of Mines in Rapid City to learn to be a mining engineer.

CHAPTER 25
Midland High, Here We Come

Julian and I shared the cot in Aunt Amanda's living room. Julian wore her black hair in ringlets that hung down her back. She tackled school with a quick smile and a ready wit. She wasn't afraid of anybody. Kenny, Orville's younger brother, was a freshman, too, and he had an immediate crush on her.

My hair was reaching for my collar. I combed it straight back. I tried not to look so fierce, but nobody had a crush on me. I wasn't exactly afraid of the boys, but I didn't know what to say to them.

Besides the Freshmen, a bunch of new students came in from the country high schools. We lost some students that moved away. South Dakota people were still heading for Oregon, California, anyplace but South Dakota's bleak prairies. My class lost seven but we gained four boys: Tom Stalley, John Gillaspie, Kenneth Anderson and Willis Drew.

Uncle Walt agreed to give us a dime for each "A" and a nickel for each "B" on our report cards. We were to pay him for each "C" or "D". On my first report card I had three "A"'s and two "B"'s. Julian had four "A"'s. Uncle Walt paid us each forty cents. After every test, we presented our report cards, and he happily dug into his pocket and paid us.

Aunt Amanda kept her clock twenty minutes fast so she could say, "Hurry up and get ready, girls, it's nearly seven o'clock." We knew the time was nearer six thirty, but the psychological effect got us moving.

We started the morning with a fine breakfast. Aunt Amanda kept sour dough starter working in her warming oven so she could make sour dough pancakes, Uncle Walt's favorite. Sour dough would work forever, if you kept it going.

My favorite breakfast was a delicious baked pudding made with eggs, raisins, cream, milk and sugar, pie without a crust.

Some days Julian and I rode Blue and Snip to school. We stabled the horses in the Douglas barn. If we got caught in a storm, we stayed at the Douglas home.

Alice Douglas was in Julian's grade, Marjorie two years younger and Audrey the little sister. The girls and their mother had fiery red hair and freckles. So did Warren who was a mechanic at Ilg's Garage. Warren was shy and almost never talked so we loved to tease him. We tried to make him talk, but he just grinned behind his newspaper. We figured Warren liked us because he always danced with us. Howard was a senior in High School and Mr. Douglas worked on the railroad, coming home weekends.

When dish washing time came, Julian and I each grabbed a dish towel. Alice and Marjorie got into a scrap over who had to wash the dishes. Julian and I looked on in amazement at those two girls coming to blows over a dishrag. Their mother stopped the fight.

Howard said, "We should put Alice and Marjorie in a cage and let them fight it out."

When Alice and Marjorie came home with us for a week end, we went riding over the hills and valleys. Uncle Walt had a gentle team that didn't care how one slipped around on their broad backs so long as they were not expected to gallop.

Julian and I saddled Blue and Snip and bridled the work horses. We boosted Alice on the gray and Marjorie on the bay. They rode bareback as we headed out across the hills. The horses broke into a trot.

Alice bounced to one side and then the other. "I'm going to fall off!" And off she went, grabbing for the mane. She slid off the horse and landed on her feet. Alice never learned to balance correctly on the horse. She fell off for no apparent reason, always landing on her feet. Then someone had to dismount and help her aboard again.

Julian and I were a spooky pair. When Uncle Walt and Aunt Amanda went to the monthly meetings of The Eastern Star, we stayed home with Aunt Amanda's 22 Special close by our chairs. Nobody came to bother us, but we kept the rifle handy just in case. We were scared of ghosts, although we knew there weren't any. We were also scared of burglars or murderers that might be lurking around to snatch us.

We knew how to handle a rifle. We all learned to shoot with the Stevens Single Shot 22 that Uncle Walt gave to Herb and Hank. We used up boxes of shells practicing. We also learned to be careful.

Mom laid down the rules. "Never point a gun at anyone even if it's not loaded. It's usually the unloaded gun that kills someone." Aunt Tina and Aunt Amanda backed her up. They told tales about people who had been accidently shot by someone pointing a gun at them that was supposed to be empty.

We obeyed the safety rules. Don't carry a gun with a bullet in the barrel. Always point the gun barrel down. "If you point the barrel down, you can only shoot yourself in the foot. You won't shoot yourself or someone else in the head." Or the heart.

I wouldn't want to shoot myself in the foot either, but I almost did. Julian and I were fooling around with the 22 Special and I shot a hole in the floor. The bullet whizzed past my foot, slammed through the rug and into the floor.

Julian looked at me, and I looked at her. The bullet hardly left a mark, but it drove home the warning about empty guns. We were worried about what Aunt Amanda would say, but she didn't notice the tiny burn mark on her dark carpet and we didn't mention it.

On a crisp fall day, we walked up Mitchell Creek. I carried the 22 Special. Julian had Uncle Walt's 22 rifle. The woods were deep and dark along the creek. Ash, elm and cottonwood trees, stark and naked, towered above us. A carpet of leaves crackled under our feet. We startled a red squirrel and he ran up an elm tree. He peeked at us from behind the trunk.

I don't know why, but we decided to shoot the squirrel. I aimed at the bright-eyed little creature and pulled the trigger. The bullet sped past the squirrel. He dodged around the tree. I shot again and missed. The squirrel skipped around on the branches and peered at us. Julian aimed her gun at him and fired. She missed. The squirrel looked as if he wondered what those silly girls were doing. We headed up the creek, glad we had missed.

We decided to explore Uncle Charley's homestead. We walked another quarter of a mile and crossed the dry creek. Across the flat was his homestead shack. We inspected the barn and the chicken house that was dug into a draw that ran past the house. The roof had caved in. Dirt leaked into the interior. We could imagine the horses snug and warm in their barn when the winter blizzards howled.

We went to the house with its front porch open to the weather. Gone were the vines that had climbed the porch. The path lined with red and pink hollyhocks had vanished.

We went into the kitchen. An ash pan from an old kitchen range sat on the floor. Boards creaked as we walked through the living room and went into the room lined with rocks that Uncle Charley had dug into the hill side. The roof had fallen in.

"I'm cold," Julian said. "Let's build a fire in the ash pan."

We gathered sticks and twigs and laid them in the ash pan on top of a few leaves. We always carried matches. We had heard horror stories about people caught in the cold with no matches to light a fire. Their frozen bodies were found too late. I scratched a match and lit the leaves. A little blaze sprang up and a little fire warmed us.

Scrunched down, we warmed our hands over our fire. Julian jumped up. "Hey, the fire is burning the floor." Smoke curled from under the pan.

I grabbed the pan and carried it outside, dumped the wood

and coals on the ground and jumped on them to put the fire out. We carried dirt into the house and smothered the fire. A square black spot was burned into the floor.

One afternoon, we walked up the creek until we came to a gorge filled with cedar trees. Aunt Amanda had told us about the beautiful Cedar Canyon. Cedar trees are unusual along Mitchell Creek. We walked into the first canyon until we were deep in a forest of cedars. The dark canyon was like a huge cathedral, beautiful and awe inspiring.

Tall cedar trees grew in the bottom and up the sides of the canyon. We followed a trail to the top of a high shale bank and looked down at the creek winding toward the Steien ranch. We never tired of going to Cedar Canyon and walking among the lofty trees.

Uncle Alvin and Uncle Albert were avid readers. Uncle Albert bought every kind of detective magazine and pulp western that Engman's Pharmacy sold. I loved the Ranch Romance stories. Uncle Albert passed the magazines on to Aunt Amanda. Julian and I looked at the gruesome pictures, read some of the stories and scared ourselves silly.

One lovely afternoon, we walked home from school, discussing the wild stories in Uncle Albert's magazines. Aunt Amanda wouldn't be home when we got there. We would have to go into an empty house. Who knew what sinister thing might lurk behind the door? What if a mean man was waiting to grab us? "If there's somebody in the house, we can run to the corral and get Blue and race away," I said. Julian agreed. We approached the house warily, opened the door and stepped into the kitchen.

Tramp! Tramp! Tramp! Someone was walking around in the bedroom. But nobody was here. I looked at Julian. Her brown eyes were about ready to pop out of her head.

"Run," I said.

We hit the back door like a team of horses going through a gate. The screen door slammed. We tore down the hill toward the corral. Blue's head shot up and his ears shot forward. We were halfway down the hill, running like frightened deer when a voice called from the back door. "Where are you girls going?"

That voice stopped us in our tracks. Aunt Amanda stood in the doorway, a fly swatter in her hand. Looking as foolish as we felt, we went back to the house.

We were adventuring in the east field when I found a rusty pistol lost by some cowboy in the early days. The walnut was gone from the handle. The barrel was full of dirt, but I was thrilled with my find.

I found a rod that was used to hold the damper in a stove pipe. This rod was about a quarter of an inch in diameter and eight inches long with a sharp point so one could puncture the metal chimney to put the damper in place.

I stuck a small piece of oiled rag in the barrel and pushed it with the damper rod. The rag stuck. I pushed and poked at the rod. Whoosh! The rod went through the gun barrel and the back of the middle finger on my left hand. I looked at the dirty, rusty rod that protruded three inches past my finger. I couldn't pull it out.

Uncle Walt sat in the living room in his favorite chair, reading the paper. I stopped in front of his chair. "Pull this rod out of my finger, will you?" I asked, pleasantly.

He looked up, saw my finger skewered on the rusty damper rod and shot out of his chair. "What on earth are you trying to do," he shouted.

I said, "Please, just pull it out."

He grabbed the handle as I braced my hand. With a mighty jerk, the rod came out. Aunt Amanda gave me a pan of water with iodine in it to soak the wound. My hand healed fine. I don't know what happened to the gun.

On a Friday night rain fell and froze. The road curving down to the corral gate was covered with glare ice. Ice coated trees sparkled like a million chandeliers.

"Wow," Julian said. "Let's go skating."

We donned shorts and sweaters, clamped our skates to our shoes and skated down the road. We whizzed down the hill.

Walking sideways, we went back up the hill to the house, slipping, sliding and laughing.

Aunt Amanda was waiting at the door, looking stern and disgusted. "You girls put coats and pants on before you catch your death of pneumonia."

"We're not cold," Julian said.

Aunt Amanda shook her head. "It's ridiculous to go outside with bare legs in winter. You'll freeze."

We dressed in pants and coats and went back to skating.

We went home for Christmas vacation with deep snow all over South Dakota. On Christmas Eve Uncle Albert drove his Chevrolet sedan from the Bad River ranch north to spend the night at Aunt Tina's house. Uncle Alvin was already there. Everyone was to come to our house for Christmas dinner.

Uncle Albert stopped at Ham McCready's house and had supper with Essie and Ham. After supper he drank a few cheers to the season before heading across the snow covered fields to the Myrland home, a mile and a half away.

He angled across the Zuchhi quarter in snow almost running board deep. The car stalled in a drift at the bottom of a draw. Uncle Albert got out of the car and shoveled snow, trying to free his car. He gave up and tracks showed him heading toward the Myrland home. The temperature was below zero. A bitter wind blew out of the northwest. The deep snow made walking difficult for a crippled man. He turned and started back toward the McCready house.

Ham McCready thought he heard someone yell. He stepped outside and hollered into the freezing wind. He listened. No answer came. He went back into the house. Exhausted and cold, Uncle Albert fell in the snow about three hundred feet from the house. Uncle Alvin found him about ten o'clock Christmas morning.

They put Uncle Albert in a car with no heater and took him to St. Mary's Hospital in Pierre. Mom and Dad and our aunts and uncles went down to be with him. Hank, Julian, Buddy, Mickey and I waited at home. The turkey roasted in the oven. Pumpkin pies and lefsa waited to be eaten. Buddy and Mickey played with their new toys. Tom Roberts came over and stayed with us during the long wait. He tried to cheer us up while we ate nuts, Christmas candy, cookies and worried.

Late Christmas night, Mom and Dad came home and told us our beloved Uncle was gone. Uncle Alvin gave each of us kids a dollar. "The Big Fellow was going to give you this for Christmas," he said. He turned away and blew his nose in his big white handkerchief so we would not see him cry.

Snow continued to fall in enormous amounts. Blizzard winds blew, blocking roads all over the country. There were no big snow plows to cut through the huge drifts. People on farms were snowbound for weeks.

Trains didn't get through. Snow was high above the train. The great cuts along the railroad track drifted full of snow. Even the huge plow in front of the steam engine couldn't push through the cuts. Men with shovels tried to free the tracks, but the cuts drifted full again. On The Burlington Road eighty miles north of Midland, the passenger train stalled on the prairie and passengers and crew nearly froze to death before they were rescued.

Uncle Walt made a valiant effort to get us to school. He built a sled snowplow with winged log runners. The wings shoved snow out of the trail. On sunny days, he hitched the team to his small plow. Riding the plow, he drove the team across the flat to the hill above town and home again, making a trail for the Model A to follow.

He would come into the house, stamp the snow off his overshoes and say, "Tomorrow, I will take you to school." Tomorrow the road would be drifted shut again. Julian and I missed two weeks of school.

After two weeks the train finally whistled into Midland. Uncle Walt drove the team to town and got two weeks worth of papers, including two bunches of Sunday's edition. He took The Argus Leader so the funnies were different than the ones we read at home. For once we had enough funny papers. We loved Buck Rogers and liked to imagine ourselves flitting between the planets with Buck and his friends.

A truck loaded with groceries and about fifteen men with shovels took supplies to the Ottumwa country.

Uncle Walt's trail stayed open. He dodged around drifts, following the high spots where the snow wasn't so deep. He cranked the Model A and took us to school. If the Model A got stuck, Uncle Walt got the scoop out of the trunk and shoveled snow away from the car.

With Julian and me pushing and Uncle Walt driving, the Model A chugged through the snowdrifts. Uncle Walt made tracks all over the flat that winter. He shoveled a mountain of snow and we pushed the Model A for miles, getting to school.

Julian and I both played basketball. We beat Okaton twice, but we never got close to Belvidere. That was the last year of interscholastic girl's basketball for many years. I earned my letter in basketball and proudly sewed it on my red sweater.

Uncle Walt often took us to the movies. We knew if a Will Rogers or Shirley Temple movie was playing, we would go. Wednesday night was bargain night with all tickets for ten cents. It was also "take a chance night", because nobody knew what the movie would be. We talked Uncle Walt into many Wednesday night movies.

One Wednesday night, Julian and I wanted to go to the movie. Uncle Walt was sitting in his wicker rocker, reading the paper. Julian asked, "Can we go to the movie tonight?"

Uncle Walt searched his pockets. "We can't go," he said. He held up his hands. "I don't have any money."

"If we can find enough money, can we go?" she asked.

Uncle Walt grinned. "Yes, if you can find the money, we'll go."

We dashed into their bedroom and rummaged through the pockets of his pants hanging in the closet. We found enough nickels, quarters and dimes to make forty cents.

"Here's the money," Julian said, handing him the collection of coins. Uncle Walt laughed and pocketed the money. Uncle Walt had gold teeth and a broken nose. The gold teeth were sharp and strange. The broken nose ruined his handsome face.

We piled into the Model A and headed for town. I always got the middle. Julian sat on Aunt Amanda's lap. Uncle Walt drove with his hands on the bottom of the steering wheel and one elbow in my stomach. I had to keep my stomach pulled in and brace for any quick turns or get a jab in the belly.

On Sunday night, we usually attended The Lutheran Church where Reverend Olson preached. I've always been thankful to Aunt Amanda and Uncle Walt for taking us to church. We seldom got to go on our own. Stores weren't open on Sunday, and our parents went to town mainly when they could do their trading. Once or twice during the summer, we went to a church over east in the Phoeba territory when they had church and a neighborhood picnic.

Most of Reverend Olson's congregation were high school kids. The students from Moenville came and Kenny and Alpha Olson. Our friends came because we were there. The only adults in church were Mrs. Olson, Steiens, Schonevilles, Jim and Rachel Nelson and Mr. and Mrs. Fennefos. Sometimes only four adults showed up in church along with about fifteen students. Two of Kenny's friends left at 7:30 to go to the movie.

I wasn't as timid my second year in high school. One day I walked down the aisle past Harold Norby's desk. Harold was engrossed in a book balanced on the edge of his desk. I barely touched the book, but it clattered to the floor.

Harold almost jumped out of his desk. Nobody thought that shy Martin girl had anything to do with Harold's book suddenly falling off his desk to wake up the whole assembly room.

That spring at the Freshmen party, we played a game in which a boy chose a girl and then everybody marched around the room, winding between the desks. Roy Schoneville, a Senior, chose me, a Sophomore in a red dress too shy to say a word. We marched silently. Julian bounced along beside Kenny Bentley, talking his arm off. Frances and Orville were at no loss for words either. I enjoyed the party, but Roy didn't dance.

Spring brought baseball for boys and softball for girls. We walked down to the diamond by the stockyards to watch the boys play. The girls didn't play other schools, but we had picnics around a camp fire by Bad River and scared ourselves with ghost stories and wild tales.

Farmers looked hopefully for a better year. South Dakota farmers had struggled against depressed prices since 1923. Would 1936 break the cycle of despair?

CHAPTER 26
A Dry and Thirsty Land

Most of the snow blew off the fields. The spring of 1936 farmers planted spring wheat in March in fields so dry the seed didn't even sprout. A few showers fell in April but didn't wet down to the seed. The crop never came up. Farmers dug down and found kernels of wheat that had not even swelled.

Dad planted milo instead of corn to foil the grasshoppers, but the milo didn't come up either. Dad dug seed out of the lister ditch that looked like it had just came from the seed sack. He showed Mom the seed and shook his head.

The Government was paying farmers to build dams on their land. Dad hitched his four horse team to the fresno and raised the grade of our dam. Uncle Alvin did the same at the Calhoun place, but no rain came to run water into the dams. The hot sun sucked out the water they had.

The grasshoppers were still with us, but not in such large numbers. They didn't cover the side of a building when they sought shade from the hot sun anymore. In fact, it looked like the grasshoppers might starve to death.

There were still plenty for our chickens, guineas, ducks and turkeys. Mickey and Buddy used them for fish bait. Catching bullheads for supper was Buddy's job. We ate eggs for dinner. For supper we had bullheads fried in butter. Buddy was eight-years-old and took his job seriously, but Mickey didn't like to sit on the bank with a line dangling in the water, waiting for a fish to bite.

Every morning they took buckets to put their fish in and

long willow poles and headed for the dam. Jack and Tippy went along. They caught grasshoppers for fish bait. A big grasshopper is hard to catch and even harder to put on the hook. Grasshoppers wiggle, kick and squirm. Sometimes they bite. A big grasshopper can bite a hole in your finger. Besides they spit tobacco juice on you. Catching the bait probably took longer than catching the fish, because the hungry fish bit as fast as the line hit the water.

Catching the fifteen or twenty fish that we needed for supper took about an hour of sitting in the hot sun. Dad cleaned the fish when he came home for dinner. He hung them in the old cistern with the milk and butter to keep cool until supper time.

We all watched for clouds. They drifted over filled with lightning flashes and rumbling thunder. The wind blew, but no rain fell. The clouds scudded along until they reached Iowa where they dumped their load on Iowa corn fields.

A blistering wind blew out of the southwest and the temperature soared to 112 degrees. The incessant, howling wind shriveled the grass that had started from the moisture left by melting snow. Cattle and horses nuzzled in the sparse grass, trying to find enough food to survive. Some grass grew in draws where snow banks had lain.

The blizzards of 1919 blew away my parent's dream of a cattle ranch. The Black Blizzards of the thirties threatened to bury us in dirt as fine as drifting snow. The Black Blizzards came year after year after year, blowing the fields away, tearing at the grass roots.

Machinery was buried in the fields. Fence lines lay beneath the sifting soil. Road ditches filled with dirt. Dust storms blew across Oklahoma, Kansas, Nebraska and Colorado into South Dakota, blotting out the sun.

Banks of dirt built up like snow drifts in front of our house. Buddy and Mickey took little shovels and tablespoons and played in the dirt. But this wasn't all foreign soil. Some of it was our dirt. Our fields were moving, eroding, blowing away.

The heat grew more intense, rising to 120 degrees in the

shade. Verna Lammon who lived six miles southwest of our place wanted to see how hot it was in the sun. She laid a thermometer out in the open. The mercury shot up and blew the top out of it.

Mom wouldn't let us go swimming until nearly sundown and even then the heat was smothering. The young chickens, ducks and turkeys sat in the shade of the house with their tongues out. They didn't even have enough energy to chase grasshoppers.

Despite the severe drought and grasshoppers, some farmers in Haakon County combined two or three bushels of wheat per acre. Top wheat was $1.18 per bushel in Midland, but the wheat was far from top. Kernels were small and withered. We had no wheat to sell. The grass was so dry and shriveled that the grasshoppers had a hard time finding anything to eat. The Midland Mail said, "The grasshoppers are drying up with the grass."

Those were days to break the heart of a farmer, or a grasshopper for that matter. The hoppers were skinny and under-fed. I don't know what our horses and cows ate. We still had our milk cows, but the Bertelson herd was dwindling. Dams were turning to mud holes. Gasping fish came to the surface, looking for air. Cows and horses waded almost belly deep in mud to get to the soupy water.

In July Hank and Glen Crawford went to The Civilian Conservation Corps camp at Farm Island near Pierre. Herb went to a camp on the Missouri River near Chamberlain. The men stayed for six months and worked on various projects. Herb worked on a resort that is now under about a hundred feet of Lake Sharp.

The CCC was set up by President Roosevelt to give jobs to young, unmarried men. They were housed in military style camps and paid $30.00 per month. Of the thirty bucks, the young man got to keep five. He had to send the rest home.

Our family got a windfall. Fifty extra bucks a month. To Julian and me, the important thing was that we could go to the dances in Midland and Hayes. We could go to Midland on Saturday night, go to the movies and the dance and get home about the time the sun was coming up. I fell into bed, went to sleep and ten minutes later, it seemed, Dad yelled, "Get up, Thelma. We have to milk the cows."

I hated to get up and milk, but Dad couldn't milk sixteen cows by himself if he wanted to get them out to pasture before noon. I grabbed my bucket and one side of the ten gallon cans and we headed for the barn. The cows were up, mooing because they wanted to get out and look for a few morsels of grass.

The worst part was carrying the milk to the house. With a full bucket in one hand, I grabbed the handle of the ten gallon can. We headed for the kitchen. If I was lucky, Dad would ask if I wanted to rest at the halfway spot. We would set the can down and have a breather. If Dad was pre-occupied, he would forget and I had to trudge on while the can nearly jerked my arm out of the socket. Naturally, I would not tell him I wanted to rest.

I helped Dad, and Julian helped Mom. She baked cakes in the temperamental three burner kerosene range. The oven was placed on top, but you had to watch those burners. They crept up, if they thought you weren't watching, and smoked up the cake. Many a lovely angel food cake turned from white to black in that little marvel. Julian rubbed and trimmed off the black and we ate it anyway.

To add to our problems, the Willis Knight died. Dad parked the majestic old car east of the chicken house and bought a gray Model A sedan. We loved the Model A. We could all ride inside of it. One day Mom asked If I wanted to drive it home from Aunt Tina's house. I knew I could. The only difference between the Model A and Model T was the gear shift. "I can drive it," I said. "I know how to shift." I proudly drove it home. There was no Driver's Ed then, no driver's license. We learned to drive at home with the prairie for a highway.

The Model A was parked on the hill south of our house so we could roll it off the hill to start. A rock kept the car from accidently rolling down the hill.

One day Mom, Julian, Buddy, Mickey and I went to visit Aunt Tina. Mom parked the car on the hill above the dam. The wind blew the car and it careened down the hill into the dam. Uncle Charley was gone. I walked home and got Dad with the team to pull the car out. Dad wasn't happy about it.

One morning when we turned the cows out, they ambled west of the house. One cow laid down on the hill and died. Dad went out and burned the carcass in case she had anthrax. No other cows died, but we had one less to milk.

I rode Whitefoot over the pasture every day, checking for dead cows. Dry hard dirt showed between each grass plant. I watched the ground, looking for arrowheads. Uncle Alvin had a cupful of them that he had found while riding. Sometimes I stopped to kill a snake.

The brown grass, the hard earth, the empty waterholes were monuments to six years of too little rain and too much wind. Fortunately I didn't find many dead cows. I often saw a thirsty jack rabbit resting in the shade of a fence post. I don't know what the rabbits ate or drank. If they found any grass, there surely was not much moisture in it.

We had a pet jack rabbit. We found him hopping around on the prairie minding his own business and brought him home. By some miracle, Peter lived and grew into a powerful jack. He grew up unafraid of either dogs or cats.

Peter drank milk from a pan on the summer kitchen floor that he shared with the cats. If angered, he could kick a cat across the kitchen floor with his strong hind legs. If he didn't like something we did or if we teased him, he dived on our feet and scratched with all his might.

Peter was free to roam outside where ever he chose to go. Jack and Tippy reluctantly learned to leave Peter alone when he adventured outside and to let him come back to the house when he was ready. He finally ran away to join his own kind.

One day Buddy got on Whitefoot behind me and we headed for Aunt Tina's house. "Be careful you don't kick Whitefoot in the flanks," I said. "If you touch her there, she'll kick up." Buddy sat behind me, hanging onto the cantle, digesting this bit of wisdom. Then the little dickens slid back and grabbed her flanks with both heels. Whitefoot laid back her ears and kicked higher than a Brahma bull.

Buddy flew into the air. On the way up, he grabbed my head and pulled himself back down. He rode the rest of the way carefully keeping his heels away from her flanks.

That summer Lee Schroader came from Iowa to visit Aunt Tina and Uncle Charley. Her father was Uncle Charley's nephew. Lee was everything that I was not. Red haired, brash, Lee Schroader wasn't afraid of anybody. She never met a stranger, and she was the only person I knew that could brag about her horses faster than Uncle Alvin could brag about his.

Tom Roberts stayed home that summer and helped his father do nothing. Nothing, that is, except milk cows. T.W. didn't even have hogs to feed.

Tom rode after their milk cows at about the same time that I rode after ours. We often met in the pasture and brought our herds home together. When we got to his gate, he drove his cattle to their barn and I headed mine down the lane to the dam. He sang hauntingly beautiful melodies to me like: "In The Valley Of The Moon," "Isle Of Capri," and "Rose Of San Antone."

We belted out our favorite cowboys songs as we rode over the hot and dusty prairie, serenading the cows with "Home On The Range," "Frankie And Johnnie," and "Red River Valley." I always sang when I rode after the cows. The music teacher didn't appreciate my voice, but the cows didn't care, and Tom never complained.

Tom told me he was going to Montana to be a cowboy. He talked about rodeoing. "I can bulldog a steer," he said.

I immediately wanted to see him bulldog something. We didn't have any steers, but I pointed out a big calf. "Let's see you bulldog that calf," I said.

We cut the calf out of the herd. Tom spurred Tony after him. The calf ran like a wolf was on his heels. Every time Tom got close, the calf dodged away. I wasn't a very good hazer, so Tom gave up.

"I can't bulldog him. He won't run straight," he said. "I could do it, if he was a steer with horns." Diving off the horse and catching that speedy calf would have been difficult. I think Tom was afraid of getting a snootful of dirt.

That summer I had my first real date. Dressed in my red dress with silver spangles on the sleeves, I went dancing with Tom. He had taken me to Rapp's Cafe for a bottle of pop at midnight and we were rapidly approaching the end of a near perfect evening. "Can I take you home?" Tom asked. He didn't have a car, so we would be riding home in his father's black Model A sedan with his mother, father and sisters.

I was thrilled, but I didn't know what my parents would say about me going with a Roberts. However, Mom said I could go.

Mrs. Roberts, Lucille, Marlys and Cleta got in the back seat of the Model A. Tom slid behind the wheel. I sat in the middle. T.W. sat on the outside, in the gate opening position.

Tom took his family home, then drove around the big draw and pulled up at our house. That was my first, last and only date with Tom Roberts. True to his word, he saddled Tony and headed west to Big Sky Country to be a cowboy.

In August the dams went dry at our place and the Calhoun place. Fish gasped and died. Buddy and Mickey rescued about a dozen small fish and kept them in a bucket.

The dams were fenced and the cows bellowed at the gates, smelling water in the stinking mud. The time had come to dig wells, and all we had to dig with was a pick and shovel.

Finding water below the ground when there is none above is a ticklish proposition. Streams run underground just as they do on the surface. If you dig a hole and tap into an underground stream, you've got a well. If you don't, you've got a dry hole. If you're digging with a pick and shovel and the sun is bearing down with over a hundred degrees of fire power, you don't want to dig many dry holes.

Several methods are used to find underground water. Uncle Albert had the gift of water witching, but Uncle Albert was gone.

314

Uncle Alvin preferred the auger probe method. He drilled down with an auger that had a long handle. The auger never lied. Either water came up the auger hole, or it didn't. You dug no dry holes.

Finding water was critical. Livestock can exist on a few mouthfuls of grass, but they will live only a few days without water. One desperate farmer knelt beside his corral and prayed for water for his thirsty herd of milk cows. A rancher chanced to ride by and saw him kneeling in the dust, crying for water for his bawling cattle. "Bring your cattle to my place," he said. "I've got plenty of water."

"Oh, thank God," the farmer said, leaping to his feet.

"You might thank me," the rancher said, "I'm the one giving you the water." Ah yes, but who sent the rancher to answer his neighbor's prayer?

Dad dug a well below the grade of our dam to get water for our cows, horses, hogs and poultry. We hauled water from Crawford's sweet water well for drinking and cooking. We couldn't drink the bitter water from our well.

Dad helped Uncle Alvin and Uncle Charley dig a well in the draw above the dam. They dug a hole about six feet square. One man hacked at the hard earth with a pick, breaking off chunks. The other men threw the dirt out of the hole.

When the hole was about six feet deep, they were too far down to throw the dirt out, so they rigged a tripod over the well and put the dirt in a fifteen gallon barrel. Uncle Alvin's old gray work horse pulled the barrel out of the well. The barrel tripped at the top, rode along a cable for about ten feet and dumped the mud, then went back for more.

One day Dad sent me down to drive the horse. Uncle Charley filled the barrel. Uncle Alvin signaled for me to pull the barrel out of the well. I drove the horse ahead, watching the barrel rise to the trip. The trip let go. The full barrel slammed back into the well. We heard it smack into the mud at the bottom.

The old horse stopped. I looked at Uncle Alvin and he

looked at me. Neither of us said a word. Neither did Uncle Charley.

Uncle Alvin looked into the well. "Are you all right, Charley?"

Uncle Charley looked up, his face white. The barrel had settled neatly in the mud inches in front of him. We went back to digging. When four feet of water ran into the hole, they quit digging and fenced it. Uncle Alvin and Uncle Charley pulled water out with a large bucket to fill a tank. The horses and cattle came to drink and emptied it several times each day. Filling the tank was hard work. That water was so alkali it would curl your hair, but the livestock had to drink it.

Uncle Alvin worried that the cattle would break through the fence and fall into the well, but it wasn't cattle that had that problem.

When a well went dry, they gathered their spades and pick axes and dug in another draw. Uncle Alvin, Dad, Uncle Charley, Ham McCready and Albert Rosy were digging a well south of the Calhoun place in a likely draw. They were down about eight feet. Water and mud mixed covered the bottom of the well.

Uncle Alvin and Albert Rosy stood on a plank laid across the well pulling out buckets of mud as Dad and Uncle Charley filled them. Ham, on hands and knees, watched from the edge of the well. With a loud crack, the plank broke, dumping Alvin and Albert Rosy into the well on top of Dad and Uncle Charley. Ham peered over the edge and fell in on top of the men struggling around in the mud.

They crawled around on their hands and knees in a tangle of muddy arms and legs. One by one, they got loose and stood up. Uncle Alvin looked at Ham and asked, "What are you doing down here, Ham? You weren't on the plank."

Ham looked foolish. "I leaned over to look and lost my balance," he said with all the dignity a man can muster when his face and clothing are slopped with mud. He hauled himself out and stood up.

Uncle Alvin threw back his head and roared. The other men looked at each other and began to laugh. They never lost their ability to laugh at the absurdities of daily living.

"Wasn't no reason for Ham to fall in the well," Uncle Alvin said. "He just looked down at the rest of us and decided to come on down."

The hot winds continued to blow. The clouds that floated over were empties. The summer of 1936 was the only summer I ever saw when no rain fell. We began to think rain would never fall on our parched land. The curly buffalo grass was gone. People said it would never come back, that the prairie would never come alive again with bluebells and sunflowers. Wheat grass would never wave in the breeze. The birds would never return to sing their prairie songs. The deer and the antelope were gone, too. I'd only seen one wild antelope in my whole sixteen years.

People were afraid of prairie fires even though there was no grass to burn. I was at Aunt Tina's house one day when Essie and Ham came riding as fast as their horses could go, which wasn't very fast. Ham rode an old bay and Essie rode a stove-up black and white pinto that Uncle Alvin loaned to her. They were carrying burlap sacks.

"There's a prairie fire coming," Essie said, waving her sack. "We came to help you fight the fire."

There were no fire trucks with water tanks. People fought prairie fires by whipping them out with wet sacks or sweeping the edges with brooms. The flames couldn't leap very high in the short grass. Fire crawled across the prairie in a low red line. "A fire," Aunt Tina said, "Where?"

"Look at the smoke," Essie said, pointing west. A cloud rolled along the southwestern horizon.

The smoke was a great cloud of dust blowing in from the southwest, more Colorado, Kansas, Oklahoma and Nebraska dust coming to bury South Dakota. If the rains ever came, our fields would be ready. We had the best soil from six states.

When Dad worked late, helping to dig wells or pull water

out of them, Julian and I milked our sixteen cows. We took our buckets and cream cans and went to the barn. Julian never milked a cow unless forced into the job so she wasn't good at it.

She grabbed a stool and sat down beside an easy milker. I wanted to be fair. "I'll take this hard milker, and you take that one," I said, pointing to the other cow that was difficult to milk. The cows placidly chewed their cud contemplating ways to keep us from getting their milk too fast.

Julian didn't care about fairness. "I'm not milking one of those hard milkers," she said, squirting milk into her bucket.

"You have to milk one," I said, trying to be reasonable.

She jumped off her stool and offered to whip me. She couldn't have, but I could see us rolling around in the manure in the gutter. I decided I would rather milk both the hard milkers, and I did.

The first part of August turned cool, a welcome change from the searing heat of July. Highway 14 into Midland was being oiled, no more driving on a dusty gravel road to get to town. They even straightened out some of the sharp curves. Deadman's Curve was no more.

A steady rain the last of August sprouted the wheat that had lain in the ground since spring. Our fields were covered with a lovely carpet of green. The cows enjoyed the green pastures.

The Government loaned farmers money to buy livestock feed. Dad bought cottonseed cake for our cows. Uncle Alvin bought a few tons for the cattle he had left. His herd was to shrink until it was a shadow of what it had been. The Federal Land Bank would have foreclosed on his Bad River Ranch if there had been anyone to sell it to.

With the coming of fall, school loomed again on the horizon. The time had come for Julian and me to trot off to Midland High while Buddy and Mickey bridled their ponies and road across the prairie to Liberty. Mickey would be in third grade because the teacher had promoted her two grades instead of one.

318

One of the first pictures taken of Mickey and Buddy Martin. It was taken in 1936. The Willis Knight is in the background. There were few pictures taken during The Depression.

CHAPTER 27
Come With the Rain

We weren't ready for school, but school was ready for us. The Midland streets were getting a face lift. The Government was putting in new curbs and sidewalks with WPA labor. The WPA had a sewing room to give women employment. Six ladies worked there, hemming towels, making quilt tops and so forth to give to the poor. The town was humming.

Julian and I struck it rich that fall. The Government was hiring students from low income families to help the teachers. The only hitch was you had to be sixteen. I was, but Julian was only fourteen.

I worked for Miss Sheggeby, the English teacher and girl's athletic coach. She was my favorite teacher, a lovely blond not much older than the Seniors. I sat in the upstairs classroom and listened to the chorus practicing in the assembly as I corrected papers. I wished I was in there singing, too.

I hadn't even tried out for chorus. The year before was still fresh in my mind. I had bravely tripped down the stairs and tried to sing "America The Beautiful," while fat, jolly Miss Ellefson tried to make the piano jump off the floor. Every student in High School was called for chorus except me and Alice Douglas. I figured we must be terrible singers.

Working for the teachers paid the wonderful sum of $4.00 per month. Sometimes I earned my money watching Miss Duryea's first, second and third grade room. I split my $4.00 with Julian since she was not old enough to earn her own. We went to

320

Engman's Drug Store to cash the check and splurge on an ice cream cone for a nickel. We used the rest of the money to buy clothes and school supplies.

I bought a yellow shirt, a blue skirt, a blue turtle neck sweater and blue slacks. Blue was my favorite color. We needed slacks for picnics and sports. We never wore them to dances or school.

Julian bought a red sweater. We also had to buy socks and shoes, caps and mittens. Every evening we sewed up the runs in our silk stockings. We each had a couple of outfits to change off wearing to school. Mom made our party dresses. She must have gotten a bargain on some forest green material because she made each of us a green skirt and tunic outfit. We put a yellow flower perfumed with gardenia at the throat and ventured off to dances, looking like twins. The outfits were pretty and stylish so we didn't care.

Herb, Clifford Stone and Clarence Petoske got in Herb's Model T and headed for Iowa to pick corn. Clarence could take a team out and pick a hundred bushels of corn a day, but Herb never got the hang of throwing that many ears into a wagon. He got a job shoveling corn into the crib from other men's wagons.

On the way home, the Model T roared down the curving hill south of Keller's corner and smashed into a cement bridge. Nobody got hurt, but the Model T was a total loss. There went Herb's profit from shoveling corn.

The first old age pensions arrived in Haakon County so Aunt Tina and Uncle Charley were happy. Uncle Charley was old enough to get $65.00 per month, a windfall for someone without any income. They jumped into their Model T and went to Iowa for the winter.

Julian loved to make speeches and debate. She was on the Debate Team with Orville Bentley and they happily argued with students from other schools in front of the whole high school. They were the best debaters Midland ever had. They won the District Debate Tournament. You couldn't have dragged me up to that podium to speak in front of a bunch of people with a four horse team.

I took chemistry which is the only subject that was so hard I could hear the gears mesh in my head when I studied. I loved Latin. Julian and Frances took Latin I when I did as well as some kids that should never have tried to crack a Latin book. I spent a lot of time showing Ramona Rank and Tom Stalley how to conjugate Latin verbs and other finer points of a language already dead for hundreds of years.

Those of us who found Latin fun ran around saying things like "amo te" which means "I love you." I think Miss Sheggeby would have been more impressed if we had spent more time on Julius Caesar and "Vini, vidi, vici," his battle cry after he fought all the way to Britain and conquered a bunch of cave men.

Mumps traveled through the school. Julian and I both came down with swelled necks at the same time. We looked like a couple of fat ladies with double chins and got to stay home for two weeks. We played cards with Aunt Amanda and Uncle Walt and proved that we could eat dill pickles.

Aunt Amanda had her troubles with us. Naturally, she didn't want us to smoke, but she was always afraid we might start the dreadful habit. When she noticed a tiny hole in my skirt, she was sure I was smoking, although neither Julian or I ever touched a cigarette in high school. We pretended she was right, which shows how ornery teenagers can be.

During cold weather, Julian and I were often late for school on Monday morning. One Monday morning dawned bright and extremely cold. Dad put on his sheepskin coat and went out and drained the oil from the Model A. He heated the oil on the back of the kitchen range and put it back in the motor. Hot water for the radiator steamed away on the back of the stove. Dad got in the car and rolled it off the hill.

The Model A rolled all the way to the bottom without a sputter. Dad got out, cussed the car and headed for the barn to hitch up Sorrel and Emmet. He hitched the team to the front of the car. I slid behind the wheel to drive the car.

Holding the cold team in check, Dad said, "Put her in low and leave her out of gear until she gets rolling." Sorrel reared and pawed the air. Frosty breath puffed from the team's nostrils. They headed down the draw as I let the clutch out. The motor sputtered, then caught and roared. We went to school.

Going to dances, movies, card parties or school doings was an adventure in winter. The driver drove slowly, one hand on the steering wheel, the other rubbing a peek hole in the frosty windshield. The passenger rubbed a clear patch on his or her side to help watch the road. Keeping the whole windshield clear was impossible.

Every car carried a scoop shovel to shovel the car out of snow drifts. The driver hit the drift hard, hoping to go through. If we got stuck, everybody except the driver got out to push. Sometimes the driver got out and ran along beside the car, steering and pushing until the car was through the drift. Then everybody piled into the car and we went happily on our way again. There were no snow plows. We opened our own roads.

Hank was our best snow and mud driver. If a car or truck could go through a mud hole or snow drift, Hank would take it through. He tore out rear ends, broke axles and burned out motors, but he got through drifts and mud holes so we didn't have to walk the last hundred feet to the house. He also left deep ruts in the prairie.

Uncle Alvin bought a second hand Dodge pickup that had been converted from a sedan. The Dodge had once been red and one window was gone. A coat or a piece of cardboard covered the hole.

If there were too many of us to fit in the cab, someone curled up under quilts in the pickup box.

Julian and I collected nickles and dimes from Uncle Walt all year. We often walked home with the Rogers girls, dark-haired Joyce and the blondes, Velda and Marsha. In May Joyce was taken to the Pierre hospital with a burst appendix. The doctors had no penicillin, or antibiotics. Joyce died. School closed and we went to her funeral to say good-bye to our small friend who died so very young. She was twelve.

In February Hank and Glen went back to the CCC camp near Pierre and worked on parks. They got in Hank's Model T and came home on weekends. By the time they bought gas, a bit of Bull Durham and a movie or dance ticket, their $5.00 stipend was shot. The girls loved to dance with Glen. I think most of us were secretly in love with him. Glen loved the girls, too.

So spring came again. Lambs gamboled beside their mothers. We had calves and colts and little red pigs. Herb went off to herd sheep for Griggs Davidson northeast of Midland in the Ottumwa country.

Herb lived in a covered wagon with plenty of groceries he had to cook himself. He had a trusty horse to ride as he herded his band of ewes and lambs. One night he bedded his sheep, staked his horse and climbed into his sheep wagon. He rolled up in his blankets and went to sleep.

He was tired. He slept hard. A storm came up in the night. Thunder rumbled, lightning flashed, and rain poured down. Sheep don't sleep hard. They rise with the sun and go adventuring to see what mischief they can get into. When Herb looked out of his wagon at five o'clock, the sheep were gone. His horse had broken loose and gone home. On top of that the ground was muddy.

He got dressed and slogged through the mud, tracking sheep up hill and down dale. The trail led southeast. He followed the tracks through several pastures as the sheep crawled through fences and left precious wool on the barbs. He found his sheep in one of Oliver Nelson's pastures. The sheep were mixed up with a herd of curious steers. The steers ran about, sniffing at the sheep, kicking up their heels. Herb ran after his herd, trying to separate the animals.

He finally got the ewes and lambs into one baaing mass. He herded them back to his wagon and ate breakfast. Some kind person brought his horse so he was a full fledged sheep herder again. He was also a more careful sheep herder.

The gentle rain fell in May and June, soaking our parched soil. Grass grew. Flowers bloomed and farmers smiled. Wheat covered fields with a soft green mat. Corn popped up in the corn rows.

We were at a card party in the Crawford house one night when clouds rolled in. Thunder rumbled and lightning split the sky. Rain fell in sheets for an hour. After a lull, rain came again in a gully washer that ran water into the dams.

One man looked up from his cards and said, "When those clouds turn around and come back they really rain." Every farmer in the house had a grin plastered on his face.

They wouldn't have to dig any more stinking wells. Cattle would wade belly deep in water. The meadowlarks would be heard again. Plovers and horned larks would nest on the prairie. Buddy could turn his captive fish loose in the dam once more.

Aunt Tina and Uncle Charley planned a party for their wedding anniversary June 14. Uncle Charley predicted rain. The Midland Mail said, "Mr. Myrland's ability as a prophet was well established that day as he foretold rain and plenty of it. It came in such quantities no guests were present."

Rain came so hard that the oiling of Highway 14 was delayed. A two inch rain washed out corn fields and filled dams to over-flowing. Mitchell Creek ran high once again. Water roared like a river around the spillway of the dam on the Calhoun place. I watched Uncle Charley wade around in the water and was afraid he would wash away, but he didn't.

Fields were lush with wheat and small grain. Corn that hadn't washed out was growing tall. Crop prospects were good for the first time in many years.

The grasshoppers hadn't all died. The Government urged farmers to poison hoppers while they were small, but it was an operation in futility. At least the turkeys were well fed.

I went to town with Aunt Tina and Mom in Aunt Tina's Model T. The Model T usually boiled at the top of the Wenger hill so we had to stop and cool the motor and add water. We sold our eggs and cream, bought groceries and headed home.

Black clouds built in the west. Wind chased the clouds across the sky while lightning flashed, and thunder rumbled and crashed. Rain fell, sheeting across the windshield until Aunt Tina could barely see to drive. The car crept along the road. By the time we reached the turn-off, the rain had stopped. Water ran down the muddy trail. Aunt Tina turned off the highway and headed west across the prairie. Behind us a rainbow spanned the eastern sky.

Gumbo piled up on the wheels of the car. The Model T chugged along in low, going slower and slower and finally stopped. We were stuck.

I got out, leaned against the trunk and pushed with all my power. The Model T began to move. I ran behind, pushing. Mud flew off the wheels and spattered over me. My shoes became great globs of mud. Mud speckled my white dress. If I stopped pushing, the wheels stopped rolling. I pushed the Model T down a hill, across a draw with two feet of water coursing down it and up the other side.

I pushed it up hill and down for over two miles to Aunt Tina's house while Mom and Aunt Tina sat inside laughing as great speckles of mud splattered me from head to foot. I didn't care. We were happy to get the rain.

Julian spent most of the summer with Aunt Amanda, except for a time when she went to work for Mrs. Eckwald. The Eckwald brothers lived on a farm six miles west of Steiens. The farm sat high on the prairie with a huge grove of trees around the farmstead, a lovely novelty at that time.

Mrs. Eckwald was a near sighted, stout lady who peered at you from behind thick glasses like a huge owl. Mrs. Eckwald bought an apartment building in Philip and took Julian to Philip to help her clean it. The apartment building got water from a well in the back yard.

When Julian pumped a bucket of water, mouse parts appeared in the clear liquid. "Don't worry," Mrs. Eckwald said.

"You just pump   the well dry. Fresh water will run in and be all right to drink."

Julian pumped the well dry, but she didn't drink any of the fresh water. She was afraid a mouse tail might float to the surface.

It was a busy summer for me. Darkie was a chunky, dapple gray beauty. The time had come to break her to ride. Essie was going to haze for me. I cinched the saddle tightly and climbed aboard. Darkie followed her mother across the prairie. She didn't know what to do about the lump on her back, but she decided the best thing was to walk or trot whenever her mother did.

I wanted to ride like a cowboy. I kicked Darkie. I hit her with the reins. She ran around Whitefoot, pushing against the old mare and shoving against Essie's legs. I tried my best to make her buck, but she didn't have a jump in her, fortunately.

Darkie became one of the best horses I ever rode. She was one of those rare horses that knew more than her rider did. She was gentle. She wouldn't hurt anyone, but she would run home to the barn with an inexperienced rider and refuse to leave again, or stand on a hill and rear until the rider got off. She was constantly outsmarting people who couldn't handle her.

Darkie was as chunky as a Percheron, but she had the heart of an Arabian. She didn't look like a race horse, but she thought she was one. She beat almost every horse she was matched against, until the day we raced her against a Thoroughbred stud. The race was grossly unfair. Darkie ran as fast as she could but he was still lengths ahead. It nearly broke her heart, and I'm still ashamed of that race.

Uncle Alvin promised me a new pair of Blucher boots like his if I would ride the pasture every day. I longed for a real pair of cowboy boots. Faithfully, I rode over the prairie on Whitefoot or Darkie, but we didn't find many dead cows. Darkie became a fine cow horse, but Uncle Alvin never found the money to buy me the twenty-five dollar boots.

Hank had gone to a CCC camp in the Black Hills. Herb was building dams for Griggs Davidson. He and Fred Holden drove Farmall F20 tractors, hitched to a fresno to build Government dams on farms and ranches.

The grass was growing tall. There was going to be hay to mow again and fat calves to sell come fall. Dad's corn grew fast. So did the weeds. He sent me to the field to cultivate the corn.

I harnessed Emmet and Sorrel, hitched them to the cultivator and headed for the east field. Cultivating was hot, dusty work. I carried a pint thermos of water with me. I hoarded my water, drinking half a cup at each end of the half mile rows. Emmet and Sorrel plodded down the rows, switching their tails at the flies. I thought about the end of the row and my cool drink of water. My feet in the cultivator stirrups guided the shovels to tear out sunflowers and cockle burrs. Rabbits dodged out of the way.

I was ready for dinner when the sun reached high noon. So were the horses. I drove home for dinner with the team at a trot. The cultivator wheels spun and rattled. At the barn, the team went through the gate and I unhitched. I drove them to the dam for a drink, then put them in the barn to eat and rest while I had dinner.

One day I drove home at a fast trot, dust flying behind the cultivator. Emmet and Sorrel were as anxious to drink and rest as I was. They whipped through the gate and turned to get unhitched instead of going straight through the gate. The right wheel of the machine caught on the gate post. The cultivator tipped over. I flew through the air, hitting the ground with a solid thud. The team looked at me as if to say, "What happened to you?"

I tipped the cultivator over and unhitched the team. I limped behind them to the dam. They took a long drink, slopping water around to brush their teeth. I drove them back to the barn and went to the house to eat dinner.

The crops promised in the spring didn't pan out. Wheat fields combined in July only made eight to nineteen bushels of fifty-two pound wheat. The Government paid farmers to summer fallow part of their land in hopes of better crops. Summer fallowing was a new concept and turned South Dakota into a winter wheat state with hardly any corn planted west of the Missouri

River.

At least we had grass for our cattle and horses and corn for the hogs and turkeys, in spite of the grasshoppers and lack of late summer rains. The drought was broken. Things were looking up.

A gang of horse thieves rode through the free range one day and picked up all the horses they found ranging the open prairie. Luckily our horses were inside the pasture, except for a trim bay filly out of Mom's old Florrie. She was missing.

I rode for many miles and many days on the free range, looking for the two year old filly. Sometimes Buddy rode with me on Star and got thirstier than a baby meadowlark on a hot day. We stopped and drank in a dam, but he wanted to ride two miles south to Owen Lohan's place and get a drink of ice water. He had been at Owen's house once after Owen had been to town and brought home a cake of ice. Buddy figured Owen, a friendly old bachelor, always had ice water at his house.

I rode day after day in sizzling heat and drizzling rain, but I didn't see "hide nor hair" of the filly. Then one day I rode to the Paulson farm to visit Ione. I put Darkie in the corral and there was Mom's filly staring me in the face.

I turned to Mr. Paulson and said, "That's my mother's horse."

"She was out south of here by herself and I ran her in," he said. "I didn't know who she belonged to." Maybe he didn't, but she had Dad's rocker open A on her left shoulder.

He had broken her to lead, so I lead her home. She was a bay beauty with large eyes, trim legs, a white blaze and a nasty temper.

I decided to break her to ride. I lead her around, petted her and tried to be friends. The high spirited filly grabbed my shirt with her teeth and jerked the buttons off. I never did break her to ride.

Uncle Charley planted a big garden of melons again. The early moisture brought his melon crop along. He carried water from the dam during the dry spell, making trip after trip in the hot sun. His labor paid off. In September he sold melons in Midland just like in the old days only now he hauled them to town in the trunk of the Model T.

With September came school. Julian and I went down to stay with Aunt Amanda and Uncle Walt again. I was a Senior, Julian a Junior. Mickey and Buddy rode off to Liberty, both in the fourth grade.

The Martins: (Back Row) Thelma, Hank, Dad, Herb, and Julian. (Front Row) Buddy, Mom, Mickey. 1938.

(Back Row) Thelma and Julian wearing the green tunic and skirt outfits Mom made. (Center Front) Mickey, paying more attention to her Betsy Wetsy doll than to the camera.

330

CHAPTER 28

School's Out

Of the eighteen students who started the fall of 1934, only four remained: Frances, Orville, Paul and I. Violet Hineline and Margaret Seidler were new. Along the way, we had picked up Harriet Olson, Kenneth Anderson, Thomas Stalley, John Gillaspie, Willis Drew and Ruby Muirhead so we were twelve.

Mr. McNally was our superintendent. The Senior Class picked Berdella Sheggeby for class sponsor although Orville told us "Seniors always chose the Superintendent." He was put out with us, but even Orville couldn't prevail against eleven other students.

I found physics to be extremely difficult. I worked hard, going so far as to take my physics book home to study because I wanted an "A". I got an "A" on my test, but Mr. McNally only gave me a "B+" on my report card. I was disappointed and angry. Mr. McNally had already made "A's" harder to get by raising the grade level.

Mr. McNally used a telephone to demonstrate the properties of electricity. The students held hands with two boys holding opposite poles to complete the circuit. Mr. McNally cranked the phone. The current shot through us. The boys held tightly to the girl's hands. The girls nearly jumped through the roof. I don't know why boys can stand more electricity than girls can, but they surely proved it.

Mr. McNally grabbed my hand and the phone wires and twirled the crank. I felt like I was getting electrocuted. He thought

331

it was funny.

Between the grasshoppers and the drought the latter part of the summer, Dad didn't get much of a corn crop. When we came home for the weekend, I helped him pick corn.

Dad hitched Emmet and Sorrel to the wagon with the high bangboard on the right side. We climbed into the wagon as the sun was rising. The team trotted to the field a mile and a half away. We headed down the rows with Dad taking the two outside rows while I shucked the corn nearest the wagon. I had to watch out that Dad didn't hit me in the head with an ear of corn.

Emmet and Sorrel moved straight down the row, never turning either way. Dad's corn hit the bangboard with a steady rhythm. My corn hit half as often as I shredded the wet husks back with my wrist hook.

By the time the sun was at high noon, my wrist felt like it was sprained. I was tired and hungry, but we weren't going home for dinner. Emmet and Sorrel weren't hungry. They picked corn as they ambled down the row. Dad didn't check his horses so they couldn't reach the corn like some farmers did. The Bible says, "Do not muzzle the ox that treads the grain," and I guess, to Dad, that meant the horse that pulls the corn wagon, too.

We picked corn until the sun went down, then rode home, hungry and tired, with the wagon box half full of small yellow ears.

Some days were cold with a skift of snow. I got so chilled I felt like a snow man. My gloves got wet from the snowy ears. My hands turned numb with cold. I was glad to see the sun go down.

I think the horses were glad to go home, too. I sat hunched down on the corn with the high bangboard sheltering me from the wind. The horses trotted home and stopped beside the corn crib.

That winter Miss Sheggeby divided the girls into three basketball teams and had a tournament. Harriet and I wanted to be on the same team, but she wouldn't allow that. She wanted the teams evenly divided. The tournament turned into a battle between Harriet's Comets and my Dare Devils. The Dare Devils won and the season ended.

I won my third "M", but Miss Sheggeby said, "Anyone who wants a letter will have to pay for their own. The school doesn't have money to buy letters for girls." The letters cost forty-five cents. I regretfully decided I had better places for my money. I was again working for the teachers and getting paid by Uncle Sam. Julian was only fifteen so she still shared my paycheck. I had to pay for my Senior Class ring which cost $8.00, four months work for me. I also had to pay for my class pictures which would ruin another eight bucks.

Early winter was cold. Aunt Tina and Essie came to town in the Model T when the temperature was twenty below. Uncle Charley had to build a fire under the car to get the engine hot enough to start.

Kenneth Doud died in December. He was twenty-six years old and had leukemia. Douds moved to Oregon. The Roberts family moved to the Doud farm. They soon left that farm and South Dakota. They piled into their black Model A and headed west to Oregon.

Mom invited them to our house for Sunday dinner before they left. They came so the hatchet was buried between our families, but we never saw them again.

January turned spring like after the cold weather. Julian and I were exempt from semester tests and enjoyed a two day vacation while unlucky students were doing their tests.

Rain fell generously in the spring. Farmers began to believe the drought had finally broken. They tilled their fields and planted their crops.

That winter Julian and I and Alice and Marjorie Douglas went to confirmation. Reverend Olson taught us The Ten Commandments, The Apostle's Creed and that God is love and sent his Son Jesus Christ to die for our sins. I went to confirmation with Ramona Rank only she went to the Catholic priest.

That year I had a boy friend. Evan was tall and thin, and a good dancer, but not a talker. We were a silent couple, gliding around the floor, saying not a word. Evan drove a 1928 Chevrolet Sedan. He got tired of waiting for me to say something and got a girl friend that would talk.

Our class loaded into three cars and spent Skip Day touring The Black Hills. We stayed in two cabins, one of them Uncle Walt's.

Frances, Orville, Paul and I climbed Harney Peak, had our pictures taken on the dinosaurs in Dinosaur Park and walked the trails of Wind Cave together. Then we went home and prepared to go out into the big world.

Julian was on the Lucky Thirteen, the highest grades in school. I didn't make it, but my grades were good enough for semester test exemption except for one thing. Professor McNally decided on a dumb, we thought, contest. He pitted the Juniors and Seniors against the Freshmen and Sophomores in a contest to see who got the highest grades. The Sophomores and Freshmen won. The Seniors and Juniors had to take the test so for the first time, Julian and I were taking semester tests, and we didn't like it.

Graduation was fast approaching. Uncle Alvin promised to give me $10.00 to buy a graduation dress. I thought he was never going to find the money, but he did. I had bought a long pink formal for the Junior-Senior banquet and I didn't have any money left.

I bought a black suit and a lovely pink dress with a pleated skirt. All the other girls bought white graduation dresses. I had looked at white dresses, but chose pink because I couldn't afford to buy a dress I would only wear once.

We graduated with the motto, "Climb though the rocks be rugged." Our colors were silver and rose and matched my dress. Orville Bentley and Kenneth Anderson were valedictorian and salutatorian and had to make speeches. I was glad I came in third. They both won scholarships to colleges they did not attend.

I was eighteen-years-old with no job and no place to find one. I went home and helped Dad milk cows. All summer I rode the range on Darkie, looking for dead cows. Golden sunflowers bloomed every where. The prairie was resplendent with green and gold. The grass grew thicker, closing the space between plants. Dams filled with water. Ducks swam on the ponds.

Emil Nemec fenced his eighty acres that had been our horse pasture and built a large dam. We took the little kids and spent many happy hours swimming with Florence Nemec. He put a boat in the dam and we rowed out to deep water and dived off. No mud. No sea weeds. Just cool water.

Dad cultivated the corn and cane fields and worked his summer fallow. He still didn't have a tractor. Buddy was our fisherman, catching bullheads for supper. He never lacked for bait. If a fish got his hopper, he could easily catch another.

That summer Don, John and Bill from over Ottumwa way found out where we lived. They rode the ten miles across the prairie to our place. Julian and I saddled Star and Darkie and rode with them.

We had a plank running out into the dam to dip water for the hogs. Bill thought the plank was a diving board. The water was only a few feet deep at the end of that plank.

Bill put on his swimming trunks and strutted out to the end of the plank. "Can I dive off this board?" he asked.

"Go ahead," Julian said.

Bill backed off, took a run and did a graceful swan dive off the end of the board. He almost buried his head up to the shoulders in mud. Lucky he didn't break his neck.

Aunt Amanda and Dad had one thing in common. They both tended to exaggerate the time so we would hurry. Dad would say, "Hurry up and get up, Thelma. It's nearly seven o'clock" when the time was nearer six-thirty. The cows needed to be milked so they could go out and make more milk. I needed a little more sleep because we had been dancing the night before and hadn't gotten home until three in the morning.

One night we were all sleeping when a loud, "Bang! Bang! Bang!" sounded on the door. Dad leaped out of bed and went to the door.

"Can the girls come out and ride around with me?" Don asked, politely. That time Dad didn't exaggerate. He roared, "No, they can't come out. It's nearly ten o'clock." Actually it was nearly midnight. Julian and I lay in our bed and tried to smother our giggles. Dad went back to bed.

Don mounted his horse, rode to the dam, watered his horse and then rode up and down the grade of the dam. Dad saw the tracks the next day and was furious. He didn't want that stupid fellow coming to our house again, but he did.

All summer I hoped for a job. I wanted to go to the University at Vermillion when fall came, but money was too scarce. I had graduated from High School with the brave motto, "Climb though the rocks be rugged," ringing in my ears, but I wasn't climbing very fast.

Half a world away, dim armies marched, armies that would cast their shadows across the ocean and change forever the world we knew. These goose stepping soldiers saluted a mad man named Adolph Hitler who would set the world on fire and change the course of history.

Post-graduation picture of the author: Thelma Martin Anderson

336

To order additional copies of **Where Coyotes Howl**, complete the information below.

Ship to: (please print)

Name _____

Address _____

City, State, Zip _____

Day phone _____

_____ copies of *Where Coyotes Howl* @ $16.95 each $ _____

Postage and handling @ $2.00 per book $ _____

South Dakota residents add 5% tax $ _____

Total amount enclosed $ _____

*Make checks payable to **Thelma Anderson***

Send to: Thelma Anderson
P.O. Box 211 • Midland, SD 57552

To order additional copies of **Where Coyotes Howl**, complete the information below.

Ship to: (please print)

Name _____

Address _____

City, State, Zip _____

Day phone _____

_____ copies of *Where Coyotes Howl* @ $16.95 each $ _____

Postage and handling @ $2.00 per book $ _____

South Dakota residents add 5% tax $ _____

Total amount enclosed $ _____

*Make checks payable to **Thelma Anderson***

Send to: Thelma Anderson
P.O. Box 211 • Midland, SD 57552